W9-BZT-692

Dear Reader:

The book you are about to read is the latest bestseller from St. Martin's True Crime Library, the imprint *The New York Times* calls "the leader in true crime!" Each month, we offer you a fascinating account of the latest, most sensational crime that has captured the national attention. *The Milwaukee Murders* delves into the twisted world of Jeffrey Dahmer, one of the most savage serial killers of our time; *Lethal Lolita* gives you the *real* scoop on the deadly love affair between Amy Fisher and Joey Buttafuoco; *Whoever Fights Monsters* takes you inside the special FBI team that tracks serial killers; *Garden of Graves* reveals how police uncovered the bloody human harvest of mass murderer Joel Rifkin; *Unanswered Cries* is the story of a detective who tracked a killer for a year, only to discover it was someone he knew and trusted; *Bad Blood* is the story of the notorious Menendez brothers and their senstional trials; *Sins of the Mother* details the sad account of Susan Smith and her two drowned children; *Fallen Hero* details the riveting tragedy of O. J. Simpson and the case that stunned a nation.

St. Martin's True Crime Library gives you the stories *behind* the headlines. Our authors take you right to the scene of the crime and into the minds of the most notorious murderers to show you what really makes them tick. St. Martin's True Crime Library paperbacks are better than the most terrifying thriller, because it's all true! The next time you want a crackling good read, make sure it's got the St. Martin's True Crime Library logo on the spine—you'll be up all night!

Charles E. Spicer, Jr.
Senior Editor, St. Martin's True Crime Library

In Clarkston, Ken Arrasmith had parked a truck filled with weaponry in front of the police department, and had given himself up while cops in an adjoining community were asking for help in finding the suspect. Arrasmith was handled gently when he was taken inside the police station. He wore a shoulder holster and a nylon belt pouch with clips of ammunition, but not steel handcuffs. After all, Ken Arrasmith was a hometown boy who had once been a deputy sheriff on this side of the Snake River, and was widely known in Clarkston and in Asotin County.

A FATHER'S RAGE

Don Davis

St. Martin's Paperbacks

NOTE: If you purchased this book without a cover you should be aware that this book is stolen property. It was reported as "unsold and destroyed" to the publisher, and neither the author nor the publisher has received any payment for this "stripped book."

A FATHER'S RAGE

Copyright © 1997 by Don Davis.

Cover photograph of Ken Arrasmith by Boston Globe Photo.
Cover photograph of Ken and Cynthia Arrasmith embracing by Barry Kough © *Lewiston Tribune.*

All rights reserved. No part of this book may be used or reproduced in any manner whatsoever without written permission except in the case of brief quotations embodied in critical articles or reviews. For information address St. Martin's Press, 175 Fifth Avenue, New York, N.Y. 10010.

ISBN: 0-312-96095-6

Printed in the United States of America

St. Martin's Paperbacks edition/January 1997

10 9 8 7 6 5 4 3 2 1

For Jill Hill

ACKNOWLEDGMENTS

This story was discovered by my dear friend Jill Hill of Clarkston, Washington, who did not realize what we were getting into when she telephoned with the suggestion. She and her mother, Nancy Woods, provided an oasis of support and assistance during a rugged month of reporting.

No book of this complexity can be written without help from many, many people. My agent Jane Dystel and my editor, Charlie Spicer of St. Martin's Press, were excellent in putting the project together and shepherding it through some dark times.

In the official arena, Denise Rosen, the prosecuting attorney of Nez Perce County, and special prosecutor Mike Kane provided extensive posttrial interviews and analysis of important points of the case. Detective Wade Ralston, the lead investigator, kept the author from wandering away from facts.

Defense attorneys Roy and Craig Mosman willingly offered guidance, suggestions and friendship throughout the case.

Trial Court Administrator Steven Caylor and his team of clerks and marshals were efficient and helpful every single day, despite having to handle a barrage of media requests.

Although the beautiful Lewiston-Clarkson area was cast in dim light by this trial, I would like to thank the many area residents and officials who made time available to talk with me, although most asked that their names not be used. In all, more than fifty people in four states were interviewed. Rilla, Josh, Jo and Deena were particularly helpful.

Cynthia Arrasmith remained charming and friendly throughout the trial. Her family declined interview requests because Ken Arrasmith told the author he was planning his own book.

Members of the press became friends as well as sources. Joan Abrams of the *Lewiston Morning Tribune* was incredibly kind in sharing her reports, sources, and thoughts. Eric Sorensen of the *Spokesman-Review* provided uncanny insight into the case. And the tenacious Lucy Kaylin of *Gentlemen's Quarterly*, with her solid professionalism, gave us all a lift when we most needed it. A talented young group of area television reporters did a much better job covering the case than did their national counterparts. A special salute goes to Lynn Rossi of KHQ-TV.

Finally, this book, like all the others, couldn't have been done without the steadfast help of my wife, editor and partner, Robin Murphy Davis. Our dog, Teddy Salad, kept my feet warm during a long winter of writing.

A FATHER'S
RAGE

1

The killer turned his ex-wife's black Toyota pickup truck onto Shelter Road and tried to ignore how much the place looked like a train wreck in a junkyard. He could not let his attention wander, although the desolation and clutter almost cried out for closer examination.

An ancient and delapidated stone building, the old Sacred Heart Chapel, with three small arched windows on each side and two more in front flanking double doors, was an indication that the area had not always been in the condition it was on this hot and muggy day in the middle of May 1995. But things change, people change and so do buildings made of stone. Once a center of worship, the church's old slate roof was broken and covered with crawling islands of green moss and lichen. Weeds at the sides reached into the abandoned chapel, and a drooping barbed wire fence warned potential intruders to keep out, as if there were some reason why anyone would want to set foot in the building. Abandoned by its congregation long ago, it had been reduced to being a lone, spooky sentinel in a grubby field at the corner where Shelter Road intersects with the main highway, just beyond the weathered sign announcing the eastern city limits of Lewiston, Idaho.

He gunned the accelerator, the big tires grabbed gravel and the truck moved easily past the church, on a road that led sharply upward. Beyond the old church was a carpet of junk. Pieces of old cars, trucks, bikes, trailers and assorted other metal objects that wore coats of rust of various thickness littered stair-step fields. In the midst of it, people actually lived in small trailers, apparently oblivious to the garbage, fluttering paper, drooping tarpaulins and mounds of dirt and weeds strewn at their doorsteps.

The killer stayed on the road, slowing as he reached a large building made of corrugated tin. It was an automobile repair shop, and it was there that he hoped to find his prey. Both of them. The man and, with luck, the woman, too.

He had waited and waited, carefully stalking them, awaiting just the right time to do what he had to do, what he imagined anyone in his shoes might do. Once he learned they were not at their home, which resembled the mess on Shelter Road, but were at the garage, he decided to move. He paused at the shop's driveway, looked around, then continued up the hill.

Once past the shop, the neighborhood improved somewhat and the trash decreased. One yellow mobile home actually looked rather neat, and at the top of the hill sat the Lewis and Clark Animal Shelter, where he turned the Toyota around. He wore comfortable sneakers, black jeans and two T-shirts. A green one was next to his body and a larger black one, imprinted with the legend *Play With the Bad Boys and You're Going to Get Hurt*, was over it. Using an ink marker, he had written some more words on it. Between the two T-shirts, over his heart, he wore a holster that contained a dull silver, heavy Ruger 9mm semiautomatic pistol fitted with a laser sight. In the truck's toolbox was a Chinese-made SKS rifle, a lethal-looking weapon that was dull black in color. He had two more pistols, and, in a slender box altered to contain it, lay a stubby, fast-firing Tec-9 semiautomatic handgun with a thirty-round magazine. All of the weapons were fully loaded, and he had a nylon pouch on his belt containing extra ammunition. In his back pocket was a micro tape recorder.

He took a deep breath, feeling the drugs work. He had been snorting methamphetamines for ten straight days, and the cumulative buzz of the speed imparted by the "crank" was still alive in his system. He adjusted his dark sunglasses against the late morning sun and headed back down Shelter Road. Across the highway, huge white clouds belched from the stacks of the Potlatch and Clearwater Lumber factories, and a giant yellow crane unloaded freshly cut timber from a string of Burlington-Northern and Union Pacific flatcars. Beyond the sprawl of industrial buildings rose the brown-green hills on the north side of the Lewis-Clark Valley. He ignored the pulp and chemical stink that wrapped the area in a smelly haze, slowed the truck and turned again into the gravel drive. He parked, switched off the key and just sat there, turning the whole thing over in his mind. Over and over and over. He felt sick and scared but was determined to press ahead.

He was startled from his reverie when a young man with dark brown hair suddenly appeared at the truck window and asked if he needed help. "Yeah," the killer responded. "Is Ron Bingham here?"

"Oh, yeah," the young man replied, pointing up to a concrete pad just behind the big tin shop.

The killer got out, the heavy pistol snug under his shirt. He picked up the thin box containing the Tec-9 and followed the helpful youngster up the driveway to the edge of the main garage. The killer quickly noted that two more people were there. A tall kid with sandy hair pulled back in a ponytail worked beneath the hood of a truck, and a woman in jeans and a light jacket looked up as he approached. He had never seen the me-

chanic before, but knew the woman, whose blond hair
was loosely tied in back. Knew her very well. He and
Luella Bingham had grown up as friends, their families
close neighbors, but they no longer liked each other. Not
at all. Hate had replaced friendliness and any childhood
fun they may have shared was buried in the distant past.

He made a casual motion with the flat box he carried,
almost as if showing her a pizza. "I need to see Ron,
he left this at the house," the killer said. Luella ignored
him.

Three vehicles were parked side-by-side on the big T-
shaped apron outside the main door of the shop. Luella
was standing beside the truck on which the mechanic
was working, and that man glanced up when the killer
spoke to her, then went back to work.

The young man who had brought him up the path
pointed to the rear of another truck, and the killer saw
a pair of legs, a stomach and part of a chest sticking out
from beneath the vehicle. A large chrome bumper lay
nearby. Ron Bingham was flat on his back.

As the escorting guide turned and walked away, the
killer took a position near the right side of the prone
man, and Ron Bingham could barely see him. He and
Ron had been wary of each other over the past two
weeks. Each knew the other carried guns. Each knew the
other was using methamphetamines, which could lead to
instant, unreasoning, paranoid behavior. Each detested
the other.

The killer braced his legs apart and slid his hand into
the opening at the bottom of the box and tightly grasped
the handle of the Tec-9. "I got something for you," he
growled. "I got something real special."

Ron Bingham was not a man who could be easily
frightened. He was short and stocky but had survived
many a fight, a term in prison and was a successful
dealer in the murky, violent drug world. "Oh, cool,"
Bingham replied with sarcasm. He didn't give a damn

about the guy standing at his feet, but when he glanced up again, he saw the dark, round hole in the end of a gun barrel pointing at him. Ron Bingham knew his life was on the line. He drew his right leg up, trying to curl away from the gun, and began to roll to his left.

The killer squeezed four quick shots, the Tec-9 hardly bucking in recoil as he pulled the trigger and the bullets lanced into Bingham. One drilled into the victim's buttocks, two others hit him in the body and one heavy 9mm slug grazed his right shoulder as he tried to flip over and hide from the fusillade. It then went into his neck, his head and brain, fracturing his skull and killing him instantly.

Then the damned gun jammed. The killer was furious and ripped the box from around the weapon. He had loaded the thirty-round magazine so carefully, but the mix of meth and excitement apparently had drained his attention and he had put one of the bullets in backward. After the trigger was pulled, the Tec-9 was supposed to eject the cartridge it had just fired and insert a new one from the magazine into the breech. The reversed bullet snagged and stopped the action. With Ron Bingham already dead, the killer jerked a small lever on the left side of the weapon and the pesky backward bullet was flung free. The gun was ready to shoot again.

While he was working to free the action, he had moved around the feet of his victim, whose still boots pointed toward the sky, aimed downward and pulled the trigger again. And again. And again. And again. Again and again. Through the fog of gunfire and the sound of his own blood roaring in his ears, he heard Luella scream, "You shot him, you son of a bitch! Somebody call the police!" He ignored her, continuing to pull the trigger, pumping more bullets into the shredded corpse on the ground.

The killer finally stopped his barrage with one single bullet still in the Tec-9, ready to fire. That simply would not be enough to finish the job, not in a way that would be certain and final. He was going to have to enter a dark place, and so would need the extra firepower of the pistol. He reached beneath the black T-shirt and hauled the heavy Ruger from its holster. As his right palm closed around the grip, it squeezed a narrow band that activated a tiny laser sight mounted beneath the barrel. The tiny red light, almost invisible in the daylight, arrowed into the distance. When he was ready to squeeze the trigger, he knew a bullet would precisely follow the narrow beam of light. It didn't matter to him that the laser, an acronym for Light Amplification by Stimulated Emission of Radiation, was a scientific marvel. He only cared that it was one hell of a good way to aim a gun.

Luella was nowhere in sight and he assumed that she had dodged into the darkened shop. There was no sign of the two other men, and since they did not represent a threat, he ignored them. He took off his shades and ran after the woman.

As he walked in, she might have been able to see him in silhouette against the bright daylight, so he dodged to the side. She would have seen him holding the Tec-9 he had used to murder her husband in his left hand, and the large Ruger pistol in his right. In the darkness of the shop, the laser beam could be clearly seen as its ruby stream of electrons roamed about, like some kind of deadly flashlight. He had to be careful, for he knew that since Ron had once served time for a felony, all of the Bingham guns—and there were apparently a lot of them—were registered in Luella's name, and she was known to carry one. He didn't want to be bushwhacked. "Luella," the killer called. "It's over with. Come on out. Don't do anything!"

Luella Bingham had no intention of going to him. The guy had just slaughtered her husband, was standing there with a Tec-9 in one hand and a pistol equipped with a laser sight in the other, and he wanted her to "Come on out?'' Fat chance. She headed through another door and hid beside a corner of the building, ducking under the level of the trucks on the outside pad.

And it was there that he found her, with her back toward him. When she realized he was nearby, she turned and as she did, saw the pistol was pointed at her. Like her husband, she was staring down the barrel of the gun that was going to snuff out her life. When she was still at a right angle to the killer, the evil ruby dot of the laser danced along her side. He fired and the heavy slug tore through her right breast, exited, then needled through her left breast. The force of the impact spun her back around to her left and she struggled to run away, but began to fall.

He extended the pistol and as the laser moved across her back, he rapidly pulled the trigger. The second bullet was a perfect kill shot, fracturing her spine, and it dropped Luella in her tracks. She fell forward, instantly dead although she was still on her feet, unable to even put out her arms to brace herself, and another bullet went through her right lung and rib cage. As she fell, more bullets tore into her, one ripping through her heart, spleen, stomach and diaphragm. Luella Bingham was already facedown, dead on the ground, when the man moved closer, stood directly over her body and pumped a final, sixth bullet into her lower back. It drilled all the way through her pelvis and into the dirt.

The job was done. The killer exhaled, looking around. He saw no one near him, no one between him and the Toyota, so he walked down to it, a weapon in each hand. He tossed the two guns onto the truck seat, pulled the little tape recorder from his left hip pocket and threw that in, too.

Then he climbed in, cranked the Toyota, backed into the gravel of Shelter Road and drove away, careful to obey the traffic laws. Obviously, someone would call the cops, so he had to get out of there. He did not want to be arrested in Idaho. On the way down East Main, he recognized police cars coming his way. They didn't know they were looking for him, so they made no move to pull him over. He headed back through Lewiston, knowing exactly where he was going.

He drove cautiously, heading west, away from Shelter Road and toward the river that marked the Washington state line.

2

The call from the police radio dispatcher came at 11: 42 A.M. Multiple shots fired. Multiple victims. In Lewiston, Idaho, a small town of only twenty-eight thousand people, it was the equivalent of a bomb being dropped.

The Sheriff's Department of Nez Perce County was jolted into action with the uncomfortable knowledge that this wasn't a drug bust or a speeding ticket, but an obviously dangerous situation. The location of the shootings was only a quarter mile beyond the city limits, not much in actual distance, but enough to put it on the turf of Sheriff Ron Koepper and not within the jurisdiction of the Lewiston Police Department. Sorting out who was in charge could wait, however, and for the moment, marked and unmarked units from several area police agencies sped toward Shelter Road.

The professorial Captain Scott Whitcomb, a veteran of almost twenty-six years with the Nez Perce Sheriff's Department, was in his office when the radio crackled with the news of the volleys being fired at 922 Shelter Road. Deputy Don Taylor, with thirty years on the job, jumped into a patrol car with him and they took off from the parking lot behind the courthouse on Main Street.

They sped through the big intersection at Twenty-first

Street, past Locomotive Park on the left, turned sharply right onto a little cutover traffic lane, went through the stop sign and were quickly on East Main, using the good four-lane road to gather speed. In a minute they saw the sand-colored Coca-Cola building on the right and the Potlatch #1 Credit Union Office on the left. Whitcomb spun the wheel left when East Main reached a dead end at Mill Road.

Just beyond the big green buildings of the wood product companies, a yellow roadside sign warned CHILDREN AT PLAY. The police car sped through the posted twenty-five miles per hour zone and Whitcomb slowed only when he saw the faded white sign that had been painted over an old Pepsi advertisment, pointing to the animal shelter. He turned right, the wheels spinning momentarily on the gravel and rocks, then headed up the hill to the big tin barn that housed Specialized Automotive. Whitcomb knew the place well because his son sometimes worked there.

Whitcomb pulled his car into the drive to block that exit and got out on the driver's side as Taylor climbed out of the passenger door, both with their pistols drawn. The radio had added a few more details during the short trip, but the first two law enforcement officers on the scene did not know if someone was still on the property, possibly with an automatic weapon. "It was a high-risk tactical situation," Whitcomb would later recall. "We didn't know what we had," echoed Taylor. "We didn't know if there was a shooter still up there."

They split up, Whitcomb heading through the left side of the cluttered lot, while Taylor moved cautiously up the right. That way they could cover each other and any threat would have to come from the front. Other deputies were already arriving and would cover their backs.

Taylor saw a blond woman, sprawled in the dirt between three vehicles and the edge of the shed. She lay motionless, her face turned to one side. Keeping his eyes on the big building with the doors still yawning open, Taylor knelt and put a finger on the neck of Luella Bingham. No pulse. She was dead.

He saw the second body and called out to Whitcomb, who had circled the line of trucks. The captain carefully examined the three vehicles to be certain no one was hiding in them, then turned his attention to the corpse halfway beneath the middle pickup truck. The first thing he noticed was the huge number of bullet holes in the man. He wasn't just shot, he had been shredded. Whitcomb put his fingers to the victim's ankle and felt no pulse there. He also was dead.

Whitcomb walked to where the woman lay and stood beside her white tennis shoes. Blood, he saw, had pooled on her back around the gunshot wounds. Whoever did this wanted these people to stay dead, the cop thought. And if that was true, then where was the shooter, and where were the terrible weapons that had left such carnage? Except for the personal weapons being carried by the police, no other guns were in sight. He began to count the bullet wounds in the woman's back. One. Two. Three. Then he shook his head. There were too many. He stopped counting.

It was almost noon and they had two dead people and a mystery. The officers carefully lifted the driver's licenses from the victims and identified them as Ron Bingham, age forty-seven, and his wife, Luella, age forty-three, both residents of adjacent Clarkston, Washington.

Another veteran law enforcement officer, Wade Ralston, was also on duty that morning, and picked up the telephone in his office when it rang. Just as the voice on the phone began to tell him of the shooting out on Shelter Road, his police radio started squawking the news that officers were being dispatched to the scene. Ralston had begun his law enforcement career in 1970, in a tiny

Idaho municipality, and had been a deputy in Nez Perce County for the past fourteen years. A large man with a slow speech pattern, Ralston was one of the two men in the Sheriff's Department who held the job of investigator, and since the shootings took place on his watch, the case fell on his desk.

He met his boss, Sheriff Ron Koepper, on the way out and they both got into a marked Ford Bronco as the radio chattered with updated dispatches. The crime was only minutes old and already they had a description of a suspect vehicle—a big blue pickup truck with two people inside. Ralston and Koepper knew there were only a few exits the killer could have taken from Shelter Road. East Main, the one they were on, was filling up with police vehicles hurrying to the site. Even so, Ralston was interested when he saw a pickup truck coming toward him that bore a general resemblance to the vehicle police were hunting. But the color, black, was different than the blue paint job described by the radio. And the dispatcher had said two men were in the vehicle, while this one contained only one man, the driver. Also, he noticed that the driver didn't seem to be in any hurry, was obeying the speed laws and driving carefully. Not exactly the profile of a fleeing, cold-blooded killer who had just gunned down a couple of people. The detective watched the truck go by and made a decision to let it pass. Less than five minutes had elapsed since police received the first call, and Ralston, knowing he was to be the lead investigator, had to get to the crime scene as soon as possible. He headed toward Shelter Road, and the black pickup truck grew smaller and smaller in his rearview mirror.

Ralston saw Whitcomb's vehicle parked in the drive, parked his Bronco on the far left edge of the property, and he and the sheriff got out. Although other officers had already arrived, the area was not yet known to be safe and clear, which meant every lawman there was walking on eggshells, their eyes roaming the piles of scrap and junk. "Things were really hot," he said. "We didn't yet have control of the site." There were simply too many places in the junked-up area where a killer could have been hiding.

Some of the nervousness vanished as other deputies and police arrived and climbed the hill, saturating the area with law enforcement badges. Sergeant Jim Colvin emerged from the large building after finding it empty, removing a major concern from the other officers who worried the killer might have been turning the tin shop into a fortress.

Within a short time, however, the initial emergency passed and it was time to launch the basic, meticulous police work necessary to catch the killer.

Whitcomb realized the need for protecting the scene from curious spectators and backed his patrol car down to block the road, then walked down to the main intersection to direct traffic.

Meanwhile, Don Taylor put away his weapon and picked his way down the grubby hillside to meet Ralston and Koepper, advising them that there were two dead bodies, a man and a woman. Not only had they been shot to death, but each had been shot repeatedly.

When Ralston and the sheriff had a look at the corpses, being careful not to step on the sprawl of loose brass cartridges, they agreed. It was more than murder, it was a massacre. "I had never seen, in twenty-five years, anybody killed like this and I had seen some bad homicides," Ralston said. "This was just out-of-control rage."

At this point, police knew only that two people had been violently murdered, possibly by two assailants who had fled in a pickup truck. It wasn't much.

But the clock had barely started to tick on the investigation when the first eyewitness arrived in the blue truck that matched the description of the suspect vehicle. The young man at the wheel stopped just behind Ralston and called out to the detective. Robert Warnock, a baby-faced auto mechanic, told Ralston he had been a witness and quickly added that only one man was involved. One shooter, not two. And the truck was a black Toyota. The dispatcher changed the information being given to patrol units.

Warnock told police he had come to work at Specialized Automotive about eight o'clock that morning, sat around and talked for a while with Ron Bingham and another guy he didn't know, then had driven into Lewiston to awaken shop owner Tony Adams. When he came back to the shop, he spotted someone he knew just across the road where a huge number of tires were stacked, and had gone over to talk with him for a while. It was during the time he was at the tire pile that he saw the dark Toyota truck come up and park in the shop driveway, and he walked back to see what the driver wanted.

He described the driver for the cops and went on to explain how the man had asked if Ron Bingham was there, and how Warnock had escorted him up to the pad where Ron, whom Warnock barely knew, was replacing the bumper on a truck. As he had walked away, Warnock heard them speak briefly, then heard the series of popping sounds as the gunfire started. At first he ran to some trailers and hid, then jumped into a truck left there by a customer and peeled out in a hurry.

The investigators listened warily, not entirely convinced that Warnock wasn't involved in some fashion, for events were only just beginning to unfold. Ralston wanted a more formal and extensive interview, and so had someone read Warnock the Miranda warnings and handcuff him for the trip into Lewiston for further questioning.

*   *   *

The story made the noon news broadcast, but only with the sketchiest of details, picked off of scanners, special radios used by the news media to monitor police. Private citizens, for a variety of reasons, also listen to scanners. One such person was Lee Mersching, who paid rapt attention to the police call. First reports said the shootings had taken place at the Potlatch company, where her husband had worked for years. She wanted to know if anyone they knew was involved.

Almost immediately after the news report, her telephone rang. It was her neighbor across the street, Linda Bartlett, cautiously asking if the scanner had anything to say about the shooting that was on the news.

The neighbors had communicated by telephone a number of times in recent years about police calls, particularly when the dispatchers mentioned the name of a frequent runaway child, Linda's youngest daughter, Cynthia. Repeatedly in the past three years, the troubled teenager had left home and official help had been sought to retrieve her. But this time, Linda Bartlett wasn't asking about Cynthia. She wanted to know if Lee had heard any further details about something that had been on the noon news, that the police were looking for a black Toyota truck. Lee asked what her interest was. Linda replied softly that her ex-husband, Ken Arrasmith, had such a truck.

Nez Perce Deputies Doug McPherson and Guy Arnzin arrived to perform two of the most curious, and most vital, tasks of the investigation. They had different assignments, but the same goal—to record and be able to reproduce the crime scene. Their work would become a cornerstone not only for the investigation, but also in court months later as lawyers would seek to recreate the event for a jury.

The tactical business over, it was time for the specialists. McPherson talked to the sheriff and some other deputies, then carefully walked through the area, making notes, taking measurements and jotting rough sketches. He would later take the information to an artist, and she would turn his scrawls into a perfectly measured drawing that showed the main elements of the scene, particularly the positions and locations of the victims.

Arnzin had been working a split shift that day and had only arrived at the parking lot of the Sheriff's Department when someone yelled for him to hurry up and change into his uniform and get out to Shelter Road. In his patrol car was an important 1990s-style police tool— a videocamera. At the scene, with the viewfinder at his eye, he was guided by Sergeant Colvin through the area, trying not to step "on bullets or bodies," he said. With Colvin narrating, Arnzin slowly swept the camera over every important landmark, with particular focus on the two bodies. At trial, those pictures would bring Ron and Luella Bingham into the courtroom and give the jurors an up close look at the bullet-riddled bodies. It would change the case from abstract idea into reality. When he was done, he turned the tape over to McPherson so the artist also could use it for reference.

Another specialist, a civilian, also came to the scene of carnage on Shelter Road. Dr. Carl Koenen resembled a gentle family physician, but he would be called upon to perform the gruesome autopsies. He examined the bodies, noticing they both had been shot a number of times and that Luella was lying with her arms crossed beneath her. That indicated to Koenen that she had collapsed, facedown, without using her arms to break her fall, and that suggested the possibility that she was already dead by the time she hit the dirt. The autopsy, which he would do over the next two days, would allow Koenen to trace the paths of individual bullets through the bodies and discover the secrets of exactly how the Binghams were killed. For now, he supervised the placement of the bodies in thick plastic bags for transport to the refrigerated slabs in his laboratory, where they would be sealed overnight.

About the time police were done with Warnock, another witness had emerged on Shelter Road. A lanky kid with a ponytail and dirty sneakers ambled up from the bushes when he saw a fire truck pull in behind the police units. Paul Sharrai explained that he had been working on the master cylinder of a pickup truck when the killer had arrived. The visitor had been a tall, slender dude. Clean-cut. Being a car guy, Sharrai was better on the description of the truck. Black Toyota four-wheel drive with a stripe on the side. Extended cab and toolbox. Wade Ralston had no doubt that was exactly the truck he and Sheriff Koepper had passed on East Main less than an hour ago.

Sharrai told the investigators he didn't think anything about the stranger who had walked so close past him. Nobody else was excited, so he had continued his work, then he heard the popping sounds. At first, he thought they were firecrackers, then he heard Luella, who had been standing beside him, start "freakin' out" that somebody was shooting. That had been enough for the mechanic, who dropped his tools and took off running, his long legs pumping hard as he headed downhill. Sharrai said he saw a thick clump of bushes and dove in, scared and breathing heavily. He remained in his hiding place even after he saw the killer's truck drive off, not coming out until the hillside was crawling with police cars and fire engines.

After he talked with the cops, Sharrai was also handcuffed and taken in for a lengthy interview.

The Bremmer Building is a two-story office building located behind the Nez Perce County courthouse and in the same complex with the Lewiston Police Department and the Sheriff's Office. Downstairs, in a back corner office, the telephone rang on the desk of Denise L. Rosen, the prosecuting attorney for Nez Perce County. A petite woman with a streak of steel in regard to crime, she had made it a policy to go to the scenes of major crimes in her area, to get an understanding of the location and be able to verbally translate that to a jury. Going out this time, however, would have to wait a little while.

The news of the shootings barely preceded an avalanche of paper that was about to descend on her.

Lee Mersching's telephone would stay busy that day. Shortly after she talked with Linda Bartlett, she had a call from her best friend, Rilla Smith, over in Clarkston. She had been listening to the scanner also and knew of the shootings, then had received a call from a friend who said two people had been killed.

Rilla normally kept her feelings tightly packed deep inside, but now she was clearly worried. Luella Bingham was her daughter and lived with her husband, Ron, in Rilla's home. Rilla knew Ron was working at Tony Adams's shop on Shelter Road. Her son-in-law was a powder keg of trouble and Rilla had a sudden feeling of certainty that Ron probably was one of the people that had been shot.

Rilla's concern now was only for her daughter. Luella had left the house only a short time ago after fixing some sandwiches to take to her husband. She had stopped by the apartment of her best friend, Deena DeSarno, on the way. Deena had heard the news and called Rilla, and they agreed—hoping—that Lue had not had time to get from Deena's place to Shelter Road.

Lee said she had not heard any names on the police broadcast and hung up knowing her friend was in great pain. She knew that Rilla Smith loved her daughter, without question—perhaps too much.

More than a dozen cars from three police agencies—the Lewiston Police Department, the Nez Perce County

Sheriff's Office and the Idaho State Police—combed the area, particularly the more isolated roads, looking for the pickup truck that had been described. People driving gray or black Toyota trucks were pulled over, questioned and released. Across the river, officers from the Clarkston Police Department and the Asotin County Sheriff's Office joined the hunt.

Another telephone rang early that afternoon, in the administrative offices at Clarkston High School. Sixteen-year-old Josh Bingham was a student at the school, a bright kid with a good grade point average. The school officials were informed of the names of the victims, but a decision was made not to tell Josh anything. For the rest of the school day, Josh Bingham felt his teachers were looking at him sort of funny. "Tweaked me out," he recalled later.

3

The killer had watched with nervous interest as police vehicles sped past him, going the other way, as he drove back into Lewiston. As a former cop, he knew things involving a crime sometimes defied logic. This must be one of those times. Instead of being pulled over and arrested at gunpoint, he had been able to drive the big Toyota right back into the center of town, which meant he was about halfway to his destination.

East Main took a sharp bend to the right at Fifth Street and became U.S. Route 12, which he then followed around the rear of the historic district. A sharp left, a sharp right and he was crossing the blue-gray drawbridge. As the truck rumbled over the span that stretched across the Snake River, he could breathe a little bit easier. He was out of Idaho and into the city of Clarkston, county of Asotin, state of Washington. The killer had safely made it back to the town where he had been born forty-four years before, grew up and attended high school, and in doing so, had automatically complicated the jurisdictional problem for law enforcement officers by adding the element of extradition from one state to another.

He didn't care. His hometown contained an important degree of safety for him. At least people in Clarkston, particularly many of the police officers, knew him and wouldn't panic because of what had just happened over in Lewiston. Back there, around Shelter Road, the nervous cops might have shot him on sight. Here, he believed, the treatment would be better. He was right.

Route 12 was known as Bridge Street in Clarkston, and the killer stayed on it for only a block before veering left up the Diagonal. When he reached the traffic signal at the Stinker Station, an independent gasoline distributor with a big skunk on its sign, he turned left onto Fifth Street and could see the big spike of the police department's radio antenna poking at the blue sky a few blocks ahead on the wide boulevard.

Past the Chamber of Commerce, he pulled into a marked parking space at the curb of the eight hundred block of Fifth Street to catch his breath before doing anything more. To his right was a series of low brown buildings with brick trim that contained the municipal offices of Clarkston, Washington. The Fire Department was the first in line, then City Hall. At the end, bordered by a parking lot, was a building that had large white letters painted on the door to identify it as the headquarters of the Clarkston Police.

The killer parked in one of the yellow-painted spaces in front of City Hall, the guns still on the seat beside him, and waited with the motor running. The truck was the only vehicle at the curb.

Like the killer, Clarkston police officer Ron Roberts had lived his entire life in the area known as Pleasant Valley. On May 17, 1995, he had been a cop for about twenty-three years and for the last dozen or so had been a plainclothes detective. Although standing only five-foot-seven, he has the build of a little linebacker. He was in his office at the Clarkston Police Department when a call came over his radio at three minutes before noon. Something was going down across the Snake

River in Lewiston. A double shooting, and the suspect
fled driving a black pickup truck. In the fraternity of
police officers, such a call requires everyone with a
badge to respond, just in case another officer might be
running into trouble. And having extra pairs of eyes on
the street looking for the killer was a normal procedure.
Roberts gathered up some gear, including binoculars and
weapons, and headed out the door, toward his police
cruiser parked in the adjacent lot.

Ron Roberts scanned Fifth Street when he exited the
building, squinting against the bright midday sun and
feeling the push against his skin of the muggy temper-
ature. Down the street sat a black pickup truck, and
while Roberts turned north to go to his unmarked blue
patrol car, he looked back at the dark truck a couple of
times. When it began to move toward him, staying in
the parking lane, a hand emerged from the driver's side.
It waved at him. Roberts stopped in his tracks.

He walked toward the vehicle as it coasted to a halt
and the driver's door opened. A slender man in black
jeans and a black T-shirt, a well-built guy with a mop
of curly brown hair and an infectious grin, got out. Roberts recognized him right away. It was Ken Arrasmith.
Hell, they had gone to grade school together, and Clarkston High School, too. They had known each other for
more than thirty years.

"Hi, Ken," Ron Roberts said. "How you doing?"

"Not too well," the man replied. He held out his right
hand, gripping the single key to the Toyota ignition, and
handed it to Roberts.

The conclusion was inescapable, but Roberts couldn't
comprehend such a shocking thing all at once. His friend
was trembling and the look on his face indicated something dreadful had left him shaken. "My God, Ken . . ."
Roberts stumbled over his words. "You're not involved
with that thing over in Lewiston, are you?"

The man replied, "I'm having a very bad day and I'd love a cold beer."

Roberts raised his radio to his lips, advising the police dispatcher inside the building to alert the Lewiston authorities to send an investigator over. Then Roberts turned his grade school chum around, and on the public sidewalk, gave him a quick pat-down. When his hand hit a bulky object, he lifted the black shirt and found an empty shoulder holster. Roberts reached into the black nylon holster to be certain it was empty.

Officers began emerging from the building and Roberts directed them to watch the truck, and he escorted his friend inside the station to a private room, where they could await the detectives from Lewiston. Arrasmith made no attempt to flee.

In Lewiston, Paul Sharrai and Robert Warnock had been put into handcuffs almost immediately, although they had done nothing more than witness a horrendous crime and report what they had seen to police. In addition, shop owner Tony Adams was plucked from his motel room in Lewiston and cuffed when taken in for questioning. Law enforcement in Lewiston and Nez Perce County were playing hardball.

But in Clarkston, Ken Arrasmith had parked a truck filled with weaponry in front of the police department and had given himself up while cops in an adjoining community were asking for help in finding the multiple murder suspect. Arrasmith was handled gently when he was taken inside the police station. He wore a shoulder holster and a nylon belt pouch with clips of ammunition, but not steel handcuffs. After all, Ken Arrasmith was a hometown boy who had once been a deputy sheriff on this side of the Snake River, and was widely known in Clarkston and in Asotin County.

Sometimes, who you know can be very important in the way you are treated.

He wasn't even under arrest and had not been given any of the Constitutional Miranda warnings. Officers would later testify that if Arrasmith had simply got up and walked away, they did not know whether they would have stopped him.

They remained helpful. Arrasmith asked Roberts about the status of the victims, meaning he wanted to know how badly they were hurt. Roberts made a few calls and determined the two people who had been shot had not been transported to the hospital, although the coroner had not yet been summoned.

He hung up and Arrasmith asked what was happening.

You don't want to know, Roberts answered.

Arrasmith insisted, and Roberts, using police jargon, replied the victims had not been transported. "We know what that means," he said to Arrasmith, who nodded. It meant they were dead.

Back across the river in Lewiston, Detective Wade Ralston was approaching Twenty-first Street, taking Robert Warnock in for questioning, when the radio in his Bronco squawked. New information. Someone who may have been involved in the shootings had turned himself in at the Clarkston Police Station. Ralston called for his partner, Don Taylor, to join him, and notified the CPD to keep the suspect safe and isolated until they could get there.

Ralston put Warnock into the keeping of other officers, linked up with Taylor and sped across the bridge to Clarkston. Upon seeing the Toyota truck, the weapons and the suspect, they read Arrasmith his Miranda rights and received a written waiver of those guarantees.

Ralston telephoned Denise Rosen, discussed the guns found in the truck and how the man matching the description of the killer had surrendered wearing a holster. Rosen started the criminal complaint required to keep Arrasmith in custody.

In quick succession, the detective obtained a search warrant for the truck, Rosen charged Arrasmith with two counts of first degree murder and Judge Carl Kerrick granted the necessary warrant citing probable cause for the arrest of Ken Arrasmith.

"To any sheriff, constable, marshal or policeman of the State of Idaho or the County of Nez Perce, GREETINGS: A complaint on oath this day having been laid before me by Wade Ralston charging that the crimes of murder in the first degree, a felony, have been committed and accusing the above named defendant thereof, you are commanded forthwith to arrest the above named defendant in the daytime and bring said defendant before me in my office in Lewiston, or in absence or inability to act before the nearest and most successful judge."

The case entered the criminal justice system and was assigned the number CR-9501-258. The rapidity of the process was demonstrated by the clerks at first misspelling the defendant's name as Kenneth Arrowsmith instead of Arrasmith.

It mattered little. Arrasmith was finally behind bars. He wasn't going anywhere.

Outside the police station, crime scene tape had been draped around the parked Toyota. The officers peeking through the rolled-up windows could see a semiautomatic pistol and what looked like a stubby automatic weapon on the front seat. To avoid contaminating potential evidence, they simply sealed the truck off for the time being, rented slot Number 135 at the Clarkston Rent-a-Space personal storage complex on Thirteenth Street and had a tow truck haul the Toyota into a temporary garage. They closed and locked the door, marking the storage space as police property. Two days later, using the Ralston search warrant, they would go through its shocking contents.

*   *   *

Josh Bingham got out of Clarkston High School at the usual 3 P.M. and drove home, totally unaware that his world was about to spin off of its axis. He found his grandmother, Rilla, quaking with nervousness. She told him about the Shelter Road shooting spree, including the heartbreaking fact that two people were dead, but she didn't know who.

Josh was engulfed by anger and fear, feeling instantly that one of the dead probably was his father. He jumped back into his car and sped to the home of family friend Deena DeSarno. "I had to know what was going on," he said. Deena accompanied him to the crime scene in Lewiston.

There, police confirmed the two victims were his father and his mother. With that news, the dazed teenaged boy began a swift fade from hurtful reality.

Linda Bartlett had telephoned Lee Mersching again to see if more details had come over the police scanner. Lee told her about the decision not to send the victims to the hospital. Linda didn't say much more before hanging up.

A short time later, Linda learned that Ken Arrasmith had turned himself in to police in Clarkston. She then made a trip that she had been hoping to avoid. Her daughter Cynthia was in the juvenile detention center in Lewiston, having been put there at the insistence of Linda and Ken, and her mother now asked to see her, in order to break the news that her father had been arrested in connection with two fatal shootings.

Guards, however, said she could not visit Cynthia immediately because two police officers were already interviewing her. Eventually, when Linda was able to meet with the teenager, the girl, weeping, said she had already been told what had happened and at first had feared that it had been her mother and father who had been killed.

Police, during their interview, had told Cynthia that

information was wrong. The victims were Ron and
Luella Bingham.

Finally on stage were most of the major players in the
tangled drama that was about to unfold. Lives that in-
tertwined, conditions and circumstances that challenged
believability and a legal battle that would be watched by
the nation inched inexorably toward collision.

After doing the paperwork necessary to keep Ken Arrasmith in custody, Denise Rosen was able to leave her
office and go to the crime scene. She was driven there
by Wade Ralston and the two law enforcement officers
talked along the way about some of the names that
were popping up in the case. Names they knew. Drug
names.

Yellow crime scene tape was up by then, cordoning
off the area on Shelter Road. Rosen ducked beneath it
and walked toward the bodies, which lay under white
sheets. The scene was cluttered, but almost antiseptic by
murder standards. Two bodies under wraps and little
cardboard tripods set up to mark the numerous 9mm
brass bullet casings that lay in the sun.

Television usually portrays such murders as very
bloody affairs, but Rosen knew that television was not
always accurate. She would later find out just how true
that was. But for now, she examined the sprawled bodies
of Ron and Luella Bingham, walked the area and talked
to the cops. She had seen a number of other murders in
her career and was able to stay professionally involved
with the living and not get overwhelmed by the dead.
As she toured the premises, imprinting details in her
mind that she might use later, she was pleased that the
police already had found a solid suspect. Her thoughts
could move beyond a manhunt and focus upon what
kind of evidence would be needed for a conviction. She

wanted to get this case into a courtroom as fast as possible.

Two days later, on May 19, Ralston, Taylor and Roberts were together again to retrieve the Toyota truck from storage and inventory its contents. The Washington license plate turned up a surprise. The truck didn't belong to Arrasmith at all. It was the property of someone named Donnita Weddle of Sunnyside, Washington. A further check yielded the information that she was Arrasmith's ex-wife. They had recently separated, a legal move that eventually would have great consequences.

The officers gave a copy of the inventory list and the warrant to Arrasmith, who was in jail, and tucked another copy into the vehicle. In a search that lasted from 1:45 P.M. until 3:10 P.M., they had found five guns:

• an Intratec Miami 9mm Luger, model Tec-9, serial number 126354, on the passenger seat;

• a 9mm Ruger pistol with a laser sight attached beneath the barrel, beside the Tec-9 on the passenger seat;

• a large black SKS military-style rifle, loaded with a thirty-four round magazine, discovered in the oblong toolbox;

• a Smith & Wesson .357 Magnum revolver, loaded with six Federal bullets, in the "jockey box," the term used in Idaho for a vehicle's glove compartment;

• a .22 caliber Smith & Wesson model 622 pistol with wooden grips and a clip filled with ammunition, also in the jockey box.

Also pulled from the truck was a large amount of various sorts of ammunition, clips to hold the bullets and nylon pouches that held the loaded clips, a Sony mini-cassette tape recorder, a cellular telephone and some miscellaneous material.

For police, the discovery represented a gold mine of evidence. Weighing the case to date, they had two vic-

tims who had been identified, a man in custody who had
turned himself in, the truck that the suspect had been
driving, several eyewitnesses to the crime and a trove of
likely murder weapons with the same caliber of the bullets that the coroner had determined killed Ron and
Luella Bingham. Arrasmith had confessed to nothing,
but the circumstantial evidence was growing high.

From an outsider's viewpoint, things were coming
along very nicely in the police investigation. Any such
feeling soon would be dispelled, for complications were
already looming. This would not be a simple case. Not
at all.

> The fleeting smiles/
>   despairing eyes
> The broad shoulders that belie
>
> The weight and struggle
>   that carries on
> When will this war be won?
>
> Battle after battle
>   fought and lost
> So appalling has been the cost.
>
> Not solely monetarily is the price
>   of liberty and justice for me.
> And then . . .
>
> Add up the years for my family
>   and the cost for me, again.
> The many lessons my son won't know
>   instead bitterness & maturity he shows.
>
> What is the value of a childhood lost?
>   tell me, what would a replacement cost?

Mom, older, shrunken and worn
   her life too is shredded and torn.
When all I wanted was to ease her days
   strife she's known so many ways.

—*Luella Bingham*

4

The Lewis-Clark Valley is so deep in the American West that the sun rises each morning out of the mountains of Montana, and it is said around here that you are not really a native unless you can brag that your great-granddaddy drowned in the Snake River.

There is no doubt that the twin towns have a history, as evidenced by their very names: Lewiston, in northwestern Idaho, and Clarkston, just across the bridge in southeastern Washington. The municipalities are named for two of the greatest explorers in U.S. history, Meriwether Lewis and William Clark, who left giant footsteps in these parts when they trekked through almost two centuries ago.

In 1804 Europe was awash in culture. Beethoven was writing his Symphony No. 3 in E Flat Major and the Piano Sonata in F Major (*Appassionata*), two of his greatest works. The German astronomer William Bessel was calculating the orbit of Halley's comet and the artist Turner completed his watercolor of The Great Falls of Reichenbach, which would become famous as the site of the final clash between Sherlock Holmes and Professor Moriarty. Napoléon crowned himself, before the Pope, as emperor.

But the United States of America was still in its infancy and centered on the Atlantic Coast, although the Louisiana Purchase had added greatly to its territories in the south. There was more land in North America yet to be opened, and a curious President Thomas Jefferson ordered an expedition to the lands beyond the Mississippi River. The mission of the exploration was to discover exactly what lay in the northwest part of what is now the United States, strengthen American claims to the rich Oregon territory and gather information about the Indians of the Far West. To lead the dramatic exploration, Jefferson appointed his private secretary, Captain Meriwether Lewis, who then picked veteran soldier William Clark as his second in command.

In May of 1804, they departed from St. Louis, heading up the Missouri River, and by the time the snows of winter flew, they had reached the Mandan villages, a settlement of Native Americans near what is now Bismarck, North Dakota. It was fortunate that the inhabitants of that area were friendly, for it was there they met the remarkable Sacajawea, Bird Woman, who was to become as famous in the West as another Indian woman, Pocahontas, became in the East. Sacajawea was born into the Lemhi Shoshone tribe near what is now Salmon, Idaho, in about 1787, but while still a child, she was captured in a raid on her home camp near Three Forks, Montana, by Hidatsa Indians from the Dakota territories.

Her captors eventually traded her to the Mandans and she became first the property, then the wife, of a French trader, Toussaint Charbonneau, who won her in a gambling game. When Lewis and Clark hired Charbonneau as an interpreter, they got Sacajawea in the bargain, and their chances of success took a turn for the brighter. For as they tramped ever westward, going farther from settled America and steadily away from their support, they were walking into the home territory of Sacajawea, who toted her small child as she kept up with the rough-hewn men. Lewis and Clark hoped the presence of her and the infant would persuade other Indians of the peaceful intentions of the white men.

Sacajawea became more than an interpreter, for she knew the people of the mountain tribes. Indeed, her brother, Cameahwait, had become a chief of the Lemhi Shoshone, and welcomed his long-lost sister and her friends. He would provide the expedition with the horses needed to cross the Lolo Trail and guides familiar with the area.

On October 10, 1805, the expedition, following the westward-flowing Clearwater River, reached a pleasant valley and set up camp at the junction of the Clearwater and Snake rivers. Today, a plaque near the Interstate bridge on Route 12 across the Snake marks the place where they rested and built five canoes to continue their voyage. From here, they followed the Snake River to the Columbia and the completion of their westward exploration at the Pacific Ocean.

Sacajawea and Charbonneau continued with the expedition until it returned to the Mandan villages in 1806, and although she remained there, the incredible historical record of the eight-thousand-mile expedition, written by the voluable Clark, forever enshrined the Native American woman as a heroine. Although she was a Shoshone, the immediate area around the valley was primarily the home of the small, nomadic Nez Perce. Today, the headquarters of the Nez Perce Indian Nation is located in Lapwai, fourteen miles southeast of Lewiston.

The city of Lewiston was founded in 1861, a child of the gold rush along the Clearwater River, and steadily sank roots as a center for supplies and shipping for the miners. Two years later, it became the first capital of the Idaho Territory, and the first two sessions of the Territorial Legislature met in a building located at what is now Third and C streets. Relics of the first Idaho Supreme Court were to be found later in the otherwise

modern courtroom where Ken Arrasmith would be tried
for the murders of Ron and Luella Bingham.

With a population of 31,437, Lewiston is the county
seat of Nez Perce County, which has a population of
37,426.

Clarkston has always been the smaller cousin. It was
not incorporated until 1902 and today is a city of 7,120
people and part of Asotin County, which has a total population of 18,475. Separated from Seattle by three hundred and seven miles, Clarkston shares a much closer
identity with Idaho than it does with the rest of its home
state of Washington.

The four-sided governmental boundaries—two adjoining cities and two adjoining counties—would con-
tinually fuzz up the legal lines in the Arrasmith case, for
his trail, and that of his victims, constantly crossed back
and forth across the jurisdictions. It gave the case a legal
complexity that few other criminal matters in the region
ever had.

Lewiston never really lost its rough-and-tumble frontier heritage. In the early years of the century, it not only
had a reputation as a shipping center, but also a notorious name for gambling and prostitution. When one particularly popular prostitute died, her funeral was held at
night so community leaders attending the service would
not be seen. Some hid behind trees at the cemetery as
this queen of the red-light district was put to rest. For
years, members of polite society on a trip to Boise, some
two hundred and seventy miles away, would avoid telling people in the new capital that they were from Lewiston.

The area to this day is a shipping and industrial center
and a purveyor of fruit, food and livestock and timber,
pulp and paper. The same rivers that Lewis and Clark
found helpful in their quest are the lifeblood shipping
lanes for the deepwater inland port facilities of Lewiston
and Clarkston.

Today, the unemployment rate is less than 5 percent, and the Potlatch Corporation, a giant pulp, paper and chemical operation, is the single largest employer, with 2,300 workers. Its sprawling plant is on the east side of Lewiston, across the street from Shelter Road, at the top of which is the Lewis and Clark Animal Shelter. The valley remains a close, tight-knit little world. The YMCA teaches classes in both line dancing and divorce.

The low unemployment rate is deceptive, for there is not much real wealth in evidence in the valley, even among professionals. A nice three-bedroom house can still be bought for less than one hundred thousand. There is enough disparity in wages and earning power that an economic chasm has developed. Those with money and security now have to work not to see the underclass that has grown up around them in recent years. It is not unusual to find junked automobiles and stacks of broken furniture tossed into front yards of homes not far from the beautiful country club in Clarkston or the delightfully restored historic area of Lewiston. The day before he was shot to death, Ron Bingham was given a summons for having too much trash in a ditch outside his home. Any idea that strong zoning ordinances might curb such behavior perishes under an onslaught of arguments about governmental intrusion into the way a person chooses to live his life.

And that idea, as much as anything, is a clarion call in much of Idaho today. A 1992 confrontation on an Idaho mountaintop known as Ruby Ridge left three people dead—one federal agent and the wife and teenaged son of alleged extremist Randall Weaver. Former Special Forces commander James "Bo" Gritz is developing what he calls a "constitutional-covenant community" near the town of Kamiah. Mark Fuhrman, the disgraced Los Angeles police detective whose racist words helped acquit O. J. Simpson, found a safe haven in an Idaho town. The week before the trial of Ken Arrasmith began,

Time magazine's cover story was "Don't Tread on Me . . . An inside look at the West's growing rebellion."

People proudly carry guns here and those sporting caps bearing the emblems of the National Rifle Association or some militia group probably equal those with Seattle Seahawks logos. At the Christmas Bonanza gun show at the Nez Perce County Fairgrounds, a yellow handbill encouraged people to "Go solo and be a VIGILANTE." In large letters, it called, "KILL A CRIMINAL!" Below, in a small box, was a warning that the fledgling vigilante should check local laws first, because "Killing criminals may be illegal in your area."

That, ironically, would be the drumbeat of the Ken Arrasmith story. Although his defenders officially had to deny it every step of the way, the romantic idea of one man being forced to step up and deliver deadly justice because the cops had dropped the ball would be the centerpiece argument that would be carried on television sets throughout the nation. It would hurl the case into a new and unexplored dimension, inflaming passions on both sides and twisting the inadequacies of the media.

And entwined with the entire situation would be the issue of illegal drugs, primarily the cheaply made and fantastically profitable trade in methamphetamines, known on the street as crystal, crank, speed and meth. The drug can lift its users to a gauzy place where reality need not apply, all women are thin and beautiful, all men are strong and brave and handsome. The police who have to sweep up the human residue of these people are used to seeing reality turned on its head by drugged-out kids and adults. At first, the drugs involved in the Arrasmith case could not be seen. Only as the layers of the case were peeled away like the skin of a particularly sour onion would the full stench of drug involvement be revealed, and the odor would reach from dealers meeting at midnight to the sanctity of the courtroom.

Just as in the hazy world of the addict, much of what would be put forward as truth in the Arrasmith case would eventually prove to be an illusion.

5

Not everyone in Pleasant Valley dates his family roots back to Sacajawea or Lewis or Clark. The family of Luella Bingham provides a good example of how the unique little valley draws people and keeps them.

Rilla Smith, her mother, was born in 1925 in the town of Nampa, some 320 miles from Lewiston-Clarkston. Two years later, her own mother died of pneumonia ten days after her sister, Jo, was born. Their father left the little girls with his sister-in-law in Camas, Washington, for a few years while he sought work elsewhere, but soon reclaimed his children and took them on an emotional roller-coaster journey through several new marriages and constant moving while he secured seasonal work.

"He was a very young-looking man, nice-looking, tall and slender with a big chest and his hair stayed black until he was about seventy years old," Rilla remembered. "And he was a ladies' man. He thought he was God's gift to women." At the age of forty-seven, he wed a girl of eighteen, and they remained married until they died. When they argued, he would shout: "Well, I guess I better go find some red-hot Momma." Despite his wandering eye, he treated his daughters well, spoiling them rather than enduring conflicts between them and whichever woman he was living with at the time.

Rilla married for the first time herself in July of 1942, when she was only sixteen years old, choosing someone who had the same kind of cheap attitude toward women as did her father. Her sister, Jo, would recall that Rilla's new husband was the first man she had ever slapped, because he grabbed her in the kitchen while she was getting bread for a family dinner. World War II intervened in the marriage, and he was whisked away by the military service before they were divorced in the summer of 1946. Although she was only twenty-one herself, Rilla had three children by then: Loretta, born in March of 1943, Jim in November 1944, and John in September 1946.

Then some sunshine entered her life. When her husband had gone to war, Rilla remained in his hometown of Gooding, Idaho, and on a visit to see her father in nearby Fairfield, she met a gentlemanly, soft-spoken mechanic named Walter Smith. Rilla was smitten and, shortly after getting a divorce, she and Walter were married. But in the postwar years, while much of America was booming economically, the future of small farmers was written in red ink. Unfortunately, Walter Smith was among those who were hit the hardest.

Rilla's father had deeded them a small house that was not paid for, and they traded it for another small home they could own outright. Working as foreman on a three-thousand-acre wheat ranch, Walter was able to bring in a salary of one hundred dollars a month, good wages for a farmer. And his skills as a mechanic had been honed since he was fourteen years old, when he had reassembled a junked Model T Ford that had wood blocks inside the wheels. But the steady ranch work and the sporadic mechanic business were gaining them nothing. He didn't own the ranch, so there was no equity to build. There were no supplemental benefits, such as medical care. Their family was growing, with the birth of another daughter, June, in 1948, and of Luella in December of 1952. They named their newest child after her grandmothers—Lulu on Walt's side, and Ella Mae, on Rilla's. With new mouths to feed, money was tight, and when they reached two thousand dollars in debt, Walt and Rilla knew the time had come to seek employment elsewhere.

He had heard that an outfit called Potlatch, a big company in Lewiston, was hiring. He got a job there at $1.91 an hour, and the $5.00 a month premium for medical coverage was a major plus. Rilla took charge of the checkbook, saving $50.00 from each bimonthly paycheck for groceries and using the rest to pay off their debt. They found lodging in several cheap places around the scenic valley into which they had relocated, and where Rilla gave birth to their sixth and final child, Edna, in April of 1954.

Eventually, they discovered a small home on a steep hillside adjacent to the cemetery in Clarkston. A dairy was on one corner, another house was in the middle of the surrounding orchard, a few more were up on an adjacent hill, and cattle grazed in a field that covered more than a mile. The house was small, but Rilla Smith determined that it was going to be her final home. She was tired of moving, tired of the impermanence that had characterized her life since childhood.

In May of 1957, she and Walt and their brood moved into 1050 Vineland Drive.

Their nearest neighbor lived less than a quarter mile down the road. While the Smiths were relative newcomers to the valley, this family had already been there for several generations. The neighbors were a nice couple who had a large family of their own. The husband and wife were named Charles and Edna Arrasmith, and they quickly made friends with their new neighbors, visiting on some evenings to play cards and getting to know each other closely. Chuck Arrasmith would hire the Smith boys to help him load hay on his truck and haul it to town for sale. Walter painted Chuck's car. Their children played together.

The Arrasmiths had five daughters, and one son, a lanky kid named Ken. A childhood friend remembered him being sullen and quiet, preferring to stay around the house with his sisters to roughhousing with other boys his age.

If the Smiths and tens of thousands of other families just like them around the country were having a rough go of things, their plight was minimal in comparison to what was being endured by a small boy in an obscure village far away.

Ronald David Bingham was born in Bussey, Iowa, on May 16, 1948, to Harrison and Thelma Bingham. When he was born, his father was already sixty years old.

He grew up in a household of one sister and two brothers, and he was almost a male Cinderella minus the happy ending. Ron changed diapers, swept floors and did much of the housework. One of his few treats would come on weekends, when he would be allowed to go across the street to visit his grandmother's home, which was also the residence of his favorite aunt, a kindly woman who pampered him.

In 1956, just before the Smiths and Arrasmiths became neighbors in Idaho, Ron Bingham was only eight years old. His childhood world was about to fall apart and forever tarnish any trust he might have for women. It was a bright Sunday morning and he was told to get cleaned up and put on his best clothes. Why? he asked. A surprise, they said, over at Grandma's house. Little Ron got dressed and stood beside the front door. "Now," they said. "Go across the street and meet your mother."

From then on, things became confused far beyond the grasp of any eight-year-old. The kindly "aunt" whom he had loved to visit was really his mother. The "mother and father" with whom he had been living, and thought were his parents, were really his aunt and uncle. His "brothers and sister" were really his cousins. And to top it all, his real father was an elderly man who had also sired twenty-six other children!

"He talked about that a lot," one friend would say long after Bingham was murdered. "He was carrying a lot of pain." From the moment of introduction to his real mother, Ron Bingham locked his heart. He would no longer allow people to get close to him, and his definition of love and relationships with women would be twisted.

The next few years, the end of his childhood, left him feeling somewhat cheated by life, with an unclear view of whatever might lie ahead. Happiness gave way to mere survival. His sexually prolific, but coldly distant father died in 1958. When Ron was only fourteen, he decided to take control of his young life, and dropped out of Twin Cedars High School in Marion County, Iowa, during the ninth grade. At the age of fourteen, in 1962, Ron Bingham went to work in a coal mine.

In Idaho, Luella Smith was having fun. A significant age gap separated her from her four older siblings, and their squabbling kept her at a distance. Lue's best friend was her little sister, Edna, and her world was a place of wide spaces and loving parents. The two little girls loved horses and other animals and would jump broomstick ponies over small barricades they would build in the fields. They spent hours playing dolls, and the ever-curious Luella would almost always be able to persuade the pliable Edna to join whatever activity Lue wanted to do. Occasionally, Edna would dig in her heels and Lue learned that when that happened, it was best to give in. It didn't happen often, but when Edna got stubborn, she had a will of iron.

The worst thing to happen to her came about the same

time that Ron Bingham, far away, was starting to hack at a coal face deep underground in a dark Iowa mine. When she and Edna were in the early grades of grammar school, they played with each other to the exclusion of all other children until teachers decided to intervene and force the sisters to reach out and get along with other kids. The girls came home in tears. "They were both terribly upset. They couldn't see why their playing together was hurting anyone else," Rilla said.

The change was significant, particularly for the rather shy Luella, who almost refused to partake of the friendship of other children. She was interested only in people she already knew, such as her family and her immediate neighbors. Always shy, she used her self-imposed quiet time being creative, drawing pictures and writing poems.

One of the few persons she knew at school was Kenny Arrasmith, a childhood playmate who rode the school bus with her and was only twenty-three months older than she.

While the younger Smith and Arrasmith children were matriculating in their middle school years, Ron Bingham was in Iowa, plunging through life. On October 10, 1964, at the age of only sixteen, he married another teenager, Joyce Ann Meyers, in Lancaster, Missouri. Less than a year later, he left her to enlist in the U.S. Army, on August 8, 1965.

Before he began his military tour, he went to visit his mother, for what would be the last time. No one knows what was said, but it had to have been a traumatic meeting for them both. Although she was to live another ten years, Ron would never speak to her again.

The army needed men because it was getting deeply involved in the southeastern Asian country of Vietnam, so they took Bingham although he was small, too young and a school dropout, barely able to meet even the lowered minimum requirements. Like so many young men going into the military service, Ron Bingham finally found some structure for his chaotic life, and suddenly, opportunities seemed to come forward, things that promised a future that was brighter than the past.

Because of his age, the army did not send him straight to combat, but instead assigned the mechanically adept private to attend a technical school and learn a specialty. Bingham was sent overseas, ending up not in some obscure military training course, but finding himself enrolled in the prestigious Bosch Diesel Technical School in Stuttgart, Germany. Riding a new wave of confidence, he used his army time not only to learn about engines, but to nurture a natural inquisitiveness and finish his high school equivalency courses.

Then the army demanded its payback. When Bingham turned eighteen, he was deemed to be of a proper age to fight for his country. He was handed a gun and sent to Vietnam. There was no real need for diesel engine technicians in Vietnam, because if a truck motor went bad, the army simply dropped in a new replacement engine. The extensive German diesel training was shelved and Bingham was reclassified to be something much more valuable than a mechanic in time of war—an Eleven-Bravo, an infantryman, or, in the vernacular of Vietnam, a grunt.

His mulelike physical build earned him the dubious right of carrying a heavy M-60 machine gun as his outfit moved into the dense, dangerous jungles. Bingham emerged from the war as another of America's stressed veterans. A bronze star, purple heart and a coveted blue-and-silver Combat Infantryman's Badge came with the additional burden of flashbacks and dealing with death, and learning again that it was better not to get emotionally close to anyone. "He learned to survive over there, feeling he was alone even when he was on patrols, and it haunted him," a friend said. When he left Vietnam, he returned to Iowa more bitter than when he had left.

On August 2, 1968, Ron was arrested on a charge of negligent driving, which was dropped, and three days later, on August 5, he received an honorable discharge.

The year 1969 was rather hectic for Ken Arrasmith as he finished up at Clarkston High School. He had been somewhat of a loner at school, not joining clubs and avoiding extracurricular activities. He claimed one year on the wrestling team as a junior, although he was not in the team photograph of *The Bantam* yearbook, and he was in the Boys' League all three years, a nonselective organization that had as its membership every male student at Clarkston High. Friends said his after-school activities revolved more around a crowd that favored fast cars and heavy partying. Fighting and drinking played a large part in the lives of that group of teenaged boys.

His senior class photograph shows a handsome youngster with piercing eyes, neat in a coat and tie, casually leaning to the right. The motto beneath his picture was, "I won't be reconstructed." The yearbook listed the senior class legend as: "My sword is my strength, my spear is strong; I challenge falsehood, fear and wrong, but laughter is my shield."

He graduated in June 1969, and took a job driving a dump truck for the Asotin County Road Department.

Luella Smith was two years behind Arrasmith in school, but she was growing up fast. Once a teacher firmly instructed her to start smiling and say hello to other students, she made friends rapidly. When she was fourteen, she bought a bottle of bleach and changed the color of her hair from its natural chestnut brown into a shining, bright blond. Combined with her dancing blue eyes and developing figure, Lue was transformed into a strikingly pretty young woman.

Back in Iowa, Ron Bingham, unhappy with his wife

and his life, encountered a new misery with the unexpected death of one of the few men he ever counted as a good friend. Instead of being around forever, the friend contracted a fatal disease and died horribly, leaving a request that his pal, Ron, take him home for burial—back home to Idaho.

After the burial, Bingham hung around the western state, wondering where his own life was heading, and decided to spend the hot Memorial Day holiday at a lake with a few acquaintances.

While there, he spotted a willowy young blond girl and decided to take a chance. He walked over and talked with the pretty teenager.

At the end of May 1969, Luella Smith, who had never dated a boy, fell head-over-heels in love.

The summer between her sophomore and junior years started a new life for her. She was invited by her sister Loretta and her family to go to a lake near Coeur d'Alene to celebrate the Memorial Day holiday, and there she met her one and only love.

He was short, only five-foot-four, but she was two inches shorter than that. He was twenty-one, older than her friends and much more mature, a wounded veteran of Vietnam. He had a ready smile and dark brown eyes that matched thick, dark hair. Easily intimidated, Luella was a pushover for Ron Bingham's volatile personality. Her sister thought the guy was a bum, but Lue could not have disagreed more.

From that first day, Lue Smith and Ron Bingham never wanted to be apart. Within weeks, their future was set, but Ron first had to clean up a legal loose end, for he was still married to another woman.

On September 8, 1969, he filed a terse petition for divorce, stating his wife "constantly nags, hectors and criticizes" him, shows no love and affection, refuses to cooperate in family matters, is silent and moody and frequently said she no longer loved him. Joyce didn't bother to contest the matter and, since they had no children and no property to divide, Judge Paul Hyatt granted the decree. Ron was free to pursue Luella, and he did so with singular determination.

6

Ron Bingham was silly in love with Luella Smith. Rilla Smith saw the inevitable and would try to coax her daughter to finish school, or at least wait a year to see how the relationship with the dynamic little man would work. But Rilla's cautions would vanish when Luella was in the presence of Ron, who showered her with attention. Even when she would baby-sit for someone, Ron might sneak into the house and, while the children were occupied elsewhere in the house, he and Lue would make out in the kitchen or a spare bedroom. Eight months after Ron's divorce, when she was only seventeen, Luella dropped out of school and married Ron on May 23, 1970, at the United Methodist Church in Clarkston.

When Ken Arrasmith was in his senior year at Clarkston High, a pretty young junior shared his history class. Linda Joyce Ann Christianson, a quiet girl with chestnut hair, began dating him in high school and they continued to see each other after he graduated and began working for the county. With spending money and a streak of stubborn maturity and a reputation for a flaring temper, he was different than the boys still in high school. He was quite handsome, standing an inch under six feet tall, with auburn hair and piercing blue eyes. Linda graduated in June of 1970 and three months later, on September 26, in Coeur d'Alene, she married Kenneth Darrell Arrasmith.

After Christmas of 1970, Ron Bingham and his new bride moved back to Iowa and set up housekeeping as farmers near the little town of Algona, close to the Minnesota border. But their existence took on strange overtones. Ron's hatred of his mother and the other females in his family, whom he felt had deceived and disowned him, boiled over. It wasn't long before he began a series of sexual excesses, inside and outside the law, a pattern that would continue through the rest of his life and eventually be the announced reason for his murder. And he brought Luella along as a willing accomplice. Years later, Rilla Smith would tearfully admit that "Ron made Luella into another Ron." They became a pair of sexual vultures earning their wings on the plains of Kossuth County, Iowa.

In the early 1970s, Jim Smith had nothing but bad luck. One of Luella's older brothers, Jim had been discharged from the navy in January 1969 and went off to make his living in the civilian world. But a broken marriage had left him with three small children and an accident over the July 4 weekend of 1971 set up a further tragedy.

He was driving from Virginia back to Clarkston and decided to stop by Iowa to visit his sister and her new husband, who were also being visited by Rilla and Walter Smith. The pride of his life, his Corvette, began having brake trouble and after working on it at a service station, Jim tried pushing the car to make it start. The physical gymnastics to push the tightly designed car and then jump inside behind the steering wheel proved to be too much, and the Corvette ran over Jim's foot, mangling it. Eventually, fifty-two skin grafts would be needed to mend the damage.

That left him in a quandary. He was due to start work soon but was now saddled with three kids and a torn-up foot. He reached out to Ron and Lue for help. When Jim Smith finally was able to drive away, he left his kids in their care on the pleasant Iowa farm. After all, with their grandparents, Walter and Rilla around, what could happen? He left and eventually, Walter and Rilla also returned home. Ron and Lue were left alone with the children—three young daughters. One was pretty six-year-old Lora.

Ken Arrasmith was settling down in the Lewis-Clark Valley with his new wife. His job was fine, but he wanted more out of life than a weekly paycheck from a company owned by somebody else. Driving trucks, which he had been doing since he was a kid, seemed to offer the way out. In 1972 he teamed up with a friend, Steve Duffie, and took out a business license to start a partnership in a trucking firm they grandly named Northwest Enterprises, Inc.

That same year, in Iowa, Ron and Luella Bingham's sexual appetites took an ominous turn. Eventualy, three women would come forward and say that the couple raped them in 1972. The Binghams had moved off the farm in northern Iowa and rented a white house in the town of Mount Pleasant, in the southeast corner of the state, near the Illinois border. Lora Smith turned seven that year, going to school each day with her sisters and watched over by her friendly aunt and uncle.

When Lora turned nine years old in March of 1975, she suddenly became the sexual target of her surrogate parents. The child was plunged into a churning hell of depravity. Many years later, she would describe some of the horrors, which ranged from Luella inserting her fingers and tongue into Lora's vagina and Ron becoming infuriated when her little body could not accept his penis. At such times he would cover her face with a pillow or slap her on the belly, she claimed. Lora had to stand in a corner, naked, and watch the couple make love, stick her own hand into Luella's vagina and participate in deep tongue kissing. When she was older, Lora would write that the one thing she remembered most about being nine years old was wanting to die. That year, she lost her virginity to a toothbrush inserted by Luella. The pedophilia atrocity became an ongoing practice by the Binghams, and Lora would later tell a court officer that she didn't tell her father, Jim Smith, what was happening because "there was something inside me that told me not to tell them even though I wanted to." In addition, she didn't want her father to know that his sister and brother-in-law were assaulting her several times a week. The practice would continue for years.

In Idaho, the marriage of Ken and Linda Arrasmith was encountering some rough sailing, although they gave birth to their first child on May 30, 1975, naming her Jennifer Lynn. While continuing to earn money as a truck driver, Arrasmith also improved his professional career by moving from Asotin County's road department to the sheriff's office, where he was hired as a deputy. He was no longer an anonymous person. The badge and pistol made him a *somebody* around Clarkston. He was a law enforcement officer.

Despite the steady income and the new child, the marriage had frayed and Ken and Linda separated. Linda explained later that they "just kind of broke up" but didn't really stop seeing each other.

After more than three years in Iowa, Ron and Luella decided to come back to the friendly environs of Washington and Idaho. Mounting their motorcycle, they rode across the Midwest during the summer, expecting the weather to be warm, just as Iowa was always hot in the summertime. They did not count on the huge mountains that stood in their way, and as they drove across the peaks, the cold weather pelting the motorcyle almost froze them. Jim's children had gone on ahead to live with Jim and his new wife, Anne, but Ron and Lue weren't through with them.

A devastating emergency struck early that year. Walter Smith, a stalwart man who brooked no nonsense, had been bothered by a recurring sore on his lip. Three times, doctors removed the troublesome thing, but on the fourth visit, physicians determined that it was cancerous. Walter began undergoing cobalt treatments in Spokane, growing frustrated that the medical staff would not clear him to return to work. He sought another opinion, from his neighbor and old friend, Dr. Haas, who confirmed the diagnosis and told Walter his working days were over. Walter Smith was fifty-five years old, living with Rilla in the little house on Vineland, not knowing that great trouble, in the form of his daughter and her husband, was heading his way on a motorcycle.

Rilla did not know of the sexual assaults but was aware that Ron and Luella practiced an unusual lifestyle. During an Iowa visit, Lue told her that sometimes Ron would bring strange women home with him and make Luella sleep on the floor while he and his new partner had sex in the bed. "It was all absolutely with her consent," Rilla recalled. She knew her daughter was bisexual, but had no idea of the assaults on her grandchild, Lora.

The sexual practices of Lue and Ron went "totally against the grain" for the older woman, but, since they were both adults, Rilla felt helpless. "All I could say was 'I don't like what you are doing.' " There was an important emotional dynamic at work in this strange relationship. For Rilla to challenge Luella was to risk losing her, for there was no doubt whom Luella would choose if she was pushed to pick between Ron and anybody else in the world.

Ron and Lue, once settled back in Idaho, wasted no time in resuming their predatory activities. Lora, of course, was around and continued to be victimized, including having to pose nude for photographs. The Binghams also made overtures toward her older sister, posing her for pictures wearing little clothing, but did not sexually molest her to the same degree they did Lora.

Then, in a story that wouldn't become public knowledge for twenty years, one night the couple surprised Anne B. Smith—Jim's second wife and Lora's stepmother—in her bedroom. She would tell national television audiences that Ron put a gun to her head while Lue performed oral sex, then Lue held the pistol to Anne's temple while Ron raped her.

And on a Sunday in June, Lue telephoned seventeen-year-old Terry Baker of Wieppe, Idaho, a young friend they had recently met. Luella invited Terry out for a hamburger at the Arctic Circle on sixth and Bridge streets in Clarkston, then persuaded the teenager to go up to the Vineland house by the cemetery to take some food to Ron. Once there, "they proceeded to rape me," she eventually told lawyers. Terry told her mother about the assault, but agreed to keep the attack secret because her parents were longtime friends of Walter and Rilla Smith. Rilla actually was employed in the automobile shop owned by Terry's grandfather. Once more, the Binghams got away with raping an underage girl.

Ron Bingham discovered a new passion—airplanes—and in 1976 decided to take flying lessons. He and Luella moved for a while to Greeley, Colorado, so Ron could attend flight school, and he eventually won his pilot's certificate. Lue was very proud of her husband.

Nineteen years after they lived in Colorado, a woman wrote Ken Arrasmith after seeing the case reported on television. Lue and Ron, using a pistol, raped her in Colorado during January 1977, she said. "They deserve to be in hell," she added.

Still another incident shocked the family. Rilla Smith's sister, Jo, said a female relative who was having personal problems moved out to Colorado to spend some time with Luella. She came back for a visit accompanied by Lue and Ron, and when Jo started to arrange sleeping quarters for the night, the relative told her not to bother about it: "We all sleep together." Jo said she was "flabbergasted" by the idea of two women and one man sharing the same bed. "I just didn't understand it. From that day on, I never had any use for him."

In 1977 when they returned from Colorado to live in Idaho, Ron and Lue parked their pickup camper in the backyard of the Smith home high up on Vineland. Now that he could fly, Ron had a special present for his favorite niece, Lora, who was now twelve years old. He took her up for a ride around the empty Idaho skies and made the terrified child submit to sex while flying in the airplane. It wasn't much better on the ground, where Luella experimented with her by putting a bottle in Lora's vagina and, on another occasion, sharing her with a red-haired woman.

Ken Arrasmith and his estranged wife, Linda, had many long and thoughtful talks to examine their relationship, particularly about the baby. They decided to try again and on November 11, 1977, they were wed for a second time. Within six months they felt they were on firm enough ground to buy a house and borrowed $50,150 from the First Federal Savings Bank of Washington to purchase a duplex apartment on Crestview Drive, not far from his parents' home in Clarkston. It was an investment that would turn sour for everyone involved.

*   *   *

Ron Bingham began an odyssey of odd jobs around the area. He spent a year working for a cattle company on the Oregon border, then went to work for a dairy for a year and a half. Luella began working in the jewelry department at a Clarkston department store. Ron bore a distinctive trait, considering his upbringing and his bizarre sexual life. He was a provider, always with a job of some sort, always pulling his own weight, never content just to sit around with his feet on the table, watching television. By all accounts, he worked steadily, at one job or another, including some midseventies work in the construction trades. He didn't know anything about construction, but with his usual confidence and braggadocio, that mattered little. "Just tell them you do and they'll hire you." He laughed at conning his way onto a work site.

His own father died in 1978 and Ron Bingham could not have cared less. However, the beleaguered Walter Smith, already fighting cancer, had more tragedy befall him. He was rear-ended by a big truck, an accident that broke his neck.

The mishap changed the dynamics around the Smith household. Instead of being the strong man, the lawmaker, Walter sank into physical weakness, leaving the opening for Ron to exert more influence on the family.

An explosion, long overdue, came at the end of May 1978.

Anne Smith, having already been raped by the Binghams but having chosen to remain silent, listened in horror one afternoon when she questioned her eldest stepdaughter about why she no longer wanted to visit Ron and Luella. The child revealed the secrets of the abuse, and Anne hurried over to the school where Lora, now thirteen, was attending the sixth grade. According to court records, the two of them went over to Swallow's Park and had a long talk. Lora, crying, detailed what had been done to her for the past three years, a catalogue of sexual molestation that ranged from Luella holding her down while Ron raped her to an enema on Christmas day to the many nude photos. The latest attack, she said, had happened only recently.

What occured next was still being debated two decades later. Anne told Lora's father, Jim, about the accusations just as he was about to leave for work at Potlatch. "I said wait until I get home," he recalled. "I'll talk to my dad." But with her own experience with the Binghams still fresh in her mind, seeing the pistol at her temple as real as ever, Anne went directly to the police. She told them about the situation involving Lora, not herself.

The police needed more than a verbal claim, and a doctor confirmed the child had endured intercourse. They hurriedly obtained a warrant to search the trailer in which Ron and Luella Bingham lived in Clarkston. It would soon be clear that the warrant was not broad enough.

A team of police officers gathered near a trailer park at 1398 Bridge Street and swooped into the mobile home parked in space number eleven. One of the people inside was Luella Bingham and she immediately recognized one of the raiding cops. The blocky deputy sheriff was her childhood chum, Ken Arrasmith.

The cops had come looking for one thing and found something else entirely. On the inside, the mobile home looked like a farm, and the single crop was marijuana. Nineteen potted plants were found in the living room alone, growing beneath the light of a fluorescent lamp. A blue ceramic pipe containing marijuana seeds was found in a cabinet and a spice jar filled with dried marijuana was taken from a pantry. Unfortunately, the warrant didn't say a word about looking for drugs, so the plants were off-limits to the searchers.

But they did find twenty-nine Polaroid photographs of nude people in a kitchen drawer and a number of pornographic books and drawings. None of these discoveries were protected by the warrant either and police did not have legal cause to seize them.

The only pictures of Lora, however, showed her fully clothed. Nevertheless, Ron and Luella were arrested, based on the victim's testimony, and charged with second degree statutory rape. Walter and Rilla Smith posted one thousand dollars bond each for them.

Then Jim Smith made a critical decision. He was aware of the trauma of a rape trial on the victim and decided that he did not want his daughters to endure that, on top of everything they already had suffered. He sent the girls away to live with their mother in Washington.

Since the family was unwilling to proceed in the case, the matter was soon dismissed. It had not put Ron and Luella behind bars, but the situation had wrecked the family. "Me and him were bitter enemies after that," recalled Jim Smith, who also stopped having anything to do with his sister, Luella.

Lue lost her job as word about the sexual abuse charges spread. To avoid the verbal taunts and jeers from their neighbors, Ron and Lue moved their mobile home out of the trailer park and parked it in the large yard behind the Smith's home on Vineland.

As the decade closed, two significant things took place in the Bingham household. Ron brought home a couple of rabbits, thinking they were of the same sex, to be pets. And Luella gave birth to a son, Josh, in April. The doctor who delivered the boy handed the infant to Ron, who proudly held him for five full minutes before letting Luella, the mother, hold her son.

Ken Arrasmith's police career seemed to be improving. With several years of street experience, he went to Spokane in 1978 and qualified in the basic law enforcement course taught at the Spokane Police Academy. Unfortunately, it was an election year and Arrasmith backed the wrong candidate running for sheriff of Asotin County.

Herb Reeves was elected, and Arrasmith and a couple of other deputies were out of jobs. Reeves would never publicly say a word against Arrasmith, although other officers would hint that the two men had clashed strongly over a number of issues. One cop and a county civilian employee who worked with Arrasmith remembered him as a hot-tempered man who had a roving eye for women. When the case involving the shooting of Ron and Lue Bingham erupted, investigators discovered that all records concerning Arrasmith's career as an Asotin County law enforcement officer had mysteriously disappeared.

Luckily, the dismissed deputy wasn't without resources. The part-time businessman went back to driving trucks for Northwest Enterprises, Inc. In 1979 he and his partner, Steve Duffie, bought more equipment to build up the business, not knowing that hard times lay ahead.

And on the home front, Linda Arrasmith had a second child, another daughter. Cynthia Marie Arrasmith was born August 6, 1979.

Events went steadily downhill thereafter for Arrasmith. On May 20, 1980, he and Linda divorced again, for the second and final time. Then bankruptcy loomed like a dark cloud over his head.

7

By the dawn of the 1980s, the tide of time was pulling Ken Arrasmith into a collison orbit with the depraved world of Luella and Ron Bingham.

Arrasmith, with his final divorce from Linda, left his two daughters. Jennifer was ten days shy of her fifth birthday, and Cynthia was only nine and one-half months old. The separation agreement ordered him to pay $160 per child per month, or a total of $320 a month. The issue of child support would become huge in coming years as he fell far behind in the required payments.

In the good days, the trucking partnership had earned him some $2,500 a month, but Northwest Enterprises had floundered and was now being pursued by creditors, including the U.S. Internal Revenue Service for back taxes. The company lost all of its equipment, including several trucks and trailers. With the business down the tubes, Arrasmith declared that he was insolvent.

He drifted, unemployed for the first six months of the year, his only address a post office box at the corner of Pine and Bradley in Anatone, a small town in the very southeastern corner of Washington. Arrasmith owed money to a number of creditors. Waggoner's Carpet Barn wanted $1,000 and the Diamond Shop had a bill for $156. First Federal still demanded payments on the mortgage of the duplex at 2053–2055 Crestview Drive, with some $44,735 still due. His total assets were listed as a 1972 Chevy pickup truck, a 1973 Ford Torino, some $5,000 worth of mechanics' tools and some personal effects. The only job he managed to get was driving for Coca-Cola at $1,150 a month.

Ron and Luella Bingham, having barely dodged a trial for sexually abusing their nieces, seemingly withdrew from public view during the early eighties. He was able to find work around the area as a general contractor, including a job helping to build a dome for an athletic facility in nearby Moscow, Idaho, which required him to have special boots built, with sturdy heels that would gain him leverage while working high in the building's steel skeleton. He also became a long-haul trucker and thought nothing of loading his wife and child into the big cab and taking off across the country. Otherwise, he lived quietly with Lue and Josh in the trailer parked on the tilted landscape behind the Smith home in Clarkston. Ron spent time expanding the house itself, looking toward the day when he, Lue and Josh would move in. They planted a large garden plot that first summer and Ron, who had farmed in Iowa, grew vegetables.

The rabbits that he had brought home as pets turned out not to be the same sex, and cages of white New Zealands began to stack up. Ever industrious, Ron quickly turned it into a business, erecting a sign at the end of the driveway: RABBITS GALORE.

Soon, people would come from miles around, bringing cages filled with rabbits to the Smith-Bingham home, and in the early morning, about once a week, Ron would put them all on a truck and trailer rig and haul a bunch of bunnies over to Salem, Oregon, where they would be shipped to California.

Another person in the rabbit business was Gary Gunkel, the sheriff of Asotin County, who sold rabbits raised by his son. Bingham became a rather socially conscious individual about this time, served with a citizens' group called the Jail Advisory Committee, and encouraging his business acquaintance, Gunkel, to run for sheriff in 1982. When Gunkel became a candidate, Bingham contributed his time and talent, painting campaign signs. Gunkel won.

The Binghams were keeping a low profile, appearing to have mended their ways, but in reality they had not changed their sexual stripes. They circulated in clubs where partner swapping was a normal thing, the groups going off to cabins in the woods or renting houseboats for their boisterous parties. Another alleged victim would later go public and say that she was raped by Ron and Luella that year. She said the attack was reported to police, who did nothing.

The Binghams were on a steady course for disaster.

A year after divorcing Linda, Ken Arrasmith was in love again. This time it was dark-haired, twenty-eight-year-old Lynn Ann Byroads and they were married on June 20, 1981. It was instant family, for Lynn already had an eight-year-old son, Michael, who had been born in California.

Still, he was hounded by debt and his only jobs were driving trucks now and again for companies in the area, including Bennett Lumber, which paid nine dollars an hour, and Clearwater Beverage, which paid twenty cents a mile. In all of 1982, he made only $4,800, and his mountain of debts did not decrease. In 1984 Ken and Lynn gave birth to a son of their own, and named him Charles Kenneth Arrasmith, after both his father and grandfather.

On February 29, 1984, there was a party at the home of Walter Smith on Vineland Drive in Clarkston. He had been born in a leap year, and the family gathered to

honor his sixteenth birthday, although he was actually
sixty-four years old. Friends took them out for dinner;
ice cream and cake were served back at the house, and
Ron rented a videocamera to record the happy event. At
one point, Ron held the camera on a long banner hanging
in the living room, declaring someone was "Sweet 16."

A few months later, newspaper readers were treated
to an in-depth story on Ron and Luella, but it had nothing to do with their predatory attacks on women. Ron
Bingham had made a name for himself in a very peculiar
business, and on July 23, the *Lewiston Tribune* wrote at
length about his seven hundred rabbits.

"If we are ever going to feed the Third World coun-
tries, we will have to do it with rabbits," the reporter
quoted Luella, who added that the family ate rabbit meat
regularly. It made her hair and fingernails grow faster,
she said. Ron reeled off a barrage of bunny statistics—
that it costs 28 to 33 cents a pound to raise a rabbit to
market size, and it sells for 60 cents a pound, and one
female rabbit can breed four to eight times a year, yield-
ing 270 pounds of rabbit meat. A reader would have
been impressed. The article had a large photo of Ron, in
overalls, standing amid rows of wire cages holding rabbits. He was a short man, with thick hair and powerful
arms, muscles bulging at the short sleeves of his T-shirt.

In two months, their world would shatter.

Ron and Luella had been married for sixteen years
and their four-year-old son, Josh, had recently undergone
surgery to correct a serious eye problem, paid for by the
local Lion's Club. When the parents went out for an
evening, they would hire a baby-sitter to stay with the
child in the trailer.

Sixteen-year-old Tina Cole was one of the young girls
who periodically took the job, and she agreed to baby-
sit on the last weekend of September 1984. Luella
picked Tina up at her home about 10 P.M. on Friday,
and took her back to the trailer. Ron was not there, but

Lue left about 2:30 A.M. on Saturday morning and returned forty-five minutes later with her husband. They went directly to bed, and Tina spent the night on a folding couch in the living room.

She skipped breakfast on Saturday morning and went to a shopping center with her cousin, another one of the baby-sitters, and little Josh. Lue drove over to meet them when they were done and took Tina's hand as they returned to the car, telling the girl that she liked her very much.

Ron and Lue went out again Saturday night about 9:30 P.M., with the blond Lue wearing a baggy balloon shirt, without a bra. With the little boy tucked into bed, Tina fell asleep on the couch shortly before midnight. Ron and Lue returned home around 2 A.M., Sunday morning. Instead of going to bed this time, they changed into robes and returned to the living room to rape the baby-sitter.

Tina Cole awoke suddenly. Ron had her wrists twisted behind her back and Luella had pinned the teenager's feet, while she unbuttoned Tina's blouse and Levi's jeans. Both fondled her breasts and vagina, ignoring her pleas to stop, Ron asking if she or any of her friends would be willing to pose for nude photographs. As Lue adjusted the girl's legs and held her feet, Ron raped her. There was no need for her to scream, they said. No one would hear her.

When they were done, they left the violated teenager on the couch, shocked at what had happened, while they went into the bedroom. Tina would testify later that they "let go of me and . . . went into the bedroom like nothing had ever happened." Luella came back a few minutes later and dropped a ten dollar bill on the girl, saying it was payment for two nights of taking care of the child.

Tina asked Lue to take her home, but the tired Luella refused, so the teenager ran down the small, sloping driveway to Rilla's home and used the telephone there. Calling her mother, Tina asked her to come get her as soon as possible, but not to ask any questions. Just hurry.

Tina Cole eventually decided not to remain silent about the attack and took her story to the police, then passed a lie detector test. Ron and Luella were arrested, and charged with second degree rape.

There was birth and death in 1985. Ken and Lynn Arrasmith had a daughter, his third, and named her Rosemary Lynn. Walter Smith died in the fall and was buried in a grave close to his home. Luella was disconsolate, spending many hours walking down the hill to visit his final resting place and talking to her father's spirit. Always a voracious reader, she had recently begun writing more poems and wrote this one for Walter Smith:

> High up in the pine tree
> Wisdom blinks his eyes
> As dusk softly settles
> He takes to the skies.
> Falling, falling swiftly
> Death he seems to dare.
> The heartbeat of his wingstrokes
> Chop the evening air.
> Suddenly his body lifts
> And soars above my head.
> His haunting call to tell the world
> The owl has left his bed.

It took almost two years for the rape case to be finalized, during which time neither Ron nor Luella, their names blackened once again by rape accusations, could get a job. For the six months prior to his presentencing report in June 1986, the family was on welfare.

As is normal in rape cases, the victim also came in for closer examination. In her own deposition, Tina admitted that she had problems, suffered physical abuse, was a runaway, a school dropout and occasionally used drugs. She had been sexually active since losing her virginity to a stepcousin at sixteen, but said, "As long as you love the person, I don't see anything wrong with it." In the words of one official report, she was "a troubled young lady."

Bingham presented a different version of the event, claiming Tina enjoyed drugs and wanted to ride in his truck to her boyfriend's place in Port Orchard, Washington. Since his wife had already gone to bed, he made a pass.

"I said, well, my truck was no charity bus, that it was either ass, grass or pass and she replied that my wife was asleep and that it was cool with her. So I went to the bathroom and changed into my robe. Came back into the living room and she was naked under the sheet. She pulled the sheet back and we had hot and passionate voluntary intercourse." Later, he told the investigator, the girl told him "she had several married lovers with kids. That they were the best kind, they didn't talk to anybody about it, unlike single guys." He told the investigator that Cole would do or say whatever was necessary to have the police shift their attention from her and her drug habits.

When compared to the patterns reported of other assaults, it is clear now that it was Tina Cole, and not Ron Bingham, who was telling the truth. Indeed, her background made her exactly the sort of lost soul the Binghams sought out as victims.

There was one final wrinkle, and it would not be ironed out until later. About two dozen friends, relatives and neighbors wrote the court to say that Ron and Luella Bingham were "exceptional" parents and "honest and reliable friends." One of the people who signed as a reference was Gary Gunkel, the rabbit-raising sheriff.

Countering the tributes was a letter to the court from

the victim, Tina Cole, who sounded an alarm that would echo loudly in coming years, that the laws protect the guilty, not the innocent. "For the last two years of my life, I have not been the same. No counselors have been able to help because they have no idea of the pains I have been through," she wrote. "Please, your honor, do them justice."

Her mother was equally prescient, writing: "I feel the only way to stop Ron Bingham is to put him away for the longest possible time . . . He's a very sick man."

A plea bargain was struck, with Ron finally pleading guilty in exchange for Luella not having to do any jail time. Facing a maximum sentence of twenty years and a fine of twenty thousand dollars, he was sent to Washington's state penitentiary in Walla Walla on July 24, 1986, for twenty-seven months, and his wife, although not in prison, went slightly mad. He would serve eighteen months.

A few months after Ron Bingham went to jail, his name hit the newspapers again. His old colleague in the rabbit trade, Asotin County Sheriff Gary Gunkel, suspended Detective Tom White, a specialist in sexual abuse, on a charge of insubordination. Robert Cole, the father of Tina Cole, wrote a letter to County Prosecutor William Acey, alleging that Gunkel had pulled White and another detective off the Bingham case before the investigation was complete and had even telephoned Bingham himself to advise Ron to destroy evidence.

White and Gunkel had been feuding for months. In a letter of reprimand, the sheriff said that White's ongoing complaints about the sheriff's involvement in the Bingham case constituted "verbal abuse and harassment" that reached insubordination. Under fire politically just as the election neared, Gunkel took the extraordinary step of showing friends confidential records in the Bingham case and said his only contact with Bingham was through the rabbit venture and the painting of some campaign signs four years earlier. Interviewed in prison, Bingham was asked if Gunkel was a personal friend and answered, "Oh, Jesus, no." Bingham brushed aside the fact that Gunkel had been listed as a personal reference during the presentence investigation.

A special prosecutor determined that Gunkel had not had any criminal intentions when he intervened in the Bingham matter, but the prosecutor did say the sheriff had been negligent. Gunkel said he had telephoned during the rape investigation only because further allegations had arisen concerning the possible sexual abuse of Josh Bingham. No charges were filed in connection with that allegation, although a social services worker interviewed Josh. Gunkel told reporters at the time he believed the child abuse allegations should be completed before his department continued with the rape charges.

County Prosecutor John Lyden, with whom the sheriff was not speaking, had another view. Lyden said Gunkel's choice of intervening made him decide not to issue a search warrant of the Bingham property because the phone call ruined any chance of finding evidence there. That had caused the prosecutor's blood to boil, because he felt the Tina Cole case was weak and that it only held up after the earlier rape case involving Bingham's niece was uncovered. Workers in the sheriff's office said that after Gunkel was elected, Bingham often stopped by to visit and also occasionally assisted in an investigation. Gunkel claimed he didn't know that his office had a file on Ron Bingham that dated back six years.

Tom White was reinstated and would, in 1995, become an important investigator in the Ken Arrasmith murder case.

The mideighties also saw Ken Arrasmith continue his downhill slide.

In a forecast of things to come, his ex-wife, Linda, who was raising his first two children, filed legal action in 1986 to force him to come up with overdue child support payments. That was followed in 1987 by a more formal action. On a court form, under the question "Does anyone owe you any money," Linda wrote that Arrasmith was in debt to her for about $10,000. The original separation agreement ordered him to pay $160 per child per month, or a total of $320 a month. Under the revised plan, to catch up on past debt, he was ordered to start paying $206 per child per month for the next three years, and then increase the payment by $50 per child per month. He had not been paying the $320 a month, and now the payments had been raised to $412 per month and heading higher. Jennifer, now twelve, and eight-year-old Cynthia were living with their mother at 2012 Birch in Lewiston.

Linda wasn't the only one demanding that Ken meet his financial obligations. The Nez Perce County District Court granted a judgment for a host of other creditors that ranged from the electric company to the Carpet Barn, who had banded together in an effort to recoup their money from Arrasmith, who had already found relief once under the bankruptcy laws.

That same year, Arrasmith was arrested for drunk driving, to which he pled guilty, and his second marriage collapsed. Two days after Christmas, he moved out, leaving second wife Lynn to raise his second set of children, Charles, who was four, and Rosemary, only twenty-two months old, in addition to his stepson, Michael, who was now fifteen.

The divorce became final on June 28, 1988, seven years and eight days after he and Lynn were married. She was left destitute, and the case was accepted by the Washington State Support Registry for enforcement and collection of child support from Arrasmith for Charles and Rosemary. Arrasmith was hit this time for $100 per month each to support his son and youngest daughter for the next four years, an amount that would then increase by $50 a month until the children reached their eighteenth birthdays.

In child support costs alone, by the end of 1988, Ken Arrasmith was obligated to write checks amounting to $612 every month. With so much debt, it was not long before those checks did not get written, angering both ex-wives, who were saddled with all the responsibilities of raising his children.

In the divorce action, he listed his only assets as a 1971 Mercury Monterey and a 1964 Chevrolet pickup. The unemployed Lynn, who stated her occupation as student and homemaker, said she owned only household goods. They had $5,644 in miscellaneous debt and an outstanding balance on an educational loan of $1,850 for a relative of Lynn's.

Ironically, while he left Lynn and the kids at a home on 307 Highland Avenue in Clarkston, his address was shown as the duplex at 2055 Crestview Drive—the place that Ken had purchased with his first wife, Linda. The mortgage now stood at $44,735 with First Federal Savings and Loan, and after August 1988, he stopped making payments on it, too.

Luella Bingham and her son, Josh, were also on welfare at that time. "I thought she was going to lose her mind," Rilla Smith recalled. The thought of her husband being beyond her reach and out of her life was almost too much for her to bear. Every Saturday, she drove to Walla Walla to visit Ron. "When he was in prison, it cost me a lot of money," Rilla said, since she paid the gas and travel bills. Ron was aware that he was a financial burden to his mother-in-law and regularly sent her hugs and kisses via her daughter. "He told other inmates that I was the best mother-in-law ever," Rilla said. "Later, when he had been out a few years, he would walk by me like I wasn't even there."

Lue poured her anguish into her poetry, becoming

adept, particularly for a high school dropout, at grasping a flair with words. On February 25, 1987, she wrote an untitled piece that exhibited that she and Ron were not only totally bonded, but not the least bit chastened by their fate, which she termed ''a silent hell.'' In fact, they were defiant and totally unapologetic.

Into a woman I have grown
   And while my innocence has gone,
My worldliness is just a facade
   In truth I've been ravaged and betrayed.

I trusted them, the truth will out!
   And I now cry and scream and shout.
But privately, so no one knows
   The depth of my anguished woes.

But it could be worse
   At least I can shout my grief and curse
What of you? In a double cell
   One of bars, one a silent hell.

Our existence is a fragile thing
   With days just waiting for the phone to ring.
Then I'll live while we share our thoughts
   The moments fly, we say goodbye, I'm lost.

My world revolves around visiting day
   I struggle to you, come what may.
The joy though is bitter-sweet
   All too soon I must leave.

They think they've got the upper hand
   And while the situation is hard to stand.
There's naught that they can do
   To keep me from staying by you.

They want to strip you of it
  Your dignity, your self-respect, your wife and kid.
While subdued you may appear
  Beneath the surface your rage is near.

Ron Bingham was released from prison on January 10, 1988, after serving eighteen months of his sentence. The experience had only one true impact: It made him mad.

The same year that Bingham regained his freedom, some rays of sunlight entered the life of the debt-ridden Ken Arrasmith. He had deteriorated into a skinny man with a strange haircut with out-of-date sideburns, long and full. At a bar one night in 1988, he met a pretty woman with brown hair who saw something interesting and special in him, a project, perhaps. She decided to take him in and polish him up.

It became more than a project. It became a relationship as carved in stone as the peculiar, long-term marriage of Ron and Lue Bingham.

But scrub as she might, the newest woman in Ken Arrasmith's life had to recognize that he wore a heavy coating of debt, a bill that was mounting higher by the month. She had some property bought with money from a modest inheritance and marrying him could entail high financial risk.

They decided the way around that uncomfortable matter was a legal agreement that would spell out that what was hers remained hers, and what was his—including his overdue debts and child support—remained his. A prenuptial agreement was signed five days before Christmas of 1988, releasing them from any community property rules.

The next day, December 21, in Spokane, Ken Arrasmith spoke the marriage vows for the fourth time, making Lapwai School District fifth-grade teacher Donnita

Carol Weddle his third wife. He became her third husband. Between them, they had uttered the marriage vows seven times.

The wisdom of the prenup agreement became immediately apparent. Within months of the marriage, the first two wives were preparing another legal barrage for overdue child support. The IRS had one tax lien of $1,902 against Ken's old trucking business and another of $12,323 on the Crestview duplex, which still listed the name of his beleaguered first wife, Linda, on the mortgage. A court foreclosed in October 1989, and the sheriff sold it at auction for $58,731.53.

Other events were at work. Even while his ex-wives screamed for overdue child support and the government and other creditors howled for the money he owed, Ken Arrasmith walked straight into a pile of cash. Even while his personal financial figures were looking more dismal by the day, he and Donnita started buying property in the area, making sure to file the legal documents that would transfer everything into her name. One such purchase was the Passtime Bar in nearby Genessee, just north of Lewiston in Idaho's Latah County. One of the sellers said the paperwork was in Donnita's name, but that they had made the deal with Ken. A little while later, the three of them would have an even more interesting conversation.

While the law had thrown a net, at least for a while, over Ron Bingham, it had raised an umbrella of protection over Ken Arrasmith.

8

Lynn, Arrasmith's second wife, began to steam when she learned that her ex-husband, freshly divorced, was accumulating money but was stubbornly refusing to pay the support he owed her and their two children. The kids were on state Medicaid and she was barely getting by. Lynn had a part-time job paying just above minimum wage that produced $185 a month, which was buffered by another $589 a month from AFDC (Aid for Families with Dependent Children) and $150 per month in food stamps. In child care alone, she paid $1,200 a year.

Legal documents showed that by March of 1990, Arrasmith had paid $5,148 and owed her $6,848. The papers listed him as driving a truck for the Coca-Cola Bottling Company in Lewiston, where he earned $10.50 per hour.

But it wasn't the job with Coca-Cola that irked Lynn. It was that while falling behind in paying the court-ordered child support, he and his new wife—Donnita—were buying property. She wondered why, if he could afford land and buildings, he couldn't pay what he owed his children? Her complaint surfaced in a handwritten note of exasperation to the court: "He and his wife own a bar in Genessee, Passtime Bar and Grill. He has transferred everything into his wife's name."

The judge ordered Arrasmith to begin paying Lynn and her kids—Charles and Rosemary—$412 a month. In addition, the amount of back child support he owed Linda and her kids—Jennifer and Cynthia—was steadily growing past the $20,000 mark, with Arrasmith making only sporadic payments.

The sale of the bar itself became an issue in the volatile subject of support and the equally controversial matter of Ken Arrasmith's temper.

The previous owners, Meradell Geltz and her husband, Terry, complained one day to Ken about how much child support Terry Geltz had to pay from a previous marriage. "Kenneth Arrasmith (said) . . . that he did not pay child support because all of the assets were in his wife, Donnita's, name," Meradell said in an affidavit. She claimed that Arrasmith offered to advise them on how to get property out of Terry's name and into Meradell's. When Arrasmith learned of the affidavit, he heatedly denied the charge, claiming the discussion was merely a chat about the general wisdom of filing a prenuptial agreement so that a party with assets would not be financially ruined by a spouse with no assets.

On the witness stand during the penalty phase of his trial, Arrasmith saw an old acquaintance from the days when he owned and ran the Passtime. Randy Hall was the mayor of Genessee at the time and one of his civic responsibilities was putting out a newsletter about what was happening around town.

Arrasmith wanted an article published about his bar, stormed into City Hall and yelled at a clerk, who called Mayor Hall. Arrasmith took the telephone and began shouting at Hall, who agreed to meet him the next day and discuss the matter further. In their face-to-face meeting, when Hall found Arrasmith was still furious, he agreed to put in the demanded mention of the bar, but still Arrasmith wasn't placated. In fact, he became abusive and when Hall placed a hand on his shoulder to steady him, Arrasmith shook it away and warned Hall that if he touched him again, "I'll kill you." Thereafter, when they met on the street, Arrasmith would taunt and shout at the mayor.

Ken Arrasmith was achieving major league standing as a deadbeat dad, and that failure to meet his debts may have played a role in the growing unstable behavior of his daughter, Cynthia. She had begun to run away from home, and her battles with her mother were escalating. The youngster's name started to appear on police reports.

While Arrasmith owed thousands of dollars to his four children, he insisted that he had no assets, that everything belonged to Donnita. They continued a property buying spree in several states and put everything they bought—including trucks for him—in her name for a minimal ten dollar fee to transfer title.

The irony of a woman who taught grade school owning a huge 1988 Kenworth long-haul rig while her debt-ridden, truck-driving husband pretended to be indigent was hard for both of his ex-wives to bear. Another irony was that a schoolteacher and a part-time truck driver could scrape together enough money to buy so much property, apparently able to get numerous mortgage loans with ease, including one of almost $195,000.

When the matter was discussed in court in 1995, it was estimated that Donnita had about $200,000 in assets when she married Ken.

Her first marriage had been to Cecil W. Weddle, who was arrested in July 1991, on a charge of manufacturing the illegal drug methamphetamine, and sentenced to prison. A pound of meth was seized during the raid in which Weddle was caught, and police said it could eventually have reached a street value of well in excess of $100,000. There was no indication that Donnita ever profited from such transactions that may have involved her first husband.

Her second husband was a school principal. She did not have a college degree when they married, and although he was not a wealthy man, he put her through school to obtain her teaching credentials.

Like her newest husband, Ken, Donnita also had a reputation for angry scenes. One acquaintance recalled that Donnita "pitched a fit" in class when she did not receive an A on an exam.

A particularly tragic incident involving drugs and this story took place on Monday, October 25, 1994, when Charlene Kay Arrasmith White, aged forty, was found dead in her Seattle home. She was one of Ken Arrasmith's sisters.

The death certificate filed in the state of Washington's Department of Health listed the official cause of death as "acute intoxication" resulting from the "combined effects of cocaine, opiate & ethanol." In layman's language, she overdosed on drugs. Authorities concluded it was probably an accident.

Ron Bingham came out of prison a bitter man with few prospects, and things only got worse when he couldn't find work. No matter what his other faults, Bingham had always had a job and now he and his family were forced to live on welfare. His temper, always close to the surface, developed an extremely short fuse.

He decided that because no one else would hire him, he would start his own business in Walter Smith's old repair shed. The army had trained him to be a diesel engine mechanic and that might be his ticket to economic freedom. He was determined to be a success despite what he felt was an outright war against him by the legal system.

By fixing up the shop and working long hours, the little business began doing fairly well, as word spread

among the car crowd that Bingham had real talent as a
diesel mechanic, but he was limited by a lack of equipment to repair and tune the delicate diesels.

As an ex-felon with a particularly nasty crime on his
record, Bingham was not even remotely the sort of person to whom a reputable lending institution would grant
a loan. But help was closer at hand than a bank.

After Walter Smith died and Ron went to prison, Lue
had moved back into the house with her small son, Josh,
and her widowed mother, Rilla. When Ron was released,
he moved in, too, becoming the head of the household.
It was Rilla to whom he turned for financial help. She
neither liked nor trusted Ron but felt she had no alternative but to help. "I felt trapped," she would say a few
years later. "I was afraid of the horror of being old and
alone, and Lue was here. I wanted Lue and she wanted
Ron." To keep her daughter close, Rilla agreed to help.

First came an avalanche of credit cards. Neither Ron
nor Lue could get them, but Rilla, who had always
feared debt, was an excellent credit risk, particularly
with a paid-off home that could be used as collateral.
She didn't even have a credit card of her own at the
time. With her making the applications, Visa, Master-
Card and Discovery cards began arriving, bearing the
names of Lue and Ron.

A spending spree followed. After experiencing self-
denial in their finances for so long, the Binghams soon
maxed out the cards and little of it went toward the business, as Rilla had been promised. Instead, Lue was sporting fancy new clothes and jewelry, while Ron lugged
home expensive electronic equipment, such as a laser-
disc stereo system.

The new source of plastic money also enabled Ron
and Lue to step up their lifestyle as sexual swingers.
Their friends would drop by from out of town and everyone would take off for a houseboat romp on a lake in
British Columbia, or a weekend at some ski chalet. In

addition to the mechanical equipment for the shop and
the clothes for Lue and stereo for Ron, the Binghams
made massive purchases of pornography and stored it in
the dozen drawers beneath their water bed. A suitcase
was filled with sex toys, such as dildos, and porno films.

The entire tenor of life changed around the little house
above the cemetery on Vineland Drive in Clarkston. Instead of a drab abode occupied by worried people, it
became a party place. Rilla, said her sister, acted like an
ostrich about the changes, just keeping her head in the
sand, refusing to recognize what was really happening
for fear of losing her Lue.

Not only swingers came by to visit, but teenagers also
frequented the place. They were allowed to crash for a
time in a 1953 GMC bus, a big blue hulk, that Ron had
purchased with the idea of converting it into an RV in
which he and Lue could tour the country. The seats were
removed and it evolved into a makeshift motel, with
young people hanging their clothes on the overhead
handrails and sleeping on a queen-sized mattress stuffed
into the back. Bare bulbs hung overhead on a wire.

Bingham, the kids thought, was a pretty cool guy. He
was short, but powerful. He had access to money, he
could fix any car that rolled and he knew where to get
drugs. The biggest downside was that he yelled a lot in
a voice that should have belonged to a bigger man.

"You couldn't let that bother you, or you'd cry all
the time," said Rilla. "But when it was over, it was
over. Once he said something to me that bothered me
for a month, but when I sat down and told him I couldn't
bear it, he laughed and hugged me, and just said, 'Oh,
Mom.' "

But the young men seemed to sink or swim with his
bizarre behavior. Ron would size someone up instantly
and there was no middle ground: You were a friend or
an enemy. Those who could get past the verbal abuse
looked up to him as a leader and a friend. The others

left. "Several of them thought he was the bee's knees, because he cared," said Rilla. "They were mostly into drugs and drinking, and he'd give them some orders. If they didn't follow his instructions . . . he'd yell at them for fifteen minutes."

As time went on, however, the kids also found that Ron was a pushover. Once past the screaming, he could be manipulated. Josh Bingham, his son, recalled later that both boys and girls came to visit, many of them just to "use his drugs, eat his food, get a bed and not want to earn it." Eventually, Ron would kick them out, always in a brutal, loud scene.

Ron Bingham was convinced, after a couple of incidents, that he was a pariah as far as the law was concerned. Rilla Smith said that Detective Tom White, who investigated the rape case, "hated him with a passion."

But the first demonstration of how far beyond help he had gone came in a routine business disagreement. He contracted to put a used engine in a truck, only to find that the engine was faulty, and he demanded a new one, which he then installed. The woman customer stormed at him for not putting in the original engine, grudgingly wrote him a check for five hundred dollars, then immediately stopped payment. Ron naively tried to bring a civil case against her, only to have it thrown out, according to Rilla, "just because he was Ron."

The second incident was much more serious. A huge Lewiston man who reportedly ran with biker gangs had a Queensland blue heeler dog named Teddy, and the dog had bitten a few people. Nez Perce County animal authorities threatened to put the animal to sleep, so the man gave Teddy to Ron. Later, at the Bingham house, Ron was severely beaten by the man, who was about twice his size. Three ribs were broken and muscles torn in his back when he was thrown against the blue bus. The matter went to court, and again the legal ruling went against

Ron. According to Rilla, the judge said the assault was justified because the Lewiston man wanted his dog back.

After that, she said, Ron Bingham, who once had been friends with a sheriff, had no use at all for law enforcement. "He decided, 'To hell with them,'" recalled Rilla.

In 1993 the small-boned Lue discovered that her hard work around the shop had worn out a joint in her hand. Doctors operated and fused the bones together, but after that Lue was hardly able to hold a pencil with her right hand and lost almost all use of her right thumb.

That meant that not only did Ron need the help of other mechanics, help that he found among the transient young men who would pass through the house, but he needed assistance on the paperwork side of the business, too. Sharing the cost with a job training program, he and Lue hired a willowy woman with long brown hair as their bookkeeper, and Deena DeSarno soon became their closest friend.

With their sexual appetites, it was only a matter of time before Lue offered to let Deena join their swingers' club. She declined, saying she valued their friendship, and was never pressed again although she was in contact with them almost daily. Other young women would also say they frequented the Bingham home without experiencing even so much as flirting by Ron or Lue. The friendship between Deena, Lue and Ron differed from the casual acquaintances who popped in and out of the house and shop. It bloomed, and when she needed a car, Ron helped her get an orange Nova. Her first comment was, "Ron, it looks like a pumpkin!"

"Well, who drives a pumpkin?" he joked. "If you're Cinderella, I must be your hairy godfather." After that, he was the "hairy godfather" and she was "Sinderella," with an *S*.

Deena found the shop was in financial shambles.

"Just when they were about to make things work, they'd get a nine hundred dollars check that bounced," she recalled. The fees charged by banks for processing the worthless checks at one point reached two hundred dollars. "The harder they worked, the more things would go bad. People weren't paying."

It was time for more money, and once again he tried the legitimate sources first, was rejected, then turned to Rilla. They made a deal in which she borrowed money on her house and gave thirty-one thousand dollars in cash to Lue and Ron. In exchange, Ron promised to make the mortgage payments and also carry a fifty thousand dollars life insurance policy on himself.

The deal was doomed from the start. Eventually, Ron stopped making the house payments and after Rilla made a few, the money was gone. Both filed bankruptcy, to the tune of twenty-five thousand dollars apiece. The deed on the house that Rilla had owned with her husband, Walter, and that had been completely paid for, was now sitting in the vault of a bank.

The bottom had fallen out for all of them. The business was floundering and the one legitimate available source of money—Rilla—was tapped out.

There was, however, another guaranteed way to make money and Ron was presented with an opportunity to establish himself in the illegal drug trade. He had dabbled in such deals for years, but now one of the boys who occasionally hung out at the shop decided to leave town. He was a dealer, and almost as if passing off a franchise opportunity, he sold his business to Ron Bingham.

Bingham was ready for the change. Drug dealers had regularly brought their cars to Ron, paying him to build them high-performance engines so they could outrun police, and he saw how much money flowed in the drug pipeline. According to his son, "He decided to get into it himself."

Certainly, he had the physical strength and courage to handle the dirty end of the business. Although he was a felon, Ron had guns, but they were registered to, and normally carried by, his wife or one of their friends so he could not be arrested on a weapons charge. His weapon of choice was a sawed-off baseball bat that he kept handy, an item that he called "the knee-breaker," laughing that he might be short, but if he whacked someone with the bat, "the biggest man will fall." A witness saw him do just that in a racetrack argument in August 1994, when he laid low a couple of punks who threatened him.

In November of 1994, Bingham stopped being merely a user of illegal drugs and became a drug dealer. His confrontative personality, his disdain for the law and his need to make a living suddenly combined into something that he was good at doing. Rilla recalled: "Before long, they were not doing anything in the shop. Traffic started about five P.M., people coming and going, and the phone rang until two in the morning."

Money started rolling in as Bingham tended his illegal business, eventually ranking among the top drug dealers in the Lewis-Clark Valley.

Rilla was only vaguely aware of what was happening, again deciding to keep her nose out of the business of Ron and Lue. She had to acknowledge the drugs finally the day her daughter telephoned in a panic and told her to look in a certain place and remove any money that was there. "I found rolls of money," she said later, "rolls the size of your fist. I knew something was going on." Actually, quite a lot was going on, and she had no idea how much. All Rilla Smith knew, as 1995 came in, was that her peaceful life had been replaced by a tenuous existence on the edge of a rowdy world in which money, sex and drugs had forever stained the little place that had been home to herself and Walter. And she knew the bills were not getting paid.

*   *   *

Ken Arrasmith also entered 1995 trying to keep trouble at an arm's length. Linda, his first wife, was after him again and this time the child support bill was truly horrendous. Without counting the amount still overdue to second wife, Lynn, and their kids, the court papers would soon show the deadbeat dad was $30,686 in arrears to Linda, and that was after his oldest daughter, Jennifer, had turned eighteen and he was no longer obliged to support her.

Arrasmith and Donnita at that point made a move that would have tremendous importance in the future. They still lived together in the town of Sunnyside, Washington, and intended to continue to do so, although he had another official address, too, at one of their many properties. Just as they had signed a prenuptial agreement before they were married, in December 1994, they now filed a petition for dissolution of their marriage, along with an agreement releasing her from community property rules. The shrewd legal maneuver, which would take several months to become official, put Ken Arrasmith even more distant, on paper, from the fortune the two of them had accumulated. No matter what happened to him in the future, the money would be secure in her name, which she changed back to Donnita Weddle, choosing to keep the name of her first husband, who had been imprisoned for drug use, and not the name of her second husband. Months after Ken Arrasmith was jailed for murder, Donnita's telephone answering machine would continue to say the caller had reached the "Weddle-Arrasmith residence."

Her holdings were substantial, according to court documents. In Nez Perce County, Idaho, alone, Donnita Weddle had property with an assessed value of $628,189. In the agreement, she would claim a living trust whose assets included thirteen pieces of real estate in Washington and Idaho, various bank accounts, retirement accounts, life insurance policies, furniture ranging from a computer to a water bed and two television sets, and three vehicles, one of them the big Kenworth truck. Later she would huff that the published accounts of her holdings did not include her properties in Arizona. The same agreement said that Ken Arrasmith owned two dressers, one television set, one microwave, one bed, dishes, towels, clothes, four sleeping bags and some personal items. She had thousands of dollars in liabilities, mostly in loans and mortgages. He listed his only liability as "alleged child support."

For more than two years, he had kept a steady job, driving a truck for Sartin Construction and Trucking in Sunnyside, Washington, but according to his legal deposition, he hardly had two cents to rub together and apparently lived out of a sleeping bag. Certainly someone that destitute could not be expected to make child support payments.

In late 1994, Arrasmith was driving a rig back from California for the Sartin Company, which had a leasing arrangement with Donnita for the Kenworth truck. According to police sources, the home office began receiving strange, "paranoid" telephone calls along the route. Arrasmith would say that he was being followed and that he had twice abandoned the truck to hide beside the road.

Finally, when he was only about one hundred miles from Sunnyside, he said he could drive no farther. The office, worried about potential insurance problems, instructed him to stop and get a room. Two men from the company went out, recovered both truck and driver and drove the rig back to their base. Arrasmith was described as being in total control of himself at the time, and passed a drug test administered immediately afterward, one of three such random tests he passed during the two and one-half years he was associated with Sartin.

His reputation for being a hothead was demonstrated

the same year when, after a minor automobile mishap, Arrasmith exploded in profanity in a car shop that was to repair what was little more than a paint chip on a bumper. Someone who witnessed the incident said Donnita was present and frustrated at Ken's temperamental display. ''She said that if people stood up to people like him, we wouldn't have as much trouble with kids today,'' the witness said.

In January 1994 a valley resident named Wes Rehm purchased an interesting weapon from an Oregon gun dealer. The stubby gun was an Intertec-9 semiautomatic, known as a Tec-9, that he kept in a plastic case. But the gun was soon stolen from his collection and the following month was purchased from someone else by a large young man who ran an automobile repair shop in Clarkston, Kyle Richardson.

Ken Arrasmith had met Kyle during the summer of 1994 while visiting the home of his second ex-wife, Lynn, where Kyle was living at the time. They became well acquainted and eventually agreed to a joint business venture. Lynn drew up a paper, dated February 20, confirming that Arrasmith loaned Richardson ten thousand dollars in cash, and noting that the funds were definitely not to be used for any illegal activity. Richardson would later testify that wasn't quite the truth. In fact, Kyle said, Arrasmith loaned him the money to buy drugs, and that Kyle was supposed to repay eighteen thousand dollars within thirty days. The note, he said, was simply an attempt to make the deal appear legal.

When time came for the loan to be repaid, Kyle had spent much of the money. Arrasmith laid claim to the collateral that Kyle had posted for the deal, much of the equipment in his automobile shop. And the well-traveled Tec-9.

*   *   *

Such was the background of Ron and Lue Bingham and the peculiar Weddle-Arrasmith relationship on February 24, 1995, one of the most important dates of the entire saga, for that was when fifteen-year-old Cynthia Arrasmith turned up on the doorstep of the Bingham home, to stay for a while.

9

As the primary events in this story unfolded, during the early months of 1995, Cynthia Arrasmith was still a juvenile, and as such, all records pertaining to her have been sealed by the courts. The author made no attempt to penetrate the wall of secrecy that protects juveniles, but the overall story relies so heavily on her actions and choices that some examination of her movements during the period in question is necessary, if the entire event is to be understood. Therefore, much of the information contained herein came from Cynthia herself and Arrasmith family members, in their comments on the witness stand, on numerous television shows, in print media interviews and communication with the author. Other information was available from people who were with her at certain important times, and many actions were observed and reported by witnesses in the double-murder trial of her father. The descriptions of Cynthia and her actions in this book have been limited to such sources.

February

Fifteen-year-old Cynthia Arrasmith and her boyfriend of the past year, Ken Rathbone, were at Mr. John's, an automobile sales lot in Clarkston, in late February 1995, looking for a car. He was tall, with shoulder-length, curly dark hair that needed to be washed, and she was also dirty, with dark bags under her eyes. They looked like a couple of street people. She had moved out of the home of her mother and stepfather, six months before, and had been living with her boyfriend at his father's place since then.

Ron Bingham, accompanied by his son, Josh, also drove up to see what might be for sale that day at Mr. John's, and Ron recognized the young man with the girl, who appeared much younger than the boyfriend. Ron knew Ken Rathbone's father through a mutual friend.

As was his practice, Ron was always on the lookout for men to help around the workshop as cheap labor, and the fact that a pretty young girl might come along interested him even more. The couple told Bingham they were looking for a place to stay, and he quickly offered the usual spread of shelter, food and money in exchange for Ken Rathbone's work as a mechanic. His young girlfriend could do chores around the house, such as laundry and sweeping. Rathbone and Cynthia Arrasmith moved into the old white trailer, which had once been the home of Ron and Lue, that was behind the Bingham house.

To Cynthia's delight, the nearest house down the hill was the home of her grandparents, her father's mother and father, Chuck and Evelyn Arrasmith. Friends told her mother, Linda, where Cynthia was and said she would be safe there. Linda was relieved, knowing her daughter was not out on the street and that her grandparents were nearby. She said that drugs had been used at Cynthia's previous residence. Linda said she frequently telephoned Cynthia, visited the Bingham home and had coffee with Lue and occasionally took Cynthia out to lunch or dinner.

Cynthia was also apparently pleased to find that she

was among people with whom she felt comfortable.
Josh Bingham, who lived in the house with his parents,
was her own age, although he still went to school,
while she was a dropout. She considered him unsophis-
ticated in the ways of the world. Rilla Smith was a
grandmotherly type, and in Luella Bingham, Cynthia
Arrasmith thought she had found a surrogate parent.
Ron Bingham, however, scared the dickens out of her
with his sudden bursts of screaming. "The first time he
screamed, she came unglued, and he wasn't even talking to her," recalled Rilla. "She cried and cried. I told
her, 'Cynthia, if you can't stand for anybody to yell,
you shouldn't be here.' "

She told everyone there that she was eighteen years
old. Her boyfriend was twenty-five. In those early days,
Rilla recalled Cynthia being immature and Josh compared her to a child. "I liked her all right, but there was
something definitely wrong," said Rilla. After a few
days on the property, Ron and Ken Rathbone planned to
go out of town to pick up a car, a job that would keep
them out almost all night. "She started to cry so much
that Ken didn't go," Rilla remembered. "Josh went instead. I thought that no eighteen-year-old is going to cry
like that when her boyfriend leaves overnight."

A few days later, Cynthia lowered her age, claiming
she wasn't really eighteen, but sixteen. "My mom confronted her about it," said Josh, who was present at the
conversation that took place a week after Cynthia arrived
on February 24. "Cynthia goes, no, I'm sixteen."

Lue pressed harder, saying that the age difference was
important, that she needed to be truthful and honest.
"Cynthia goes, all right, I'm fifteen, but my birthday
will be in August."

She had another surprise for them. The fifteen-year-
old girl said she was pregnant.

March

Cynthia would later testify that about March 1, only a week after she arrived at the Binghams, Lue invited her into the bedroom to try on some clothes, shut the door and raped her. The girl told no one at the time.

Almost from the start, Ron had a hard time dealing with Ken Rathbone, whom he didn't think was carrying a large enough share of the work in the shop to earn his room and board. The young man spent most of his time working on the trailer in which he lived with the teen-aged Cynthia. Ron ordered him to do his work in the shop first and work on the trailer in the off hours.

In mid-March, two weeks after the couple arrived, Josh Bingham awoke in his back bedroom, hearing strange noises from the front yard. Looking through a window, he saw Cynthia, wearing only a nightie and panties, out in the cold, "tweaking out by the house."

Although he was almost used to the sudden mood swings of the young girl, he thought she was halluci-nating in a particularly bizarre way. She poked an empty box with a stick and told the cat she saw at her feet to go get some mice inside the box. Josh thought that strange because the cat was inside the house with him. He went out to try to bring the girl inside, only to have her resist. She didn't want to go in, not with all those spiders. What spiders, Josh wanted to know. She pointed. Those big spiders that were crawling up the outside the window, over the top and down inside the house. "Omigod, it's so sick," she wailed. The window did not have an open top and there were no spiders. Eventually, Josh got her inside, dressed and warmed. "But she would still tweak out and think she saw some-thing," Josh said. He did not find the girl attractive. "After that I was repulsed," he said later.

After three weeks, Ron told Ken Rathbone to hit the road, not because of a lack of work, but because Bingham thought Rathbone had hypodermic needles. Bingham did many things, but for some reason that Rilla Smith thought dated back to the untimely death of his best friend, Ron Bingham hated needles. Although Cynthia would confirm that she was doing drugs while she was at the Binghams', she insisted that both she and her boyfriend had stopped using them prior to moving into the trailer.

"Cynthia agreed with my dad (about firing Rathbone)," Josh remembered. "She told him (Ken) to get the hell out herself." Ron and Lue did not force the pregnant teenager to also leave. In the trial of her father, defense lawyers would paint this situation as a classic case of predators grooming a vulnerable young girl to be a sexual conquest. Her boyfriend was gone and she was now on her own, relying upon people whom she thought were her friends.

After Rathbone left, Cynthia did not want to be alone in the trailer and began to switch back and forth between the bed in the blue bus and the couch in the living room of the house. Her mood changed rapidly. "Most of time she was happy," Josh said.

Part of that could be tied to the relationship she developed with Luella. Although she was a chronic runaway from her own home and her father had lost track of her for more than a month, there apparently was a mutual chord of affection between the wayward teen and Luella, although according to Cynthia, she had already been raped by Lue.

"She gave my mom hugs all the time," Josh said. "She gave me hugs. She was happy that she had found a place to stay with somebody who cared about her. My mom cared about her because my parents couldn't have kids after me. She always wanted a daughter, so Cynthia was the daughter she never had." Rilla Smith also said that Cynthia would frequently hug Luella Bingham and happily call her "Mom." Another source said that when she first met Cynthia, Lue actually introduced the girl as being her daughter.

Cynthia would confirm that during those early weeks, Luella bought her clothes, gave her money and told Cynthia she was the daughter Lue never had. Josh said that several times while Ron was off on an all-night errand, Cynthia would sleep with his mother on the water bed, not on the living room couch.

The girl was not alone. The Bingham home had become a hive of activity. Ron and Lue would run their shop during the day, Josh's school friends would hang out in the afternoon and the drug trade would start in the evening. The result was a constant going-and-coming of people on the property. Josh would testify that Linda Bartlett, Cynthia's mother, made several visits to see her daughter, the girl's friends also came by, and several times Cynthia walked down to visit her grandparents, once to have her picture taken with her father's new long-haul trucking rig. "They made out like Cynthia couldn't get away from here," Josh would recall bitterly. "She could have walked out of here at anytime she wanted."

Cynthia was temperamental with some of the other visitors and would "get pissed off and cry" when she had a fight with another girl, Josh related. She would pout for a few days around the house, things would get better and she would get into another squabble. Every day she consumed some sort of drug, and witnesses would later testify Ron Bingham regularly had her take a Valium, a drug considered a relaxing "downer."

Meanwhile, Ron's drug business apparently was falling apart, possibly because he was using too much of his own product. One of his customers had been Kyle Richardson, the drug dealer who had recently defaulted on his deal with Ken Arrasmith and given up his Tec-9.

Kyle had hired Josh to work on a car, then only paid him half the agreed price. Ron wanted nothing more to do with him after that, not even dealing in drugs. "The phone would ring and I'd tell Ron. 'It's Kyle,' " Rilla would later say. Bingham would growl back a terse, "Fuck Kyle." The two drug dealers drew apart. Richardson no longer needed Ron to be an older influence in his life. He had met someone he looked up to, almost as a role model—Ken Arrasmith.

10

April

On April 3, the dissolution of the marriage of Ken Arrasmith and Donnita Weddle became final. It did not matter that they were still together, their fortune was safely squirreled away from the child support demands of his other pesky ex-wives.

Rilla Smith was in an inextricable bind that seemed to be drawing tighter around her. She was shocked to discover that Ron had stopped making payments on the fifty thousand dollars life insurance policy, which lapsed. That had been his collateral to her on the mortgage loan deal. Remembering the fist-sized rolls of money she once found stashed around the house, she went looking for more. All she could find was "a teeny roll of ten one hundred dollar bills in a sealed container." Ron might have had drugs buried in sections of plastic pipe in the backyard, but money was running short.

Cynthia's pregnancy was becoming a concern for all of the adults involved, although perhaps not as much for the teenaged mother-to-be. In fact, one woman said the girl seemed "overjoyed" about being pregnant. Cynthia happily told her, "We're going to have babies!" She saw a local doctor for prenatal care and talked with Lue and others about becoming a mother at such a young age. At one point, she asked Lue, "Do you want to be a grandma?" Then, finally considering reality, they started to talk about abortion.

One day in early April, Luella, wearing her favorite grubby sweats, had a premonition. She confided to her friend Deena: "If I die, I hope somewhere in my life I made an impression . . . to make someone's life better." Perhaps, but her actions of the next few weeks certainly did not improve the life of her "daughter"—Cynthia Arrasmith.

Ron Bingham found still another lost soul on Friday, April 14, a rotund young woman who had been sitting daily beside a fresh grave in the cemetery at the foot of the driveway for a week. When approached, she said she was watching people and cars coming up out of the grave of her recently deceased boyfriend and that every day she would climb down a ladder to tidy up the place. Patti Mahar Johnson entered a situation that was already boiling.

It was the long Easter weekend, and Ron took Patti to the Quality Inn Motel beside the river in Clarkston. Lue brought Cynthia over later. Before long, a scene of depravity took place as Ron and Lue had sex with both Patti and Cynthia, an episode that would be recounted in graphic detail in the trial of Ken Arrasmith. Cynthia, on drugs, was sodomized and had sex with both Ron and Lue. In the bizarre assault, Ron Bingham shaved off her pubic hair and put it in a container to save as a souvenir. But once again, although she and Patti stayed awake and talked during the night while the Binghams slept, Cynthia said nothing to anyone about the assault.

*   *   *

During the Easter holiday, while Ron took Patti along on a run into the desert to buy drugs, Ken Arrasmith came to Clarkston to visit his parents. While there, he heard that Cynthia was living with the Binghams, and although he would say he did not approve of that, the place was better than the girl "running in the gutter" with druggies.

He had already met Ken Rathbone on an earlier trip, when Cynthia introduced them in a brief meeting at a telephone booth, where he gave them ten dollars. Arrasmith felt that Cynthia living with Ron and Lue, a few minutes from her grandparents, was a good alternative to her running off to California with her older boyfriend.

Arrasmith had a brief meeting with Cynthia over Easter and even drove her back to the Binghams. She didn't mention a word about any assault.

Meanwhile, things were in motion concerning Cynthia's unborn child. She had backed out of one planned abortion, but on April 17, her mother signed a letter giving Lue and Ron permission to make medical decisions for her minor daughter. An appointment had been made to take her to an abortion clinic in Spokane.

The Quad Cities Task Force is an assemblage of law enforcement officers from several neighboring municipalities in Washington and Idaho, among them the border towns of Clarkston and Lewiston. On April 18, officers from all of the participating police agencies gathered at the Clarkston Police Station with the objective of raiding the home of one of the larger drug dealers in the valley—Ron Bingham.

They need not have bothered, since the raid was compromised before it even started. What followed was a Keystone Kops episode in which the suspects ended up chasing the police.

To keep watch on the house in the hours prior to the

raid, a plainclothes detective in an unmarked car had eased into the graveyard late on the night of April 17, turned off his lights and settled down to wait. Cynthia Arrasmith was inside, along with the entire Bingham family and two visiting young men. She had no intention of sleeping, because, according to Josh Bingham, "She didn't like to sleep. Day or night didn't matter to her."

About nine o'clock, Patti Mahar Johnson, the newest recruit at the Bingham place, heard a twig snap and since almost everyone in the house was paranoid anyway, Ron Bingham, Luella and Patti grabbed their guns and jumped in a car that was already pointed down the sloping driveway. As the stakeout policeman watched in horror, the car's lights went bright and headed straight for him. Luella was shining a handheld spotlight out her window.

Panicked, the cop took off in his own car, with Ron Bingham right on his bumper. The policeman grabbed his radio and yelled for help and other police units converged on the area. Bingham, however, swiftly figured out what was going on, and passed the escaping red four-door sedan as the two cars headed into Clarkston, and exclaimed, "Oh, shit. It's a cop." He let the red car disappear.

Moments later, a uniformed patrolman pulled over the Bingham vehicle. The two women told the questioning officer that they were carrying weapons, but he didn't seem concerned about that. Instead, he carefully explained that the car they had been chasing had been that of someone who had gone to the cemetery only to grieve over the death of a relative. Right, Officer, replied Ron.

The police car pulled away, his ridiculous story trailing behind him like a bad smell. Ron found the first telephone he could and started calling back to the house, giving orders on how the people still there should dispose of the drugs stashed around the place. Move fast, he told them. Do it now. The cops are coming.

For some reason, the eight policemen on the strike team were still confident five hours later as they came up the narrow driveway to the junk-cluttered yard that surrounded the little home. One had the search warrant.

Lights burned brightly in the living room and the officers could see the silhouettes of people who were still awake in the earliest hours of the new day. It was known that Ron Bingham was a dangerous man when angry, so they drew their weapons and split into teams to cover the back door as well as the front. Music and the sounds of people moving around inside the house could be heard, and one raider saw a curtain move and someone peek through the window, almost as if whoever was inside was expecting visitors at that odd hour.

At a nod from Joel Hastings, the officer in charge of the case, a deputy sheriff yelled a warning and six officers, guns drawn, poured through the front door. Two more deputies came in through the back, their guns also ready. The twin tactics of a lot of noise and the display of weapons normally combine to throw surprise and fright into suspects in such a case, but the two young men and one young woman sitting in the living room were not in the least alarmed. In fact, they almost seemed amused. Even the two dogs on the premises, a large rottweiler and the lean Queensland blue heeler, were taking things calmly. They didn't even bark at the intruders.

A cop rushed into a back bedroom and hauled a teenaged boy wearing only undershorts out of his bed and he was ordered to lie facedown on the floor alongside the two young men and one girl found in the living room. Josh Bingham remembered looking at a clock and noting it was exactly 2:10 A.M. An older woman was found in another of the back bedrooms. A policeman took up station at the door to the room, alternately watching Rilla Smith huddled beneath the sheets, as if wrapping herself in a cotton cocoon, and watching the young people in the living room.

Ron Bingham and his wife, Luella, were nowhere to be found. He was not in the house, not in the big automobile repair shop, not in the bus, nor in the trailer in the rear of the house. However, another man was found asleep in the trailer and he was also hauled down to the group gathered in the living room and handcuffed.

The police began their search for drugs and quickly found some. They riffled through the pockets of a coat on the floor and found a small amount of methamphetamine. One of the men on the floor, Lyle Stevens, admitted that the coat was his. He was placed under arrest.

A small can filled with a crystalline powder was discovered in a pocket of Todd Reed, and when a field chemical test determined that substance was "meth," Reed was also arrested.

So far, so good. They were barely inside the door and already they had two people in custody, more in cuffs, the lady still cowering in her bed and some small amounts of illegal drugs. But they had come for Bingham and his large cache of drugs, and so far, they had found neither. Things looked bleak for the Quad Cities Drug Task Force.

Little did they realize that they were perched on the threshold of the most publicized crime—one of an entirely different nature—that had ever struck the region.

The trouble that night would not begin with drugs or with Ron Bingham, but with the petite girl who had been allowed to sit on the sofa, her wrists still bound behind her by steel handcuffs. She wore a tattered denim jacket, cutoff jeans and a blue shirt and the cops thought she looked dirty. Unkempt brown hair hung straight to her shoulders, framing a youthful face that seemed to the police to hold a combination of arrogance and laughter. On close inspection, her eyes seemed clear and she gave no indication of being on drugs. Detective John Kelley began asking her questions and was shocked when the uncooperative girl told him that she was only fifteen years old.

Her name, she said, was Cynthia Arrasmith.

When asked about her parents, the child replied that her mother lived across the river, in the Orchards section of nearby Lewiston, but could not be contacted. What's her telephone number? She doesn't have one, the girl told them. How about your father? She replied she knew where he had been last night, when they had spoken on the telephone, but didn't know about tonight. He was a truck driver. Could be anywhere. She was sullen.

Hastings and Kelley held a whispered conference and made a decision. No matter what else was done that night, they wanted to get the kid out of there. The idea of leaving a fifteen-year-old girl in a drug dealer's house, accompanied by men who were quite a few years older, was abhorrent to the cops.

Her behavior confused them. She showed no sign of distress, calmly telling the cops she had been living there for about two months. She did not ask for their help, and, in fact, seemed to mock them, as if she knew something they didn't. Using a Polaroid camera, Kelley snapped her photograph and, when the picture rolled from the camera a few moments later, he wrote her name and age on the front of it, and her birthdate of August 6, 1979, on the back.

The search then turned up a bombshell discovery. The middle bedroom was a trove of pornography. Investigators found stacks of adult magazines and dozens of photographs of people engaging in sexual acts. With the door closed, they examined each of them, trying to determine if the underage girl in the front room was shown performing a sexual act. Without the warrant specifying that they should find and remove the teenager, the police needed concrete evidence that she was being mistreated. They could not find that.

Eventually, Ron Bingham came home with Lue and Patti. After they were also handcuffed, they pointed police toward the guns they had left in the automobile, explaining the weapons were legal and owned in the name of Luella, because Ron, a felon, was forbidden to have guns. There were no drugs to be found on them.

Patti Mahar Johnson had something to show the police and led them down to the cemetery. She complained that someone was desecrating the grave of her late boyfriend. Crying, she said nothing about a sexual assault. "A babbling idiot," was the conclusion of one witness to her actions.

The police turned to removing Cynthia but were quickly thwarted there, too. Lue unzipped her fanny pack and handed the cops some papers. The documents, she explained, were a permission slip for medical care signed by the girl's mother, Linda Bartlett, and a Medicaid coupon to pay for an abortion. The date on the note was April 17, only the day before the raid. With that documentation, combined with the girl's insistence that she was fine and wanted to stay where she was, the police finally threw in their cards. No drugs. No girl. Ron Bingham had beaten them. They left.

Lue, Cynthia and Josh all went to Spokane the following day and the abortion was performed at a clinic. While she was being examined, Lue joked with the doctor, asking how he liked Cynthia's haircut: She was referring to the pubic area that had been shaved the previous weekend. After the exam, it was determined that the girl probably had been pregnant since late January, before she got to the Binghams.

According to sources who met her afterward, Cynthia "was so happy, bubbling in the bedroom" while she recovered from the procedure. Lue confided to a friend that Cynthia puzzled her, that "the minute we left, she was overjoyed."

The next day, April 20, Patti bailed out. In a strange episode during which she admitted she was high on drugs, she donned an all-black costume and ran, after dark, down the hill to the country club, demanding that someone call the police. She then hid in some bushes until a patrol car came along and took her to jail. She was babbling and almost incoherent, but had at least one interesting thing to say, and officers at the jail telephoned Detective Tom White, the sexual assault expert within the Asotin County Sheriff's Department. As soon as he heard the name ''Ron Bingham,'' he paid attention.

But not only could he not understand Patti that night, he was not officially on duty. White instructed them to keep her overnight. Questioned again the next day, Patti claimed she and another girl were raped at the Quality Inn, but her comments remained almost incoherent. Police put Patti on a plane to her sister in Portland, Oregon.

A week later, on April 29, Ron and Lue took Cynthia back to the Quality Inn and staged another sexual marathon.

Detective White returned from vacation, only to hurt his back while performing routine patrol duty at the county fair. He was sent to bed for two weeks to recover. That would be a critical turning point in the case.

11

Saturday, May 6

Cynthia left the Bingham house to spend some week-end time at the home of her mother, Linda Bartlett. Their relationship had been strained for years, and she had moved out of Linda's house the previous September, but Cynthia still maintained contact. Now, after the two sexual sessions at the motel, the additional assaults by Ron and Lue, the continual use of drugs and the emotional experience of the abortion, Cynthia was barely able to function. She had no energy reserves whatever, and in that weakened condition, the awful truth finally popped out, unbidden.

She arrived at Linda's and almost immediately plunged into deep sleep. She slept all day, then all night and most of the next day. Her mother was concerned and would shake Cynthia awake periodically to ask her if she was okay.

Eventually, Luella Bingham telephoned and grew angry when she was not allowed to talk to Cynthia, because the girl was still asleep. Luella said it was time for Cynthia to come home. Linda and her other daughter, Jennifer, discussed the troubled girl and decided to try and convince Cynthia that she still had the alternative of living with them, and not outside the family unit.

When the conversation finally took place, Cynthia stood shakily behind a rocking chair, gripping it tightly.

"You don't have to go back to the Binghams," Linda coaxed her daughter. "You can stay here."

Cynthia, choked up, answered, "Mom, I can't."

"Why?" the puzzled mother asked.

The girl broke into tears. "I have to go back. You don't know what they do to me," she wept. "They make me sleep with them."

Linda Bartlett made up her mind instantly. "You're not going back," she said. "You're staying here."

"No," Cynthia insisted, fearfully. "They'll kill me. They'll kill you and they'll kill Taylor (Jennifer's child)."

Linda was adamant. "No. I won't take you back to that place."

Her daughter resisted even more, warning her mother not to call the police. "I'll go back and they won't know anything," she said. Instead, Cynthia called the Bingham house and asked Josh to come pick her up. When he got there, Cynthia was not quite ready to go, and Josh waited for about thirty minutes as she gathered some clothes.

"In the car, she seemed upset, but she wasn't crying," Josh would testify later. In fact, he testified that she gave him an entirely different view of what she was feeling. Josh said that Cynthia had some "waviness" in her voice, but told him she was upset with her parents, particularly her mom. Josh stated that Cynthia repeated a comment he had heard from her many times before: "She told me she hated her parents."

Nevertheless, her comments to her mother and sister had already triggered the avalanche that was soon to bury the region.

Immediately after the confrontation, Jennifer went to

a pay phone and placed a call to her father's home in
Sunnyside, Washington. Donnita answered and told her
that Ken wasn't there. He was in his truck, hauling a
load back from California. Jennifer redialed.

Ken Arrasmith answered the next call on his cell telephone and Jennifer told him there seemed to be a problem with Cynthia, possibly a sexual assault. He would
say later that he was not really aware of what was going
on, only that his daughter might be in trouble. He
mashed the accelerator and the big Kenworth truck
leaped forward, chewing up the miles toward his home
in Sunnyside.

Sunday, May 7

Once there, he made more calls. Both Linda and Jennifer gave him detailed explanations of what Cynthia
had said. Then he called people he knew in the valley,
and they confirmed there was word out concerning Cynthia and the Binghams. His friend Kyle Richardson responded with caution, "I'm not sure what's going on,
but I have heard something." Kyle refused to discuss it
further over an open telephone line. Arrasmith, troubled,
blurted: "I gotta come down there." About midnight on
Sunday, he rolled into Clarkston, 181 miles from Sunnyside.

In a half hour meeting with Richardson, Kyle revealed
that he had learned from Lynn Kohl—the latest name of
Ken's second ex-wife—that either Jennifer or Cynthia
was being raped and kept on drugs by the Binghams.
Arrasmith appeared overwhelmed by the news. On the
witness stand, Richardson had particular recall of one
Arrasmith comment about Ron Bingham: "He said he'd
like to kill that motherfucker."

*   *   *

The first item of importance was to remove Cynthia from the Bingham house.

That had already been done, and another, unexpected factor had entered the equation. Ken Rathbone, Jr., Cynthia's old boyfriend, who had been thrown out by Ron Bingham, was back in town. Ron had loudly protested his reappearance and refused to allow him in the house. That meant that if Cynthia wanted to see him, they would have to meet elsewhere.

In what would later, at the trial, be depicted as a daring escape, Linda Bartlett picked Cynthia and Rathbone up at a Southway gas station and tried to talk the girl into coming home with her. When Cynthia refused, Linda drove them to the home of Tracy Anderson, a young woman who also had stayed at the Bingham place for about a month. She was pregnant at the time and testified she used meth while there. After observing a number of Ron's tirades, including him shouting at Cynthia about Ken Rathbone, Tracy and Cynthia discussed leaving. Tracy moved out.

Linda said she thought Cynthia would "be safe" at Anderson's house. Tracy was surprised at Cynthia's unexpected appearance on her doorstep, noting later that the girl "was crying, scared, upset and looked terrible." Tracy certainly didn't want Ron coming around hunting Cynthia, so she drove the young lovers to the Hollywood Motel, a low-rent operation just across the street from the Flying J truck stop and bus station, and bought them a room for the night. Cynthia and Rathbone spent Sunday night there. The truck stop was important. Cynthia told Tracy she wanted to go with Rathbone to California, to hide.

The sequence would later raise the question whether Cynthia was running away from the Binghams, or toward a new life with her boyfriend. As a chronic runaway for years, she had repeatedly demonstrated she had no desire to stay. Only fifteen years old, she was about to get on a bus with a man ten years her senior, the man with whom she lived when she became pregnant, the man both her parents would say they disapproved of, while continuing to allow her to be around him.

Ken Arrasmith, while his daughter slept, had gone from Kyle's shop to the home of his second wife, Lynn, who confirmed she had heard reports of Cynthia being sexually assaulted by the Binghams. Ken learned the girl was out of the Binghams' clutches and at the motel and felt that she was temporarily safe and there was nothing more he could do that night. His long, exhausting day came to an end and he decided to confront Cynthia the next morning and order, not ask, his daughter to make a choice—either go back home or be locked up by the police.

Monday, May 8

Linda Bartlett went to the Lewiston Police Department the next morning, saying that her daughter was in danger and they needed to intervene. Cynthia, she said, was in the company of an adult male and would attempt to board a bus for California. She testified that their response was not one of urgency, and they told her to file a runaway report. Actually, since they had heard Linda tell them many times that Cynthia was in trouble, this new claim was akin to the fable of the boy who cried wolf. To them, it might have been just another entry in the thick log of Cynthia Arrasmith's runaway record. Linda dutifully filed the report at 11:40 A.M. Officer Nick Krakalia, at the front desk, radioed another policeman to meet him at the Hollywood Motel.

Interestingly, the conversation between Linda Bartlett and the police focused upon Cynthia being in the company of Ken Rathbone, and not about any sexual assaults involving the Binghams.

Meanwhile, Linda's ex-husband drove his black Nissan pickup to the Hollywood Motel, braking to a stop in the parking lot when he saw Cynthia standing outside with Rathbone. He waved for her to get in the truck for a talk, and she reluctantly complied. When he asked what was happening, she replied, "Nothing, really." Their conversation devolved quickly into a quarrel and Arrasmith exploded, saying, "Cynthia, don't you think some of this is your own fault?"

She got mad and stepped out of the truck, her father calling after her: "I'm going to have you picked up as a runaway!" He telephoned the Lewiston police on his cell phone and was told that his ex-wife had filed the necessary report and officers were on the way.

Officer Nick Krakalia and Corporal Dave Meyers arrived about the same time, in marked patrol units, and pulled into the Hollywood Motel parking lot to find a rather confused scene. Ken Arrasmith was in his black truck in the rear of the parking lot. As he dismounted to meet them, the young couple walked out of the motel room. The father and his daughter stood about a dozen feet apart, separated by police officers, in a strange, tension-filled confrontation.

Krakalia spoke with Ken Rathbone, who confirmed that he was twenty-six-years-old, matching the complaint that the girl was with an adult male. The cops had only seen him exit the room with the teenager and had not seen anything that may have happened inside the room. In addition, both Cynthia and Rathbone denied engaging in sex. Meyers talked with Arrasmith, who wanted Rathbone arrested for rape, but the police explained they had no probable cause to do so, particularly when the alleged victim was insisting nothing had happened. The girl seemed to be in good shape and the only problem she expressed was antagonism toward her

seething father: "She didn't want to go with him," said
Krakalia.

Rathbone, who was calm throughout the questioning,
was allowed to walk away. The officers explained to the
upset teenager what her father wanted, then placed her
in custody and took her to the police station.

Again, in hindsight, the situation was peculiar. Arrasmith had roared almost two hundred miles to reach his
troubled daughter when he thought she was in danger
from the Binghams. But in the presence of two policemen, according to his own testimony and that of the
cops, he complained only about Cynthia being involved
with Ken Rathbone, whom he had known about for
weeks. Not a word about the Binghams.

Linda Bartlett was waiting at the Lewiston Police Department when Cynthia and her father arrived with the
officers. At first, Arrasmith told the police he wanted to
have custody, but the girl remained hostile, refusing to
go with either of her parents. She denied having sex with
Rathbone, or with anyone at all! Arrasmith realized the
futility of releasing Cynthia. He told the cops she would
run away as soon as she was out the front door of the
police station, and he and Linda wanted her kept in custody. At the parents' insistence, Corporal Meyers put
Cynthia into juvenile detention. She was taken to a cell
and quickly fell into a deep sleep.

Again, a golden opportunity was there for the parents
to demand action on the central issue—the assaults by
the Binghams—and they kept silent.

Forty-five minutes later, Arrasmith telephoned the
Asotin County Sheriff's Office and talked briefly with
Captain Watkins, finally shifting the focus back to the
Binghams. Watkins gave him an appointment for four
o'clock the following day.

After lunch, Arrasmith then drove up to the Bingham
house, determined to collect his daughter's belongings.
Lue invited him inside and Ron appeared a moment later

and Ken braced them, saying Cynthia was claiming they fed her drugs and had sex with her. Watching their faces, he was convinced that she was right, even as Ron vehemently denied it. He would later testify that he became skittish, and backed off, fearful of Ron. He collected her things and then asked Ron for a tour of his automobile shop. Lue was crying, asking how Cynthia could make such accusations.

Once outside the house, Ron began to brag about how tough he was, and Ken responded that if Cynthia was correct, he would be back out to visit, with the sheriff. "You come back here and you won't be leaving," was Ron's response, according to Arrasmith's later testimony. "I'll kill you." Ken Arrasmith drove away. Throughout this and following confrontations, the facts are blurred, because they rely mostly on Arrasmith's own testimony, since Ron and Luella Bingham, the only other participants, were dead and quite unable to give a differing version of events.

Luella's brother, Jim Smith, had predicted years earlier that someday the abusive, aggressive, unreasoning and violent Ron Bingham was going to meet up with someone who was his mirror image. That meeting had just taken place, and there was no doubt that danger was hanging thickly in the air.

That Sunday evening, two important things happened. Ken Arrasmith took up temporary residence in a trailer behind his parents' home, just down the hill from the Binghams, and he also made further contact with Kyle Richardson at the Clarkston shop. Richardson would testify that Arrasmith visited him every day, and every time they were together, they would consume methamphetamines. Arrasmith denied this on the witness stand, although other people would also testify that they saw him snort meth during the time in question. If true, as is probable, not only would his mind have been awhirl with the situation involving Cynthia, but his thinking would have been muddled by a constant use of drugs.

Ron Bingham began to have fits of anger and depression. At one extreme, he drove to Tracy Anderson's house and yelled at her, saying he couldn't believe Cynthia was accusing him of rape. At the other, he worriedly visited Deena DeSarno and began transferring the titles on fifteen vehicles he owned into her name, with instructions that if anything happened to him, she should dispose of them for Josh.

He also knew a very special day was approaching. On May 23, he and Lue would celebrate their twenty-fifth wedding anniversary, a remarkable period of staying together, considering both the circumstances of their lives and the modern statistics that said many marriages are doomed to fail. Ron told his wife to go out and buy a ring, something special, and Lue ordered one laced with hearts and diamonds. They agreed to put it on the installment plan, with easy monthly payments.

Tuesday, May 9

Cynthia came to court wearing handcuffs and shackles, a waif in irons. Despite her age and circumstances, however, her attitude toward her parents remained defiant, even argumentative. She was angry at her mother for filing the runaway report and at her father for both directing her arrest and hinting that she was partly responsible for her problems at the Binghams.

The hearing on whether she should remain incarcerated began at 8 A.M., and Arrasmith and his ex-wife, Linda Bartlett, found they had to be very persuasive to convince the court to keep Cynthia in custody. If she was dismissed, they said, she would run away again. Again the focus was on keeping her locked up, not on pursuing the claims against the Binghams in front of a

judge. Although not yet recovered from her apparent
drug hangover, Cynthia was becoming more lucid and
told her mother she didn't understand why she was the
one in jail. "I didn't do anything," Cynthia said. "They
did it to me."

From the courthouse in Lewiston, Arrasmith and
Linda hurried across the river to the police station in
Clarkston. Arrasmith was once again convinced he was
being followed, this time by a couple of grungy char-
acters whom he had first spotted at the courthouse. At
10 A.M., Captain James Watkins invited Linda and Ken
into his office for a talk.

The first comment that Cynthia had made about being
assaulted was to her mother on Saturday, May 6. Her
father was notified by telephone immediately thereafter
and rushed to Lewiston. Only after having waited almost
three full days, the parents finally talked to police about
the possible molestation. Their own delay would make
their later accusations of police inactivity ring hollow.

They advised Watkins that Cynthia was now in juvenile detention and Watkins requested, and was given,
their permission to interview her. He then revealed that
he already was aware of allegations that the Binghams
had sexually abused Cynthia. In fact, he said, producing
a document, he had actually interviewed a woman who
claimed to have witnessed the assault at the Quality Inn.
He read them the shockingly explicit report.

The sheriff's captain also told them, however, that the
witness wasn't the most reliable and "appeared to be
coming down off a high" when she gave her statement.
Nevertheless, he had followed up somewhat on her report and interviewed one woman Patti Mahar had
named, and had obtained motel room records that proved
the Binghams were there at the time in question. Still,
Watkins explained, he was not the sexual assault expert
in the Asotin County Sheriff's Office and would turn the
information over to Detective Tom White, who was ex-

pected back at work within a few days, after recuperating from an injury.

Watkins then gave Arrasmith a mixed message that would have far-reaching repercussions. While they were discussing the next step in the investigation, Watkins apparently hinted that he really did not have the expertise to handle this case and did not expect to have much luck on the street talking to drug users about the Binghams. The sheriff's captain gave Arrasmith permission to pursue the investigation on his own. "I told him he would possibly be able to get information a lot easier on the street," Watkins would testify later. Watkins specifically warned Arrasmith not to contact the Binghams directly to avoid jeopardizing the case. Arrasmith testified later that he left the meeting believing he could once again act like a cop, that he had been unofficially deputized to pursue the investigation on his own. In reality, police considered him just another informant, no different from any other snitch a cop could use as a backchannel information source.

When Ken Arrasmith and Linda Bartlett walked out of the Asotin County Sheriff's Office, neither had expressed any displeasure at how the case was being handled.

Linda Bartlett and Watkins then drove back across the river to interview Cynthia at the detention center in Lewiston. By now she was ready to speak of her ordeal and began the long and devastating story of what had happened to her in the company of Ron and Lue Bingham. She confirmed Patti's statement and added gruesome details about how she was drugged with Valium, how her pubic hair had been shaved, how she had been raped by both Ron and Lue. Once she finally began to talk, Cynthia had a lot to say, but much of it was fuzzy or contradictory. She would testify in court that she told her parents different things on different days.

But on that first day, she gave Watkins and her mother

vivid description of one incident that would have a direct bearing on the eventual murder trial of her father.

According to Cynthia, Ron Bingham had gone to the Asotin County Court House in answer to a recent legal complaint, determined that he would never go to jail again. When he returned home, he made Cynthia touch the outside of his shirt and she felt bulky objects beneath the cloth. Ron, she said, bragged that he was wired with C-4, a plastique explosive, and had vowed to blow up the entire courthouse rather than face another prison term.

In coming months, Cynthia said she was afraid that Bingham would tie on the explosives again and come visit her at the detention center and blow up the building and her along with it.

The tale was never proven but was scoffed at by people who knew Ron Bingham. "Ron was too important to Ron" to kill himself, said one. Josh Bingham said that his father always kept him informed of the location of every weapon and every cache of drugs, and never mentioned having C-4 explosives. Others said it was simply Ron bragging, trying to impress a young girl. But with his reputation for violence and a hair-trigger temper, Cynthia certainly was within her rights to believe his claim. In any event, Watkins apparently took that report with a grain of salt, knowing the girl was in safe custody behind several guarded and locked doors and that any visitor, particularly a nonfamily member such as Ron, would have a difficult time even gaining permission to see her. In fact, even Cynthia's parents were denied permission to see the girl several times before working out a system in which Linda would come by in the morning on visiting days and her father would meet her in the afternoon. Between sessions, Linda and Ken would have lunch next door at the Dairy Queen.

The primary reason Watkins wasn't worried about Ron becoming a walking bomb, intent on demolishing a courthouse, was Cynthia's attitude. "She said she wasn't afraid of the Binghams," he recalled. "She said they were probably more afraid of her because of what she could do."

12

Ken Arrasmith's terrible temper wrapped him in its unrelenting grasp, a snare that was fueled by drugs. In the second week of May, his behavior became steadily more bizarre as his frustration mounted. He wanted action, and in his view, the police were doing nothing. Granted what he considered to be the unofficial permission of Captain Watkins to perform some undercover cop work, Arrasmith started down the road toward murder.

He later recalled talking to street people and learning that "everybody had a tale" about the Binghams and his teenaged daughter. In court, he appeared to be defending drug users and pushers by saying they weren't really bad people. "Everybody wanted to help," he said.

He returned their kindness by almost selling some of them out to police.

On May 11, Arrasmith, who only a few days previously had insisted that the cops arrest Ken Rathbone, now escorted the young man to the Asotin County Sheriff's Office. Instead of asking that Cynthia's older boyfriend be arrested, he arranged an interview between Rathbone and Captain Watkins. Meanwhile, a surprised Sheriff John Jeffers saw Arrasmith standing in the lobby, his face twisted with emotion, and invited the man, whom he knew, into his office for a talk. Arrasmith admitted to the sheriff that he had used drugs and even transported some to Clarkston. But now, with events spinning out of control, he told Jeffers he was considering turning in some of his meth-snorting associates. Later, it would be learned the people he wanted to squeal on were his second ex-wife, Lynn, and his pal from the garage, gun and meth scene, Kyle Richardson.

Throughout the next few busy days, Arrasmith would be in frequent contact with one law enforcement officer or another, and they would keep him closely tuned to the ongoing investigation. It would not be until he began organizing his defense that he would express dissatisfaction with their progress.

Among the officials with whom he spoke was a man who knew Cynthia Arrasmith well. Alan Johnson had been her social services caseworker for a long time, and now was meeting with the girl and her parents to determine the next step concerning the teenager. The day after her father's tearful, rambling meeting with Jeffers, plans were made to send Cynthia off to a treatment program, on May 22.

Meanwhile, the world of Ken Arrasmith became ever more strange. Hanging out with Richardson and some of his drug-dealing cronies, he used meth and plotted his next move. Fueled by drugs, he boasted that he was going to march up to the Bingham house and demand that Ron give him the container that held Cynthia's pubic hair. He would just go up there and take it!

The drugs hadn't totally divorced him from reality. A police officer later observed: "Ken knew better than to confront Ron in anything like a fair fight. Ron would have killed him." So instead of making the demand, he tucked a pistol beneath the front seat of his truck, and with a pair of binoculars, went out to spy on the Bingham place. With him was his best friend in Clarkston, Kyle, who didn't know Arrasmith was thinking about turning him in to the cops. Richardson said he went along to protect Ken because they thought a thug was living at the house to be a bodyguard for Bingham. Talking brave was one thing. Squaring off against two people who were meaner than they were was something else entirely. Instead, Arrasmith and Richardson drove up Valley View Road to a hilltop and settled down to watch the Bingham home. They saw nothing of interest but did begin making a list of the many vehicles around the place. It was Sunday, May 14, Mother's Day.

At night, Arrasmith would eventually go into the trailer behind his parents' home, just down the street from Ron's, build a barricade and sit there with his loaded guns and his dark thoughts. He would testify much later that he expected, at any moment, Ron and his bodyguard might kick down the door to the trailer and open fire. Or shoot him from a distance. Or booby-trap his car. Or kill him in a drive-by shooting. And Ken Arrasmith continued to use more drugs.

Ironically, Arrasmith was driving Ron Bingham crazy at the same time. Ron knew he was being stalked and he knew who was doing the stalking. "Something is going to happen and I'm probably going to die," he told Deena DeSarno one evening in the middle of May. He sat immobile in an overstuffed chair in her living room, having turned off all the lights but one dim bulb. When she asked what was wrong, he whispered: "Beware the arrow that is silent." Deena felt a grip of terror, for she had never seen Ron Bingham scared of anything. The brash macho image was evaporating into a hopelessness about the future. Just as Arrasmith spied upon him, he had spied right back, driving frequently past Richardson's shop, keeping an eye on things.

Bingham handed DeSarno a .25 caliber pistol and told her to go to the police the next day and get a concealed weapons permit. Carry it at all times, he warned. They know you are our friend. Lue echoed the fear, saying they were being stalked and they were worried about her. As they left, Bingham told her once again, "Beware the arrow that is silent."

Kyle Richardson was doing his part to help his friend. Not only did he supply Arrasmith with drugs to snort, but he tried to recruit friends into an assassination. One day in his shop, he held out a big rifle and offered two pals $2,500 to kill someone. They refused. Soon afterward, he began working the telephones, seeing if any of his gun-loving pals might happen to have an extra thirty-round clip for a Tec-9. On a dull afternoon, he and Arrasmith mounted laser sights on their pistols. With such aiming devices, which paint their targets with a dot of red light, the bullets truly follow the narrow illuminated beam.

Detective Tom White finally returned to work on May 15, after being off a month with a combination of vacation and injury days. As the sexual abuse expert in the Asotin County Sheriff's Office, he found his desk heavy with work.

Three cases demanded his immediate attention, two of them urgently, for the girls being molested were still around the suspects who were assaulting them. The third case involved Cynthia Arrasmith, who was locked up tight in juvenile detention across the river in Lewiston. White knew Ken Arrasmith, having joined the sheriff's office only a short time before Arrasmith quit, and had frequent conversations with him. White's impression was that Arrasmith was satisfied with the investigation, because Ken was not like ordinary civilians who would not know how police procedures worked. Arrasmith had once worn a badge and was familiar with things like warrants and conferences with prosecutors. Anyway, Cynthia was out of danger and the other two girls were still facing their abusers. White assigned the three cases their proper priorities, and Cynthia was at the bottom of the list.

May 16 was Ron Bingham's birthday, and the Health Department gave him his first present—an order that he clean up the trash around his property that was growing from large heaps into small mountains. He cursed and shoved the notice in a pocket.

He vented part of his fury on a couple of the usual transients, demanding that teenaged Tara Lebold's boyfriend get the hell off his property. The boyfriend left, but unlike the parting of Cynthia and Ken Rathbone, Tara left with him. They took their dog, too, and adjourned to the home of the boyfriend's stepfather, where they would spend the night. That decision, made so easily by Ron Bingham that morning, would assume huge importance in the months to come.

One of the street "informants" with whom Ken Arrasmith was dealing was Otis Nixon, who was providing his stepson and Tara with temporary lodging. In a conversation at Kyle's shop on May 16, Otis told Arrasmith that Ron Bingham was working at a shop in Lewiston. Arrasmith went to Nixon's house that evening and glanced in the bedroom, where a young blond girl was asleep. Nixon said her name was Tara Lebold and that Bingham had just kicked her and her boyfriend off his property. Later, Ken would say the mere sight of her resting there spurred him to vow to protect all women from the pair of sexual predators that had violated his daughter.

However, at the time, Arrasmith uttered no warning to police, to Nixon, to the boyfriend or to Tara that the girl might be at risk if she returned to the Binghams.

Ken Arrasmith had also met for a while that day with Alan Johnson to again discuss details of the treatment program planned for Cynthia. During the conversation Arrasmith confided that he was helping police gather evidence against the Binghams. Kyle Richardson continued working the telephones but was unable to find an extra Tec-9 clip. Richardson said that he and Arrasmith once again shared some lines of meth.

Ron Bingham rode his big Kawasaki motorcyle over to Tony Adams's auto shop on Shelter Road. His back hurt and he walked stiffly as he worked throughout the afternoon. When night fell, he got behind the steering wheel of a truck, lay back and closed his eyes for a nap.

Luella picked up Deena, driving perhaps the biggest, meanest car in the Bingham herd of vehicles, a diesel-powered Pontiac Grand Prix. It was a muscle car and Ron told her it could outrun anything on the road. Lue told her passenger that Ron thought people were following them, and the car was protection. Josh was in the backseat, and after arriving at the shop, he rode the Kawasaki home and went to bed.

Deena walked through the shop and found Ron asleep in the truck. Resting her arms on the frame of the open window, she quietly began to sing, "Happy birthday to you, happy birthday to you . . ." She would recall the moment later. "He didn't open his eyes, but this big shit-eating grin spread across his face."

When she finished singing, Deena handed Ron a birthday card. It was addressed to "My Hairy Godfather," and was signed, "Sinderella." Ron unfolded from the truck seat, stretched to work out the kinks in his muscular body and hobbled with her into the garage. He, Lue, Deena and the few guys who were there celebrated Ron's birthday, some of them snorting meth. As she left that night, Deena felt, despite the dope and the impromptu party, Ron seemed distant and preoccupied.

Although she never finished high school, Luella Smith Bingham was an avid reader. Fiction, technical manuals, romance novels, poetry and magazines passed rapidly through her hands as she devoured their words, ideas ⟩ and feelings. On the morning of May 17, her son, Josh, on his way to school, stepped into her bedroom to say good-bye. She was cuddled beneath the covers, reading a book. Lue smiled and gave him a peck on the cheek and returned to her pages as he left.

She rose late, padding to the kitchen in robe and slippers, and chatting with her mother. Rilla was dressed the same way, although she had risen earlier. The two women were alone in the house on the hill.

About ten o'clock, after making some sandwiches to take to Ron at the shop on Shelter Road, where he had spent the night, Lue dressed in jeans and a light shirt, then pulled on a pale blue windbreaker. She piled into the big Pontiac and drove to Deena's first, then headed over to the shop to deliver lunch to Ron. Looking back on the morning several months later, Rilla Smith could only say that it seemed no different than any other morning. Just another normal day.

About the time Lue was leaving her house, Ken Arrasmith was on his cellular telephone, talking to Detective Tom White, who at that moment was standing in the office of the Asotin County prosecutor, ready to present evidence that could result in the arrests of Ron and Luella Bingham. Arrasmith thanked White for the information, told him, erroneously, that another young girl, meaning Tara Lebolt, had been moved into the Bingham home, then hung up.

He drove the black Toyota extended-cab pickup truck down the road from his parents' home to the Clarkston shop of Kyle Richardson, stopping there long enough to slice some holes in a slender cardboard box and fold it around the Tec-9 semiautomatic rifle. He borrowed a black T-shirt bearing the "Bad Boys" logo from Kyle and pulled it over his head, covering the Ruger 9mm pistol that bulged a holster at his left shoulder. On the

T-shirt, he wrote in ink: Don't Touch Our Daughters. Three other weapons, all fully loaded, were stashed in his truck, and he also had a small microcassette tape recorder. Before he drove away, he gave his wristwatch to Richardson.

Minutes later, he drove onto Shelter Road, killed a prone Ron Bingham with a fusillade of bullets from the Tec-9, then hunted down and repeatedly shot Luella in the back with the Ruger.

13

The transformation of Ken Arrasmith into a folk hero avenger began immediately. The authorities, at first glance, should have been satisfied with the investigation. After all, they had eyewitnesses who saw Arrasmith pull the trigger and they had found the murder weapons in his truck. Murder cases had been successfully concluded with a lot less. But they had not counted on the impact of words and images. They were about to be buried beneath a story that would assume a force all its own as a gullible media transformed Arrasmith into a symbol, a champion of true justice, a child-protecting vigilante.

The first volley was fired four days after the killings. On May 21, Robert G. Hough, a brother-in-law of Arrasmith, told a reporter that "Ken's goals are to make this a safe place for girls and boys to live." Hough, the family spokesman, modestly added, "In no way does Kenny or the family take this as heroism . . . Ken said he wants to send a message to the nation."

Another four days and the message had solidified. In a Speech 101 college class, one of Arrasmith's sisters, Marlene Thornton, dedicated her homework assignment to her incarcerated brother. In a brief speech entitled, "Protect Our Kids From Sexual Offenders," she laid out the exact road map of the eventual defense strategy.

She said the law "protects the sex offenders" and disclosed the dark background of Ron and Luella Bingham. Then she assessed "victims' rights" and described how Cynthia was placed in the juvenile detention center "to protect her from further abuse. Meanwhile, Ken Arrasmith is being accused of murder. If the laws and the red tape did not slow down the investigation process, this may have been prevented." She closed by asking for contributions to a special defense fund at the Sea First Bank in Clarkston.

Had the prosecutors and investigators heard what was being said in Jacob Watson's classroom, they would have had an idea of what was to soon overwhelm the case. Marlene Thornton's speech was a quiet rumble of distant thunder.

Still, it established the pattern. The law was at fault, not the man who pulled the trigger. The victims in the case were not the people Arrasmith shot, but the people that Ron and Luella had sexually molested. Cynthia had been locked up to protect her from abuse, not to keep her from running away to California with her much-older boyfriend. While the Binghams' background was examined in lewd detail, there was no mention at all of Arrasmith's own background, including his temper and drug use. Certainly, not a word was mentioned that he was more than thirty thousand dollars in arrears on his child support payments. The financial sleight-of-hand by which he and Donnita piled up a small fortune also wasn't part of the speech.

The emotional presentation was only half a loaf of information. It worked in the classroom that day and, tightly honed, would work even better in months to come when reporters and television personalities, who should have known better, repeated the intentionally distorted version. A songwriter named Grady Shawver wrote a long ditty dedicated to Arrasmith that warbled: "He did what any good daddy would do."

In a television interview from jail, Arrasmith stared solemnly into the camera and asked, ''What would you do?''

Arrasmith needed a lawyer. As the weeks progressed, he began running a small, but important, business from his cell. Throughout the case, it would be Ken Arrasmith calling the shots on everything. But with the defense pattern already established, the first item on his agenda was to obtain legal representation. Actually, he had no trouble at all. With the story already gathering publicity, lawyers from all over the surrounding region and as far away as Seattle were calling him. The prisoner had the unique opportunity of picking almost anyone he wanted. Any good defense lawyer loves a challenge, and if the case involves a highly publicized trial, so much the better. Arrasmith, starting his pattern of running his case from his jail cell, quickly eliminated the ambulance chasing variety of attorney in favor of a reputable firm.

Roy Mosman, sixty-three, and his sons, Craig and Wynn, veterans of the court system and possessing impeccable credentials, were asked to come to the jail for a talk, and after interviewing Arrasmith, they liked what they saw: a sincere man who insisted he was forced to defend his daughter. They agreed to represent him.

Their reputations were formidable, their manner casual and their tenacity remarkable. In a trial in Los Angeles, a couple of big-city lawyers who had just been squelched in a case by the small-town Mosmans walked away muttering, ''I think we've just been 'Aw, shucksed' to death.''

Roy was a former Nez Perce County prosecuting attorney, a former state senator for Idaho and a current member of the state school board. He had overcome a tough childhood in Boise, where friends said his dream was only to become a beer truck driver. A football scholarship made college possible, but a leg injury thwarted that and he finished on a financial shoestring. Along the way, he met and married his wife, Barbara, who took him to services at a Mormon temple, where Mosman finally found direction in his life. He became a devout member of the church, as would his family members, and eventually rose to become a bishop.

He and his wife chose to have a large family and all of their children became successful, most in the practice of law. As the Arrasmith case dawned, Craig and Wynn were in practice with their father, Mike was a lawyer in Portland after service as a clerk in the Washington Supreme Court, and daughter Jill was married to a Boise attorney. Only son Matt sought another horizon, becoming a computer expert in Portland.

Craig, thirty-six, who would share the Arrasmith defense with his father, was also once a prosecutor and was considered an expert in the arcane laws involving the sexual abuse of children. A graduate of Utah State University and holding a law degree from the University of Idaho, he had been practicing law for ten years and had a flair for the dramatic defense. With a mild temperament and an efficient manner, Craig had once been groomed for political office before illness forced him to abandon such a career.

Wynn, thirty-one, another University of Idaho graduate, would tend the family law business and do background work on the cases while his brother and father handled the courtroom duties in Idaho v. Arrasmith.

Watching with some dismay as the Mosmans signed on was Denise Rosen, the current Nez Perce County Prosecuting Attorney, who had begun her law career as a legal secretary for ten years after graduating from high school, rising to become the chief deputy clerk for the state of Washington, before going to college and getting her own law degree. Becoming a lawyer in Lewiston meant a pay cut for her from her executive duties with Washington. She eventually won her courtroom spurs and was appointed to the county prosecutor's position in 1992 to fill out an unexpired term, then ran and won the office outright in 1993. She was slight in build and small in stature, but just as tenacious as the Mosmans. In the small world around the valley, Denise Rosen, a native and resident of Lewiston, had known the Mosmans much of her life. She had attended school with Mike, worked with Craig on sexual abuse issues and now held the same prosecutor's office once occupied by Roy.

Tiny but unafraid, she regularly handled murder cases, including the recent incident of a triple homicide that occurred only four houses away from her own home. Killer, kidnappers, rapists and other violent felons would find that, as mean as they thought they were, little Denise Rosen was their worst nightmare.

She respected the Mosmans but did not fear them as courtroom adversaries. As prosecuting attorney, Rosen could command the efforts of a number of state and local experts, including policemen and deputy sheriffs. These officials dealt with crime on a daily basis. While others might be building Ken Arrasmith into mythic hero status, one confided, "To me, he's just another scumbag." And at the top of the heap on this case would be a tough, veteran deputy who was a very careful and thorough investigator, Wade Ralston. He had been a cop for twenty-five years and had spent the last fourteen in the Nez Perce County Sheriff's Office. Ironically, in one of the many twists of fate in this case, Wade Ralston had grown up in the same farming area as Donnita Weddle and had known her since childhood.

A third important member would soon be added to the prosecutorial team. Rosen told the County Commissioners she would need special help on the complicated Arrasmith case. To keep the office running smoothly with the rest of the county caseload, she needed a teammate assigned just to the complicated Arrasmith matter. The commissioners agreed and allowed her to hire a special prosecutor, Michael Kane. A New York native who had moved to California, then Idaho as a child, Kane had practiced law for fifteen years and had spent most of his professional career as a county prosecutor and with the state criminal investigation division. He had handled high profile cases from one end of Idaho to the other and this one didn't particularly impress him as being filled with deep moral issues. "This had nothing to do with frontier justice. It was a sordid killing in a squalid case," he would say when it was finished.

Now it was time for the Mosmans to react. Having the experienced Kane at her side definitely strengthened Rosen's hand. The Mosmans launched a fierce campaign to keep him away from the Arrasmith case, but failed.

Observers felt the defense and prosecution matchup was about even, joking that tickets should be sold to the trial. It would prove something to watch, indeed.

Josh Bingham had despaired when his parents were killed. He challenged death by challenging life, going into denial and immediately journeying to Seattle for a Led Zeppelin concert instead of sitting at home, grieving. He eventually came back, to flounder in his misery and smoke marijuana. However, his friends at school worked hard to keep his spirits up. Anyone who became accusatory toward Josh soon found themselves facing off with a number of his protective pals. Whatever Ron and Luella had done, they said, had nothing to do with Josh.

Only two days after the shootings, he was summoned by a teacher who told him an anonymous donor was offering him a fully paid two weeks at a Christian camp called Malibu, north of Vancouver, in Canada, as soon as school was out. No one there would know anything about what had happened to his parents. Josh accepted the offer and would later say the retreat changed his life. "It got me away from this place, gave me a chance to be by myself and think about some stuff. A couple of weeks after I got back, I stopped doing drugs.''

Meanwhile, the investigation began with the most rudimentary steps. A bond hearing on the day of the shootings resulted in a $1 million bail figure for Ken Arrasmith, and an extradition order shifted him back across the river to Nez Perce County, lodging him in the third-floor jail of the Lewiston courthouse. He was charged officially with two counts of murder in the first degree.

On May 23, Deputy Wade Ralston got a picture of the prisoner and asked his secretary to search the police files and find five other photographs of men with similar facial and physical characteristics. Seventeen-year-old Robert Warnock, who had been a witness to the shootings, was brought in again, this time voluntarily and without handcuffs, and shown the photo montage. Ralston emphasized there was no significance to any of the photographs, but Warnock immediately put his finger on Photo Number Five—Ken Arrasmith. That job was done. The witness could pick out the defendant, something that always causes police to hold their breath.

That same day, the jeweled ring that Ron and Luella Bingham had purchased to mark their twenty-fifth wedding anniversary was delivered to the house. Rilla Smith sent it back.

A week later, on the last day of May 1995, the unofficial defense strategy was set. Arrasmith would be portrayed as a hero, not a double-murderer. The trick was to put the Binghams on trial. Only three people really knew what happened in those few violent moments on Shelter Road, and two of them were dead. Dead people cannot testify or throw into doubt the version of the live defendant.

The team went public on May 31 with a news conference at Beachview Park in Clarkston, where questions were answered by Bob Hough and the suave, gray-haired Roy Mosman. The attorney said, ominously, that Cynthia couldn't be there with them because she was in a hospital being treated for things "that can't be fixed with a scalpel." The teenager's drug and runaway problems were not mentioned.

"I think that Ken Arrasmith is not guilty," declared Roy Mosman, to a round of applause. Another attendee at the gathering said, "I think someone should pin a medal" on Arrasmith. Many wore burgundy ribbons and buttons bearing the message, "Protect Our Children." Hough announced that a legal defense fund had been set up and volunteers would be collecting money. There was no hint of using any of Donnita's money to defend the man she still unofficially claimed was her husband, the man with whom she had continued to live until he was arrested.

Mosman claimed that Denise Rosen had overstepped the boundary on this case and should reevaluate the charges because "she didn't know all the facts." Contacted later, Rosen responded that she had plenty of facts to charge Arrasmith with two counts of first degree murder. It was only the beginning of the legal tennis game between the Nez Perce County prosecutor and the man who had once held the same position. They would not be friends when the Arrasmith case was done.

A preliminary hearing was held June 7 and a magistrate bound Arrasmith over for trial before a district court jury on the two murder charges. Some two dozen of Arrasmith's supporters and family members crowded the courtroom, and during breaks, the prisoner held hands with Donnita and once kissed the hand of his mother, Evelyn.

Denise Rosen put young Robert Warnock on the witness stand to identify Arrasmith as the triggerman. It should have been one of the easiest steps of the entire proceeding. But on this day, Arrasmith was well-

scrubbed and dressed in a dark blue suit, looking more
like a lawyer than a killer. Warnock failed to identify
Arrasmith, as he sat between his two lawyers, who also
wore suits. Only after Rosen prodded the witness could
he say that the man in the suit resembled the man whose
picture he had picked out of the police photographs. Rosen breathed a sigh of relief as the case held together
enough to be sent to the 2nd District Court of Judge Ida
Leggett. A bit of optimism bloomed at the defense table.

Actually, there was reason for optimism and it had
nothing to do with the memory of Bobby Warnock. Ever
since the Mosmans had taken the case, they had been
deluged with communications from other women who
had been molested or raped in the past by Ron and
Luella Bingham. A shocking number of victims who had
been silent for years suddenly decided to step forward
in support of their new hero, Ken Arrasmith, who had
killed their abusers. With those developments, nothing
less than media dynamite, it was time for the defense to
turn up the heat.

14

Until now, the story had been almost totally local in its coverage, with some regional newspapers in Idaho and Washington running occasional reports. That came to an abrupt end on Friday, June 16, when a lengthy story was carried in the prestigious *Boston Globe* newspaper, written by none other than Stan Grossfeld, a winner of the Pulitzer Prize. Craig Mosman, considered an expert in cases of child sexual abuse, had a wide net of contacts in that field and one of those sources learned of his latest case and contacted the *Globe* reporter. Thus, Stan Grossfeld, the sophisticated East Coast writer, journeyed to the heartland of Idaho to blow the lid off the Arrasmith case.

Grossfeld's lengthy story was a colorful and one-sided representation of the case, featuring an exclusive jailhouse interview with the defendant, who confided to the Boston writer that "I'm not a hero. I'm a dad." It was a masterful piece of what political consultants call "spinning" a story, by presenting exactly what favors one point of view and squelches the opposition. It was quite easy to suppress the contrary view because the police and prosecutors, trying to prepare their case for trial, would not comment on specifics of their investigation. That left the field open to the vocal supporters of Ken

Arrasmith, who smothered the man from Boston.

Although the report carried a couple of comments from people on the street and some terse comments from officialdom, Grossfeld bought the attractively wrapped, easily presented Arrasmith package. He wrote extensively of the Binghams' background, but nowhere in Grossfeld's long *Globe* piece was any mention of the public records, available for the asking, concerning the background of Ken Arrasmith, their family and friends.

Denise Rosen told him, "This case will be decided in a court of law by a jury of twelve people, not the media." Eventually she would be proven right, but the media coverage was just beginning.

The *Globe* story launched the Arrasmith saga, a harrowing tale of frontier justice in which lazy cops forced a loving father to protect his innocent child, onto the national stage. Newspapers were not the best vehicle to carry the load on this one, but merely the agent to thrust the story before a much larger audience—the television talk show. Therein lay the trigger, because while you cannot find a *Boston Globe* to purchase anywhere in the Lewis-Clark Valley, almost everyone has a television set. In the vast audiences that watch talk shows would be many Idaho residents who might some day be called to jury duty on the case of Ken Arrasmith. The *Globe* piece mirrored the defense blueprint and it was merely a ripple in the media river. Wire services picked it up and television producers, ever eager to grab something sensational for their viewers, noted it with great interest. The storm was approaching.

The judge picked to hear the Arrasmith case, Ida Rudolph Leggett, was an anomaly in the Idaho court system. First, she was a woman. Second, she was short. Third, she was black. But Ida Leggett was one tough cookie.

Leggett had come from a schoolteacher mother and a

sawmill worker father in Alabama. As a black in the South she had been subjected to discrimination and was well aware of injustice. ''I remember what it was like to be a child who loved to read but couldn't use the public library,'' she told an audience years later. A family friend was shot for trying to use a public rest room. The family lived in a small house that rented for six dollars a month and lost even that when the company evicted its workers during a strike. Living on her mother's salary, the family survived.

Leggett was refused financial aid when she first tried to attend college because an adviser claimed that married women had already made their choice of career. She got into school a few years later, graduated from the University of South Florida in Tampa, and earned a fellowship to the law school at Gonzaga University in Washington, on the other side of the country from Florida. Divorced and with three kids, the first thing she did was get a map and find Washington. The law degree led to a job with the U.S. Attorney's Office in Spokane, then to a valuable clerkship with the Washington Supreme Court and a later job with a major law firm in Seattle. She then moved to Coeur d'Alene, where she practiced for about ten years, discovering that racial discrimination was still a part of her life, thanks to white supremists in the region. In 1992 she was appointed by the governor to a 2nd District Court vacancy on the bench. Her practice focused on civil litigation to prevent conflict with her service on the Idaho Commission of Pardons and Parole. She dealt with all kinds of people but had never presided over a murder trial. Arrasmith would be her first.

She would run a level trial, but observers would comment on how she must really feel about the case. One of the things that encouraged her to pursue law was watching attorneys try to collect support payments for her children. The fact that Arrasmith was more than thirty thousand dollars behind in his child support for his four kids would not win him any points with Judge Leggett.

The judge was also well aware of the media frenzy that was about to break over the case. With the infamous trial of athlete O. J. Simpson fresh in the mind of every judge in the country, Leggett determined that her court was not going to become a stage. No television cameras would be allowed inside, and only one still camera would be permitted.

The Intertec-9 semiautomatic rifle of the sort Ken Arrasmith used to riddle the body of Ron Bingham is an interesting weapon. It is a small, lightweight, snub-nosed, fast-firing gun that has the dubious distinction of being among the few weapons banned by the federal Brady Bill. That is due less to its lethalness than to an unusual exterior texture that refuses fingerprints. Police who recovered the weapon from Arrasmith's truck knew it would be difficult to prove that he had handled it. The problem didn't really materialize, one officer said, because "the dummy's fingerprint showed up on the clip."

Nevertheless, police needed to find out how each of the murder weapons came into Arrasmith's possession. The Ruger 9mm pistol was soon traced to a gun shop, but the Tec-9 would cause the police endless frustration. The first call was to the U.S. Bureau of Alcohol, Tobacco and Firearms, which matched the serial number with a weapon that went from the manufacturer to a store in Oregon. Immediately, the trail went freezing cold. The store had long since closed, the salespeople didn't know who the gun was sold to, and all records for that sort of weapons had been sent back to the ATF, where they vanished. Dead end.

Time was not on the side of the investigators. Arrasmith had been arraigned and pleaded innocent before Judge

Leggett, who turned down a request to free him on bail and set the trial date for November 6. He again wore his blue suit to court, and there was a tearful reunion with Cynthia. Now out of the hospital, she rose from the front row and wrapped him in an emotional hug. Naturally, the camera caught the magic moment. It would become a standard feature of the media portrayal of the story.

Soon afterward, Arrasmith granted the *Lewiston Morning Tribune* an interview from the jailhouse. Normally, defendants charged in serious criminal matters do not speak with reporters for fear of jeopardizing their case. Ken Arrasmith, however, was intent on getting his message out and ignored his lawyers' advice to be quiet. He would talk to almost anyone, and particularly welcomed calls from reporters and producers. Then, in a twist, he actually began calling *them*. Reporter Joan Abrams of the *Morning Tribune* became familiar with a tinny voice in her telephone addressing her sweetly, "Joanie." Arrasmith always used his interviews to polish his mantra. "When it comes time for everything to come out at the trial, a lot of people will get sick. You can't believe the sickness that will come out," he said. "It turns my stomach." If a reporter sought to shift the discussion to points other than the almost scripted recitation, Arrasmith would not answer. "We've got to stop these predators from feeding on our children," he would say. "I'm not a martyr, I'm no hero. I'm just a dad."

He responded in a consistent manner, with Question A receiving a carefully crafted Response A. Reporters found that it was impossible to steer him off the practiced line. If they pushed too hard, he would say he couldn't discuss some matters because of the pending trial. In his numerous interviews, however, Arrasmith never admitted guilt or took responsibility for the brutal deaths of Ron and Luella Bingham.

The choir of his supporters was persistent and united. Tina Cole Turner voiced her outrage that she had not received justice when the Binghams raped her. She blamed the law, even though it was the decision to remove her from the state that prohibited a trial. Cynthia was available for comment, and Donnita was always at hand for a few words. The fact that the Binghams were guilty of reprehensible crimes themselves made it all that much easier for supporters to crown Arrasmith with a halo of vigilante justice.

While the supporters could paint such a picture in the media, Arrasmith's lawyers carefully kept away from that scenario. Using the avenging father tactic would backfire in the legal arena, since it would mean that Arrasmith had planned to kill Ron and Lue with clear premeditation. Revenge meant murder.

Sometimes luck favors those who are persistent. The investigators got a break when Deputy Wade Ralston, refusing to give up on tracing the Tec-9, managed to contact the man who had been head of security for the store that originally had sold the weapon. Wait, the guy said, all of those records weren't destroyed, no matter what happened to them at the ATF. He had personally kept photocopies. Give me a few days, he promised. I'll see what I can find. Eventually, he came up with a name. Police were suddenly one important step closer to putting the gun into Arrasmith's hands.

The first media coverage immediately after the arrest of Arrasmith had been an amateur production, with only nine family members and close friends welcoming a few reporters to the Arrasmith backyard. Along with their story, they offered refreshments and soft drinks to the media. Within weeks, the organizers had accelerated their efforts and had become very smooth at handling the press, particularly after the *Boston Globe* article had generated cash donations from around the nation. The biggest event was on Saturday, July 22, at the Asotin

County Fairgrounds, where a "spaghetti feed" was held to raise money for the Arrasmith Defense Fund. For five dollars, people got a ticket for food and soda pop in Floch Hall, as well as a chance to participate in an auction of items ranging from a used snowmobile to a stuffed dog to a pair of dinners at a local restaurant. A dance followed the auction and the pink-buttoned "Protect Our Children" team called for people to come and help "a great cause." The defense fund soon had more than seven thousand dollars in its treasury, meaning that Arrasmith and Donnita still did not have to reach into their own pockets for money.

Then began the summer of televised discontent as the Arrasmith supporters found the weak point of television. They could provide producers with a couple of emotionally hot topics—sexual abuse of children and vigilante justice—true villians, an attractive hero, crying victims who were young and pretty, and outraged townfolk. Not only talk shows, but the television seminews programs usually considered more responsible soon marched in lockstep to the jailhouse door of Ken Arrasmith, ready to report his side of the story, and only his side.

The feeding frenzy exploded at the jail one morning, with CBS creating a predawn fiasco. The CBS morning show had arranged with someone other than the Nez Perce County Sheriff, Ron Koepper, to interview Arrasmith live at 4:15 A.M., with another crew from the network downstairs to interview Tina Cole Turner, who would wear her "Daughter of Ken Arrasmith" button. The Turner interview, however, had been moved to the second floor, one floor below the jail by the time Koepper found out what was going on and erupted in anger. The outraged sheriff felt his jail was being turned into a television studio, and when the crew would not stop broadcasting at his request, he pulled the plug midway through the interview and CBS went dark.

Meanwhile, in the parking lot, another camera crew,

from another network's newsmagazine, jumped into action as soon as they learned of the CBS debacle. They tried the doors, which were locked, then scrambled up the outside fire escape to the third floor, trying to get into the jail through the kitchen. Deputies swarmed out and chased them back down the metal stairs.

The media relations, already one-sided, turned even more sour.

Next came the ABC newsmagazine show *20/20*, with superstar personalities Barbara Walters and Hugh Downs. Experienced reporter Tom Jarriel journeyed to the valley for the assignment. The cameras were allowed to interview Arrasmith, his blue eyes peering into the lens from behind bars. Outside the jail, the camera caught pictures of a group of demonstrators carrying signs calling for Arrasmith's freedom, and of Cynthia waving from the sidewalk to her daddy, who flashed a mirror in response.

The story followed the now familiar track, with interviews of the Binghams' victims and Arrasmith family members. Copies of courthouse files detailing the background of Ron and Luella Bingham were shown. It must have made the Arrasmith team rejoice, for Jarriel didn't even come close to exploring information about the background of Arrasmith, which was available from exactly the same source. The nationally viewed show failed to scratch the surface of anything that would disturb the slant of the Arrasmith story and presented a distorted image of the facts. Hugh Downs, at the end of the piece, was barely able to contain his outrage over a child's sexual abuse forcing her father to kill people. "God," he said, with a shake of his carefully groomed head.

The show was dreadful. The image of an outraged town totally supporting Arrasmith's actions was nothing but a performance by a small band of demonstrators marching in a circle before the *20/20* camera, the only day they marched in front of the jail at all. The other side of the story could have easily been discovered with a little bit of basic journalistic investigation, but the court clerk said that no one asked for any records regarding Arrasmith. The episodes were shallow and sensationalist—and that was the quality of work being done by the *responsible* television network shows.

Then Cynthia and Donnita flew out to appear on the *Montel Williams Show*. It was the first major talk show for the team, but not the last. Before things cooled, Cynthia would appear on *Oprah*, *Donahue*, *Leeza* and others, and they all made the same mistake. The problem with such shows is that young producers who handle the booking of guests are hundreds, if not thousands, of miles away from Idaho. Since they are not journalists in the first place, they had no one in Clarkston and Lewiston digging for background. The clever supporters of Arrasmith therefore were able to serve up their ready-made package, while the prosecution side could not furnish nifty clips and tearful interviews, nor even discuss the case in-depth without jeopardizing evidence and witnesses.

So the producers took what they could get and rushed away to begin work on some future show. Guests normally meet the hosts and hostesses only on the set of the show, and the people who lend their names to the telecasts have little contact with the real story. They merely pilot the ship and try to create an interesting half hour of television.

So it was with Montel Williams, who went a step beyond the norm by putting Cynthia on the show alongside former Miss America Marilyn van Derbur Atler, a champion for victims of incest. "When these women say they are afraid for their lives, believe them," Atler declared.

Tina Cole, Cynthia, Donnita and Lora Smith unrolled the vile tapestry of the Binghams' sexual behavior and, since almost every charge they made was true, the picture was bleak indeed. Donnita said the prosecutor was "treating Ken horribly," as if there were something wrong with putting someone charged with two murders in jail. Montel bought the whole line and repeatedly ran the address, Post Office Box 575 in Lewiston, to which people could send donations to the Arrasmith Defense Fund.

Ken, from jail, asked Williams if justice doesn't protect children, who will? "You're right," thundered the outraged TV *talkmeister*. "I believe Ken should be free!"

He added that Ken was "a good family man." He either did not know, or ignored, the fact that the oft-married Arrasmith was more than thirty thousand dollars behind in child support. With Williams hooked, Arrasmith began to slide in "known facts" about the case that were questionable, but went out on national television.

The subject matter, boldly called "Survivors of Terrorists of Children," so touched Williams that he decided on stage to extend the program for another hour. The extra edition was shown the following day and was more of the same, with the women sitting side-by-side, holding hands through the ordeal. Williams agreed that the police were lazy in the case and hinted at dark dealings within both the law enforcement agencies and the local media. "The town of Lewiston, Idaho, is trying to shut this down," Williams declared. It seemed the *Montel Williams Show* host and producers had been used and were either unwilling or unable to present anything but a lopsided, tear-jerking saga.

The final media shoe dropped when *People* magazine devoted a major story to the Arrasmith saga, entitled "Rage in a Small Place." The usual pattern was followed, accompanied by slick color photographs of Lora and Donnita, with one shot of Tina and Cynthia together and smiling at the foot of the Bingham driveway. The interview with Arrasmith ended with his trademark question: "What would you do if it was your daughter?" The reporter was one of the few who actually interviewed Rilla Smith and the story even contained a few paragraphs that centered on Arrasmith's legal and police record, although not in-depth, such as failing to give the huge amount involved in the "nonpayment of child support." When the cops wouldn't talk about the case that had not yet been tried, the reporter wrote there were "no answers" to some questions. Actually, there were answers, but they would only come out later in court.

Reporter Judith Valente of Chicago said later she "haunted" Denise Rosen's office in hopes of an interview to balance the story. Law enforcement personnel by now had grown thoroughly distrustful of the media and reluctant to deal with any reporter. That played into a weakness of the print media that was almost as bad as the teardrop-stained packaging so beloved by TV tabloids and talk shows. The print media has deadlines and cannot wait for the conclusion of a trial to report on the crime. *People* was published the month before the trial began, and since the prosecutors weren't giving interviews and wouldn't divulge evidence, the story favored Arrasmith and his supporters, who were only too happy to assist the magazine writer from Chicago.

One item that particularly galled prosecutors was the magazine's quote from Arrasmith that when Cynthia appeared in juvenile court she was thinking, "An adult raped me and I'm the one locked up." The reporter did not know, so could not write, that Arrasmith himself was the one who insisted that his daughter be arrested.

Another section dealt with the "mystery" of why police who participated in the drug raid didn't call Cynthia's mother and father or Child Protective Services. Again, the reporter did not learn that Cynthia lied to police about the telephone numbers and strongly insisted that she had permission to live at the Bingham home and wanted to stay there. She was also unaware of the existence of the medical permission slip signed by Cynthia's mother.

Throughout the summer of 1995, the media portrayed a biased picture of Ken Arrasmith, a white knight, riding to rescue his abused daughter. Meanwhile, he still did not admit that he had killed Ron and Luella Bingham.

Even as the shows went on and the newspapers and magazines published their articles, the police investigators plodded ahead with their jobs. There were two important developments. The Tec-9 had been traced through more than a dozen owners and finally led back to the valley. And throughout the investigation, one name began to surface frequently—an overweight drug dealer named Kyle Richardson.

15

By September 26, Detective Wade Ralston had heard enough to ask Kyle Richardson to come in for an interview. His name had popped up through talks with others who had been interviewed. An anonymous caller claimed that Richardson had actually been involved in the killings, and Richardson admitted he knew Arrasmith, and sometimes visited him in Sunnyside.

As he began talking to Richardson, Ralston immediately homed in on the question of the Tec-9. Kyle replied that he owned one, but it was in Oregon with a friend he knew only as "Bill." He began to dodge when the deputy started asking whether Richardson had been looking for a clip for the Tec-9 and the SKS rifle just before the Binghams were killed. Richardson said that Ken had fired and liked Kyle's Tec-9 and had been looking in stores for one to buy. "We both like guns a lot so we looked at a lot of guns," he said. The interview gave away nothing of importance, and Richardson did not link his Tec-9 to Arrasmith. But Ralston knew more. "The pieces were starting to fall together," he recalled later. "I know he's in."

The Defense Fund, riding the wave of sympathetic publicity, was continuing to grow and would soon crest the thirty-thousand mark. Some two dozen merchants had donation cannisters in their shops. The image was slightly tarnished, however, at the start of August. Cynthia ran away from home again, and Linda Bartlett filed a new runaway report with the police. Cynthia returned home later and Arrasmith would insist that the event was a minor disagreement and was being blown out of proportion. "I don't want people to think she's a juvenile delinquent," he told a reporter. Official sources maintained that although the furor quieted quickly, it was serious.

Not everyone in town was on board the Arrasmith bandwagon, particularly the editorial writers of the local newspaper, the *Lewiston Morning Tribune*. Close to the scene and able to separate the truth from the fiction, the *Tribune* ran a scathing editorial in late August that said Arrasmith's defenders "are trapped by their own argument. If you don't really require a trial to kill people who have been molesting someone you care about, but can grab a gun and do the job yourself when you're sure the molesters are guilty, then the same treatment is relevant to Arrasmith.

"It doesn't matter that he has pleaded innocent. If practically everyone is pretty darn sure he did it, then why waste money on a trial? Just send a mob over to the jail to cart him off to the state prison."

It was not the sort of coverage the defense enjoyed, because it exposed the weakness in their presentation. All of Lewiston and Clarkston were not behind Ken Arrasmith. In fact, just as many people were speaking out against him as were for him.

The offices of the sheriff and the prosecutor were being deluged with calls and reporters began receiving anonymous tips. "I was getting calls from all over," Denise Rosen would recall later. Of course, the anonymous tipsters only made their claims in secret, then vanished from view. None could be proven and the authorities paid them little mind, for the allegations had nothing to do with the two murders on Shelter Road.

The reports, however, did show that Lewiston and Clarkston were not united behind Arrasmith. From the media reports, one would have expected to see banners and buttons and bumper stickers in support of Arrasmith throughout the region. In reality, they were rare. The picture was distorted because people with negative things to say didn't have the media fawning over them.

Denise Rosen had finally had enough of the pro-Arrasmith publicity binge. Contending the defense was trying to "impassion and inflame" the public with media hype, she warned the court that it might soon prove impossible to find a neutral jury. The prosecutor asked the court for a "gag order" to prevent Arrasmith, his lawyers and all witnesses from speaking to the press about the case.

That motion, which would be denied, was merely a fragment of what was going on in the rough-and-tumble legal world. Judge Leggett did hand down an order of rigid rules of behavior in and near the courthouse during the trial, barring the wearing of the pink buttons and burgundy ribbons and ruling the media could not conduct interviews on the courthouse grounds. No demonstrations would be tolerated.

Behind the scenes, a major legal point was being hotly debated. The Mosmans were fighting hard to be allowed to introduce the murky past of Ron and Luella Bingham to the jury, knowing that a litany of some twenty Bingham victims, repeated to the point of horror, would be too much for any juror to ignore. Rosen and Kane argued back, just as hard, that the Binghams were not on trial and that the past behavior of victims is rarely allowed into a courtroom.

*   *   *

Ralston and Mike Kane interviewed Kyle Richardson again on October 3, only a month before the trial was to start. When questioned about the Tec-9, Richardson stuck to his story that Ken was not seriously trying to persuade Kyle to give him the gun. "It was kind of a joke between us," he told the special prosecutor and the deputy sheriff. Richardson also said Arrasmith didn't come by the shop "on a regular basis."

"There is no way that you ever saw this Tec-9 that was used in the shooting?" asked Ralston.

"No," said Richardson.

"There is no way you assisted him in getting that Tec-9?"

"No."

Then Richardson dodged the issue of whether Arrasmith knew that Kyle dealt drugs, although Ralston dropped the nugget of information that Arrasmith had hinted to Sheriff Jeffers that he was ready to turn in some people that were using meth. "I think that probably he was maybe thinking about turning you and his ex-wife in. It's my supposition," Ralston said.

Finally, the deputy made one more try with the Tec-9 question. "No way, no how was that gun . . . did you know anything about that gun?" Richardson shook his head and said "Uh-uh," meaning no.

Richardson was lying. He knew it and the investigators knew it. The next day, Ralston interviewed Wes Rehm, who had paid $350 for the Tec-9, only to have it stolen from his house, allegedly by the son of his girlfriend. And the day after that, the deputy talked with Jerry Jobe, who said he had bought the weapon from the person that Rehm believed had stolen it. And Jobe dropped the hammer on the case.

He told the detective that, not only did he sell the Tec-9 to Kyle Richardson for some cash and drugs, but that his uncle, John Sweat, had visited Kyle's garage later, met and snorted meth with Ken Arrasmith, and had been handed a big rifle and offered $2,500 by Richardson "to take a hit on a couple people."

Jobe also said: "Kyle proceeded to say that Ken Arrasmith is real bummed out because his daughter keeps running away and going over to these people's houses where there was drugs involved and she was doing it, and Kyle Richardson said that Ken Arrasmith told him that his daughter was taking payments of crank for sleeping with these people and stuff." Sweat was interviewed the same day and supported Jobe's statement.

Kyle Richardson had another interview on the afternoon of October 11, and still seemed unable to understand his dilemma. This time, Prosecutor Denise Rosen increased the pressure on the young man and his interrogators were Russ Reneau and Scott Birch, a pair of criminal investigators from the office of the Idaho Attorney General. After Wade Ralston had set the table, Reneau and Birch were about to dine.

The two investigators went over the familiar ground first, that Richardson had met Arrasmith through Ken's ex-wife, and the two men had become friends. Richardson hemmed and hawed, being unclear on his answers, saying he and Arrasmith spent most of their time of the critical week in May "just going out and goofing around." He did describe helping Arrasmith spy on the Bingham residence, but began to shy away from direct answers when Reneau brought up the subject of the Tec-9.

The investigator said he had the receipt from the pawnshop where Richardson had purchased the Tec-9 that Kyle had insisted vanished with his mysterious friend "Bill" three months ago. Reneau pushed: "Did you ever simultaneously own more than one or two at the same time?" Richardson denied it.

In was a classic interrogation. Based upon what Ralston had pulled from the reluctant young man earlier,

Reneau nudged Richardson toward a legal cliff. He said the police had good information that Kyle "did in fact purchase another Tec-9 shortly before the murder." They had the names of the people involved, an eyewitness to the purchase and the serial number. "I honestly don't remember that," Richardson lied.

"This gun was stolen, it was sold to someone else by the thief," Reneau continued, unperturbed, laying out corroborated fact. "That person said he sold the gun to you. We can establish . . . the serial number on the gun that was stolen. We can walk that gun through every person who had it until you got it. Okay, do you follow me?"

"Yeah."

"All right," Reneau said. "The gun that was seized from Ken Arrasmith's truck when he was arrested bears that same serial number."

Kyle Richardson suddenly saw the box into which he had walked trying to shield his friend. His stammering answer was erratic. "Well, I can't . . . I own a Tec-9, but I . . . I know I got it . . . an SKS, not too long before, uhm, that happened. I don't remember a Tec-9 getting . . . getting a Tec-9 right before that happened."

There was more desultory talk and Reneau said, "We have got it going from Jerry Jobe to you. What we need to figure out is how it gets from you to Arrasmith." Richardson said he didn't remember and needed to sit back and think for a while. "There's . . . a lot . . . a lot . . . you know, a lot of stuff going on . . . just kind of . . . my mind is not too intact."

The investigators could almost smell blood in the water and soon moved in harder, saying they weren't trying to build some dinky drug case. "This is a double murder case," Reneau said when Richardson hedged on giving the names of some vague people he mentioned. "We have got two people who are dead, one person who is going to go to trial for killing those two people. We are

beyond whether or not people want to become involved." And, frankly, Reneau said, a lot of what Kyle
was telling authorities "doesn't make a lot of sense."

Their patience wore thin and a few minutes later Scott
Birch decided to spell things out perfectly clearly when
Kyle once again skated around remembering whether he
got the Tec-9 from Jerry Jobe. "Are you going to go
through your entire life forgetting things, Kyle?"

"No. I hope not," the large young man replied.

"I hope not, too. Particularly something that could be
as important to your life as this is. If you got the gun
from him and gave it to Ken or sold it to Ken or Ken
asked you to get it, then, damn it, let's get it out and
find out about it now. Because it's gonna come out,"
Birch told Richardson. "And you can either be a willing
participant in it or an unwilling participant in it. You
know, and that's what we're here for is to get at the
damn truth and get, you know, take care of it up front.
Now what happened with the gun?"

Kyle held his ground. "I don't remember. I don't remember ever dealing with Jerry on a Tec-9."

Soon, there was the following exchange as Kyle
stepped deeper into trouble.

Russ: Do you know whether or not Jerry Jobe knew
Ken Arrasmith?

Kyle: Uh, I don't believe he did.

Russ: Okay, so it doesn't seem logical that Ken Arrasmith would buy the gun from Jobe if he didn't know
him.

Kyle: It doesn't seem logical, no.

Russ: But we know that he did come into possession
of it somehow—that's a given.

Kyle: Uh-hun (meaning yes).

Russ: Okay, and we know that Jobe says he sold it to
you. What's wrong with this picture? Where does it
leave you?

Kyle: Kind of sittin' here lookin' stupid, I guess.

The questioning continued and Kyle became evasive again. Birch explained that investigations eventually take on a certain momentum and that if Kyle didn't talk, he soon might lose the opportunity, if the cops found the needed information elsewhere. "You're connected tightly to a gun that was used in a double homicide. That's not a very good place to be," Reneau observed. "And it's even a worse place to be if you don't give any explanation as to how you find yourself there."

Kyle hesitated, saying that the whole thing "is pretty mind-blowing."

It could not have been spelled out any clearer, but Kyle Richardson left the two-hour interview holding to his line that he didn't know anything about the Tec-9 that wound up in the truck of his friend, who had killed two people. The fat man was on thin ice.

A week later, Kyle Richardson ran out of time. Word was on the street that he was preparing to leave town and the trial was simply too close to let him dance away. Denise Rosen determined there was enough evidence to charge Richardson, and Wade Ralston went out at 3:15 P.M. and clapped a set of handcuffs on the reluctant witness and read the required Constitutional guarantees. The charge was a heavy one—conspiracy to commit murder in the first degree. The criminal complaint said he provided the Tec-9 to Ken Arrasmith, offered someone $2,500 to murder people, tried to obtain a magazine for a Tec-9 so "a friend . . . could take care of some people because one clip was not enough," and participated in spying on the Bingham house. Kyle Richardson said he wanted to talk to a lawyer.

16

The legal footwork escalated from the tempo of a leisurely waltz to that of a fast-moving, hip-hop beat in October as the November 6 trial date approached. Strategies became clear and both sides faced a couple of major hurdles.

The prosecutors needed to crack stubborn Kyle Richardson and keep the trial focused on murder. The defense had to get Judge Leggett to buy several substantial items: that no one should be put in legal jeopardy for protecting himself or others, that the jury should be allowed to know the background of the murder victims, and that the numerous women raped by the Binghams should be allowed to testify to show a pattern of behavior. "The jury needs to know this threat of imminent danger was there," Craig Mosman told Leggett in a pretrial hearing. "If (it) is not admitted, it will, quite frankly, tie the hands of the defense." Craig Mosman was betting most of his chips on Idaho Code 19-202(A), a self-defense statute that had never been tested in court, and which some lawyers maintained had a section that would cover such cases as Arrasmith.

Mike Kane made his debut for the prosecution during that hearing, arguing that since Cynthia was locked up at the time of the shootings, she was in no imminent

danger and that it was "ridiculous" to think that Idaho
law allowed someone to be killed because they had committed a crime in the past.

Judge Leggett ruled swiftly, and most of it was bad
news for Arrasmith. Any evidence of past bad acts by
Ron and Luella would not be allowed at the trial. Mosman responded angrily, "There is no defense [now].
They denied me my trial." He hotly accused Denise Rosen of masterminding a "horrible scheme to allow these
kind of monsters to survive in our society." Rosen didn't
respond.

Leggett, looking strictly at the law, was totally un-
moved by such outbursts or the ongoing drumbeat of
publicity the case was drawing as more and more Bingham victims stepped forward, willing to recount their
experiences in court. The judge kept things in perspective: "Ronald and Luella Bingham are not on trial in
this case." She said she saw no proof that Arrasmith
was threatened by the Binghams, nor that the couple
could attack him at the time of the killings. "The general
rule is that even in a self-defense or defense of others
case, evidence that the deceased was a violent or dangerous individual is admissible only when it explains or
gives meaning to his or her conduct at the time of the
killing. There must be some preliminary proof that, at
the time of the homicide, the deceased made some hostile demonstration in connection with his or her known
character or reputation to arouse a reasonable belief on
the part of the defendant of imminent peril to life or limb
from the deceased." Since no weapons were found at
the scene, Ron was beneath a truck and Luella was shot
in the back, the imminent peril argument was difficult to
make.

And as for having the rape victims testify, the judge
said, "Even if the court were to find this evidence relevant, it is so highly prejudicial that its exclusion is war-
ranted. The jury . . . could conclude that the deceased

'got what they deserved' and acquit for that reason.''
She wanted facts in her courtroom, not emotion.

Leggett also didn't buy Arrasmith's argument that the
fact that another girl, Tara Lebold, had stayed with the
Binghams, had placed her in imminent danger. The
judge said the "protection of others" defense did not
hold up when the so-called protection came "days,
weeks or years" before the shootings.

Shortly thereafter followed a distasteful episode. Ken
Arrasmith said he was broke and could no longer afford
to pay for his lawyers. "The defendant does not have
sufficient funds or property to continue to pay his attorneys or to pay for the other costs of his defense," read
the motion.

Denise Rosen immediately countered by claiming Arrasmith was hiding assets in an attempt to avoid paying
overdue child support. She said Donnita Weddle and Arrasmith had purchased numerous properties together and
that Donnita now owned property worth $626,189 in
Nez Perce County alone. "I think these are things that
should be considered in determining (the defendant's)
indigency," the outraged prosecutor said, adding that
Arrasmith was trying to defraud the court. Actually, the
prosecution had been taken by surprise. Until the motion
was filed, they were not even aware the marriage had
been dissolved back in April.

This time, Craig Mosman had the law on his side. He
pointed to the dates of the prenuptial agreement and to
the dissolution of the marriage. He said Arrasmith "described accurately" his financial situation. Donnita said
afterward, however, that "in my heart I still feel married
to Ken." The heart is different from a legal document.
And suddenly, first wife Linda Bartlett began saying she
and Ken were getting along fine and discussions were
underway to settle that child support debt. The front was
united and growing stronger.

Mosman also used the indigency hearing as an opportunity to again appeal to the judge to allow the past bad acts of the Binghams. Leggett denied him once again, but the issue would resurface repeatedly in weeks to come. It was too important for the defense lawyers not to press for it.

Judge Leggett, who once went through the agony of trying to collect child support payments for her own kids, had a thorough dislike for deadbeat dads. But in this case, her hands were tied. Any interest Arrasmith might have in a transaction had been immediately transferred to Donnita by a quit claim deed that would "disabuse others of the notion that some interest in the property is in fact held." The dates were firm and the law was the law. The judge said there was no hard evidence to counter Arrasmith's contention that he didn't have any money. "The Supreme Court has held that mere innuendo, suspicion or conjecture that a defendant may be able to secure or advance costs is insufficient," she wrote. She authorized the use of taxpayer funds to pay the Mosmans sixty dollars an hour to defend Ken Arrasmith. Once again the law raised a protecting shield over Arrasmith, who had constantly cried the law was unfair.

In an accompanying written decision, Judge Leggett knocked down the latest effort to get the Binghams' past into the courtroom. She ruled again that there was no evidence to back up the claim that Arrasmith believed he or anyone else was facing imminent danger.

With trial only a few days away, the judge was under other pressure. This time, the defense team wanted to bring in a Denver psychologist, Lenore Walker, to testify about Arrasmith's state of mind during the killings. Craig Mosman had used testimony by Walker the previous year when he successfully defended a woman accused of murdering her abusive husband while he slept. She also was an author of books on spousal abuse and had even interviewed O. J. Simpson for his Dream Team lawyers, concluding after fifty hours of talks and tests that Simpson was not in the classic mold of abusers who kill.

Denise Rosen countered that Walker's opinion was irrelevant and would only confuse a jury. She wanted the intentions of Ken Arrasmith to be shown by his acts, and not by some hired shrink brought in by the defense. Rosen argued that Walker's opinion "has no basis in science and is nothing more than a veiled attempt to improperly vouch for the defendant's credibility."

This, too, would become a running fight during the trial, but Walker was barred from the witness stand.

At the last moment, the Defense Fund, operating outside the courtroom, muddied the jury selection process by purchasing large newspaper advertisements in several cities. Having already determined that an impartial jury would be hard to find in Lewiston, Judge Leggett decided the search for jurors untainted by the publicity would be held elsewhere. The location was to be kept secret.

It was not too secret, however, for the defendant had a legal right to know the location, and Ken Arrasmith obviously knew how to use the jail telephone. The day that the jury selection process began in the southern border city of Twin Falls, there was a pro-Arrasmith ad in the local newspaper, paid for by Arrasmith's supporters and, according to police, charged to the credit card of Linda Bartlett. It contained the usual fiery comments and pieces of information that the judge had already ruled would not be admitted into the trial. Judge Leggett was furious and said in a hearing that the ad "cannot be viewed as anything other than an attempt to get to potential jurors. This is a serious matter and this court is not going to put up with attempts to make light of this case," she wrote. The Mosmans denied having anything to do with the ad and Roy Mosman said that he received evasive answers when he talked with Linda Bartlett and Donnita Weddle about it.

The prosecution wanted the entire trial to be moved to another city. Leggett denied the request but granted a week's delay in the start of the proceedings for both sides to get their acts together.

Actually, the two days of jury selection left the Mosmans feeling rather buoyant. They had been able to comb carefully through the pool of prospects and have them answer such questions as "How serious is the crime of rape?" and "Have you ever attempted to get the police to do something, but they wouldn't?" and "As a parent, have you ever had a rebellious teenager?" Among the jurors picked was a woman who had once been a rape victim. Another was the mother of eight children. And there was one steely eyed cowboy who Roy Mosman believed "would do the right thing" if he had been in Ken Arrasmith's boots. The prosecution would need a unanimous vote for conviction. The defense only needed one holdout for a hung jury.

It was time to go to trial, and Kyle Richardson was still on the sidelines, holding to his story that he really didn't remember very much at all.

17

On Tuesday, November 7, a stiff "Arctic Express" wind slapped Lewiston after dropping overnight temperatures to only four degrees above freezing. Banks of scudding gray clouds caused a light rain to fall over the region. Voters going to the polls in local elections had their spirits dampened not only by the drizzly weather, but by the knowledge that the sale of alcohol is prohibited in northern Idaho on election day. National headlines showed the stock market had taken a 16.98 point nosedive, the White House and Congress were having one of their seemingly eternal battles over the Federal budget and the famed Landmark Hotel in Las Vegas, a huge saucer atop a 356-foot tower, was intentionally destroyed in a spectacular explosion.

Dismal weather cloaked the Nez Perce County Courthouse, a stone building constructed in 1889 that once served as Idaho's first Supreme Court. Out front sat the statue of a Nez Perce Indian astride an Appaloosa pony, crumbling and badly in need of repair.

Inside, excitement built for the dual appearances on tap that morning—Arrasmith in Courtroom 1, and Kyle Richardson down the hall in Courtroom 3. The front door of the courthouse was closed and locked, requiring everyone to queue at the single door in the rear and file through a Garrett metal detector. Deputies checked everyone whose passage made the machine beep, which was almost one hundred percent of the people filing through. The detector was set so low that even small metal blouse buttons and shoelace eyelets set off its buzzing alarm and flickering red and green lights.

Cynthia Arrasmith was not allowed in the courtroom on the first day because she was scheduled to be a witness. In a worn denim jacket and loose cotton pants, she prowled the hallways, bubbly and basking in the spotlight of attention. Her father would go on trial momentarily for killing two people with whom she had lived, but her main topic of conversation that morning was that she had found a wandering kitten with two different colored eyes and she was working on the grown-ups to let her keep it.

Steve Caylor, who had knit together the arrangements to handle the expected crush of media representatives, the emotional families and the anticipated throng of interested observers, was just outside Courtroom 1, overseeing the distribution of color-coded, clip-on credentials—purple for the press, orange for the relatives and yellow for the public. As the time for the trial neared, he was suprised to find that the big courtroom would not be packed after all. There were actually seats left over, particularly in the press section. The monstrous amount of attention that had been showered on the case earlier was absent when it came time for networks to write the big money checks to commit crews and correspondents to cover the Arrasmith trial as a real news story. With the exception of Geraldo Rivera, who tagged a few minutes of coverage onto the end of each nightly broadcast on CNBC, the silence from the major media was astonishing. They had tasted the gravy and simply were not interested in the meat, content to let their distorted view of the matter stand as truth.

Once the crowd was seated, deputy sheriffs brought

Ken Arrasmith down the stairs outside the main door. He wore a striped shirt and dark tie under a powder blue sweater that bulged slightly at the waist from his months of eating fatty jail food and getting little exercise. His dark brown hair was curly, thinning on top and in the back. He wore his trademark enigmatic half grin as he took his place between his defense lawyers, Craig Mosman on his left and Roy Mosman on the right.

Sergeant Jim Colvin and Deputy Sheriff Scott Storrs took their places on either side of the courtroom, clerk Teresa Hildreth settled behind her computer terminal, and court reporter Nancy Towler prepared her transcribing machine.

Marshal Tommy E. Williams, Jr., a former professional football player, opened the door on the far side of the court and escorted in the jury. The previous day they had been ordinary citizens living their lives in Twin Falls. Since then, they had been snatched into serving on a jury that would occupy them totally for several weeks to come, given tiny "JUROR" buttons to wear, and had spent their first of many nights across the street on the third floor of the Riverside Inn. Five women and one man took seats on the first row of the jury box, two women and four men filing in to sit just behind them. Two alternate jurors, both men, were placed at the left end of the jury box. All of the jurors were white. Notebooks and sharpened pencils lay on each seat.

Boxes and notebooks and briefcases, all crammed with papers, were pushed against the railing behind the prosecution and defense tables, broad wooden surfaces which were separated by the width of a single chair. The people trying to keep Arrasmith behind bars and the ones trying to set him free would be within touching distance. Clear plastic jugs with pink tops had been filled with water by court personnel and were in strategic places. That chore had been handled by jail trustees until one

took his revenge on a judge who sentenced him by filling
the jurist's jug from a toilet.

Judge Ida Leggett burst into the courtroom promptly
at nine o'clock, a bundle of energy and confidence, ready
to get the trial started. She took her seat beneath the
Idaho Great Seal, flanked by flags, and got down to business. For fifteen minutes, in a clear voice, she read page
after page of instructions to the jurors.

Donitta Weddle and the Arrasmith family occupied a
number of seats on the right-hand side of the courtroom.
Across the aisle, Rilla Smith sat with her sister.

The double murder trial of Ken Arrasmith was finally
underway, with the defendant appearing almost cocky.
He smiled and tried to make eye contact with the jurors.

The Arrasmith trial began like a well-oiled engine starting to hum, while just down the narrow courthouse hall-
way, in Courtroom 3, the preliminary hearing for Kyle
Richardson began with a lurch.

First, all charges against the burly defendant were
dropped because that important initial hearing had been
delayed beyond the fourteen-day limit required for a
speedy trial without the consent of the defendant. The
deadline had passed on November 3 because the magistrate scheduled to handle the case was William Stellmon, whose wife is related to the Mosmans, who were
defending Arrasmith. To avoid the appearance of a conflict of interest, Stellmon was out, and the system had to
come up with another judge on short notice. The delay
resulted in the cancellation of the charges and brought
hopeful gasps from Richardson's family.

It was mere legal hoopla. New charges were filed immediately accusing him of conspiracy to commit first
degree murder. Clearwater County Magistrate Judge Patrick Costello took over the case and the hearing resumed
forty-five minutes after the original starting time. The
large twenty-five-year-old man was staring at a possible

maximum sentence of life in prison without parole, perhaps even the death penalty, and he was continuing to hang tough, admitting little and frustrating investigators. But his reservoir of resistance was evaporating.

With Deputy Prosecutor Jamie Shropshire at the helm, the state of Idaho began laying out their evidence to convince the court to bind Richardson over for a full-blown trial. Craig Mosman would come into Courtroom 3 briefly, to report to the judge that his client, Ken Arrasmith, would refuse to answer any questions in the Richardson matter, based on his Fifth Amendment Constitutional right against potential self-incrimination.

That left Richardson out there alone. He knew his buddy had once thought of turning him in to police for dealing drugs, and now Arrasmith was refusing to testify in his behalf—pulling the rug from under the friend who had remained stalwart under police interrogation. In one of his many telephone conversations with *Lewiston Morning Tribune* reporter Joan Abrams, Arrasmith had said that Kyle Richardson had nothing to do with shooting Ron and Lue Bingham. Saying it on the telephone to a reporter was one thing, saying it under oath on the witness stand was another.

Judge Costello decided to continue the hearing for a few weeks, giving the Arrasmith trial time to conclude, then requiring Arrasmith to take the stand in the Richardson case and personally state his refusal to testify.

Normally, defense lawyers and their clients use the preliminary hearing process to discover the depth of the evidence against them. Like so many other things in this case, however, the defense team learned something entirely different—that what they had counted upon so heavily, Arrasmith's comment exonerating Richardson, had vanished from their grasp. By refusing to testify, Arrasmith hung his buddy out to dry.

Kyle Richardson knew police could put the gun that killed Ron and Lue Bingham into his hands, and the witnesses at the preliminary hearing showed that the case that would be presented against him was very strong.

So strong, in fact, that after the hearing, Richardson and his lawyer, Scott Chapman, decided to look again at the deal that prosecutors had been offering for some time. Kyle could plead guilty to a lesser charge and receive a much lighter sentence in exchange for testimony that would show the jury how the Tec-9 got into Arrasmith's possession and detail drug usage and deals made in the car shop.

The choice was to talk and get a good deal, or say nothing and probably get a life term in prison. It was what police called a "Come to Jesus" time for Kyle Richardson, and he got religion quickly.

Meanwhile, back in Courtroom 1, following the instructions from Judge Leggett, the case against Ken Arrasmith finally got down to business.

Denise Rosen had been waiting edgily for months for this moment. Shackled by the need to keep silent to preserve evidence, the prosecutor had been vilified on national television and subjected to letters that dripped with acidic denunciations by people who believed everything the Arrasmith defenders were peddling. On the other hand, her morale had been boosted by steady telephone calls, and letters and notes of support. And on her desk today, she found a single red rose, from an anonymous person seeking to give her encouragement. Finally, after the networks and talk shows had feasted upon the alleged inaction of the law enforcement officers in Clarkston and Lewiston, someone was going to be able to speak out to tell the other side of the story.

At 9:21 A.M., she rose. In a neat blue suit, with her sandy hair swept back, she focused the jury's attention squarely on their job. "There are two murder cases before you today," she told them, adding that not only did the state claim that Ken Arrasmith murdered Ron and Luella Bingham, but that he "cleverly" hid his weapons

Ken Arrasmith confidently awaits the beginning of his
trial. (*Lewiston Morning Tribune*)

Ron Bingham surrounded by his rabbits.
(Courtesy of Rilla Smith)

Luella Bingham.
(Courtesy of Rilla Smith)

The auto shop on Shelter Road where Ron and Luella Bingham were murdered. (*Courtesy of Robin Murphy*)

Kyle Richardson is asked to identify the TEC-9 that was used as a murder weapon. (*Lewiston Morning Tribune*)

Cynthia Arrasmith on the stand.
(*Lewiston Morning Tribune*)

Cynthia breaks down.
(*Lewiston Morning Tribune*)

Arrasmith ex-wife #3, Donnita Weddle.
(*Lewiston Morning Tribune*)

Arrasmith ex-wife #1, Linda Bartlett, testifies for her ex-
husband. (*Lewiston Morning Tribune*)

Patti Mahar Johnson recounts life with the Binghams.
(*Lewiston Morning Tribune*)

Lewis-Clark Valley, on the Idaho-Washington border.
(Courtesy of Robin Murphy)

Luella Bingham with her mother Rilla Smith.
(Courtesy of Rilla Smith)

Ken Arrasmith glares at the camera during a conference
with his lawyer, Craig Mosman.
(*Lewiston Morning Tribune*)

as he approached his victims, then shot Ron twenty-three times and shot Luella seven times, including six times in the back.

Since there was no way for Rosen to leave Cynthia Arrasmith out of the equation, she went back in time to the April 18 raid by the Quad Cities Task Force on the Bingham home in an effort to show the girl had been presented with more than an adequate chance to obtain police protection, but refused. The first witnesses would be policemen who were on the raid.

In one exceptional statement, Rosen claimed Cynthia told the police gathered in the living room on that night that she worked as a prostitute in Spokane. According to the prosecutor, the officers, curious about the presence of the underage girl in a house being raided for drugs, asked the whereabouts of her parents, and Cynthia replied they could not be reached, that her father was a trucker and her mother moved from motel to motel.

Then, Rosen continued, Cynthia mentioned a medical form signed by Cynthia's mother, Linda Bartlett, that gave permission for the girl to be in the Bingham house. Rosen also said that Luella produced the form. The prosecutor claimed a "belligerent and ornery" Cynthia "insisted" to the cops that she had a right to be there. Because of her attitude, the parental permission slip for a medical procedure and the absence of a cache of drugs on the premises, there was no reason for the police to remove the girl, Rosen said.

At the defense table, Craig and Roy Mosman were delighted with that declaration. In their view, the prosecution's introducing the jury to what was and was not discovered in the raid would fling open the bedroom door and allow the introduction of the dirty pictures and sex toys. As Ken Arrasmith sat between them, a blank look on his face, the father-son defense team glanced at each other, passing their own silent verdict on Rosen's performance—she'd gone too far.

Denise Rosen moved ahead to April 20, when a "very disoriented" Patti Mahar Johnson wanted to give the Clarkston police information about drugs. Her stories about drugs and a sexual encounter involving Cynthia and the Binghams at the Quality Inn, however, were muddled by her inarticulate ramblings. "She was unable to focus, she was not with it," Rosen said. The cops decided to let her rest overnight and try again the next morning to make sense of her tales, knowing she had not said anything to them about either drugs or sex when they talked to her during the raid two nights before. They remembered that Cynthia had not said anything about a molestation but decided to check out the story anyway.

Rosen then had to discuss how police became bollixed up in who would deal with the case, and how it fell on the desk of Captain Tom Watkins because Deputy Tom White, who ususally handles sex cases, was out due to a combination of injuries and vacation time. Watkins, she said, was handling about twenty other cases at the time.

The prosecutor let that point rest now, having cast doubt on the credibility of an "ornery" Cynthia Arrasmith and a "disoriented" Patti Mahar Johnson, who muttered to police about strange people coming in and out of a grave.

She moved forward again to May 8 and sketched the scene at the Hollywood Motel, where two Lewiston police officers responded to a call about a runaway teenaged girl. They found Ken Arrasmith there, angry because he thought his daughter was having sex with a twenty-five-year-old man. The police found Cynthia hostile not only to them, but also to her father, and denying having sex with her boyfriend, with whom she had just spent the night in a motel. "Her parents tell the cops they can't control her and are afraid she'll run," Rosen said, and at the parents' request, Cynthia was arrested and placed in juvenile detention.

It is during that incarceration that "for the first time," she mentions that the Binghams had sex with her, but "she in no way gives any indication that she is afraid of them," Rosen told the jurors. However, the prosecutor revealed the girl described having her pubic hair shaved by Ron Bingham at the motel, and that was the first time the police had heard from Cynthia "that something is going on." In an important point, the girl told police that no drugs were involved in the incident.

Captain Watkins told the parents about the interviews and "they give him no cause for concern." Between May 7 and May 17, Cynthia remained in detention. "There is no danger to her at all," Rosen declared.

"During this time, the defendant is planning his revenge," the prosecutor said, shifting the case back to murder instead of sexual escapades, a job that would be her top priority throughout the trial. Ken Arrasmith, she said, gathered his deadly package of weapons even while he was talking to police, and "not one time did he express any dissatisfaction" with the way law enforcement was handling the case. Instead, Arrasmith even escorted Ken Rathbone, whom he had thought was having sex with his teenaged daughter, to a police interview.

Then, in a moment Rosen had been anticipating for a long time, she played the drug card against the defendant. "Ken Arrasmith tells the sheriff he has been involved with drugs," she told the jurors, adding that he promised to turn in a couple of people whom he knew were also involved in the drug trade. It was the first, but not the last time in the trial that Arrasmith would be tied to the valley's prospering drug trade.

Rosen was just beginning to strip Arrasmith of the righteous cloak of a father who was forced to kill two sexual predators who had raped his daughter. Just because the television shows liked to spin the story that way didn't mean it was true, and Denise Rosen had gathered a rather large stack of stones to throw at the glass house that had been built by the media and Arrasmith's savvy supporters.

Meanwhile, she walked the jurors through the days just before the killings, tracing how Arrasmith stalked the Binghams at the same time he was talking to police. On May 17, she said, Detective Tom White told him by telephone that the case was about to be laid before the Asotin County prosecution attorney, and Arrasmith said nothing to indicate he was concerned about a delay in potential prosecution of the Binghams.

Arrasmith was losing some of his stone-faced demeanor at the defense table as Rosen rolled along. His hands fluttered nervously, silently tapping his fingertips on the slick tabletop and squaring the yellow legal pad that lay before him.

Then she described how Arrasmith went to Shelter Road and was led to where Ron Bingham was working beneath a truck, with Luella nearby, and how he deliberately shot both of them to death. "I've got something for you, Ron. I've got something special," she claimed the defendant growled before emptying most of a thirty-round clip from a Tec-9 "mini-machine gun" into him. As for Luella: "She was trying to get away from the defendant. He hunted her down and shot her in the back."

Rosen paused and heard nothing but silence in the big courtroom. Satisfied with her preliminary sketch, she sat down, glancing at the clock with eyes that sparkled with excitement. It was 9:48 A.M. After being muzzled for months, she was finally able to give people something to talk about.

There was little percentage in the Mosmans presenting an opening statement, which would only serve to expose their game plan to the prosecution. Ron and Craig Mosman chose to save their opening statement for when they began their own case. They were eager to let the prosecution bring on the first witnesses.

18

Four witnesses, all law enforcement officers, would take the stand on the opening day of testimony, but the detailed recitation of their actions and observations would take a backseat to the real drama. The Mosmans ambushed each cop in turn, but regularly collided with Judge Leggett and her decision to prevent the introduction of Ron and Luella Bingham's checkered past concerning their sexual assaults on young women.

The judge held tightly to her pretrial decision not to allow such evidence, but as the day progressed, she was finding it more and more difficult to swat down the Mosman's attacks. Whatever her ruling on an objection concerning the Bingham background, the Mosmans appeared to interpret her firm *"No!"* command as merely permission to try again.

The first witness was Joel Hastings, a Clarkston officer with seven years of police experience. Importantly, he was also a member of the Quad Cities Task Force and had served the drug bust search warrant at the Bingham home on April 18.

Mike Kane unfolded his lanky frame from his chair at the prosecution table and rose to do the questioning. He hoisted a three-by-five-foot section of white poster board on his shoulder like a piece of lumber and carried it to the witness. A huge map was pasted to the board and Hastings used a red marker to denote some of the relevant addresses involved—the Bingham house and the adjacent graveyard. In a bit of violation of courtroom turf, just enough to show the prosecution wasn't cutting the defense any breaks today, Kane leaned the board against the defense team's table so the jury could see it better. With his dapper and polite appearance, and a calm, confident manner, Kane was sending a ''Trust me'' message to the new jury.

Hastings, who had been in charge of the raid, described how his drug task force team stormed the Bingham house and found two young men and an even younger girl sitting in the living room. Josh Bingham, in his shorts, was pulled from his bed, handcuffed and put facedown on the floor. Rilla Smith was awakened but left in her bed, under police watch. While another officer interviewed the girl in the living room, who was identified as Cynthia Arrasmith, Hastings guided the rest of the search. When it was determined that she was only fifteen years old, a police radio crackled with the request to check records to see if she might be wanted as a runaway.

A can in Todd Reed's pocket was found to contain a powder identified as methamphetamine, and Reed was placed under arrest, Hastings said. Lyle Stevens was arrested after admitting ownership of a bindle of meth found in his wallet and some marijuana in his coat. Jim Bartwell, found asleep in the trailer, was hauled inside and a drug-sniffing police dog lurched around the cluttered property, but found nothing.

In fact, Hastings testified, ''We came up empty.'' Instead of finding a major drug operation, the Quad Cities raiders found ''no evidence for other arrests.''

Meanwhile, Cynthia was emphatic that ''she didn't want to leave'' the house. Hastings said the girl appeared fine, did not seem to be on drugs and, overall, was not a problem for the police.

Hastings said the Binghams showed up some thirty to forty minutes after the police had entered the home. They were handcuffed and questioned as the search spread farther into the house. A plastic Baggie was found in the bedroom of Ron and Luella that seemed, at first glance, to contain mushrooms, which could have narcotic qualities. Hastings, the veteran drug-enforcement policeman, disagreed. "It looked more like garlic to me," he said. But outside, in the old bus, police found a set of weighing scales and a cache of Baggies, some razor blades and a flat surface—items normally associated with cutting up narcotic powders. Still, no drugs were found. Without the end product, the scales and other such items were just so much junk.

The search had taken a bizarre turn, the policeman said, and was made even stranger by the babbling of a woman who came home with the Binghams. Patti Mahar Johnson told the cops about what she thought was a real problem—a trapdoor out in the nearby graveyard and a ladder that led down to some mysterious place. They should check that out, she insisted. The chattering woman appeared either high on meth or mentally disturbed, and they decided to leave her alone.

Meanwhile, officers focused more on the presence of Cynthia in the house, and one indicated to Hastings the kid should be removed. "He had told me she was out of here," Hastings testified. But things changed rapidly when Cynthia told them the Binghams actually had permission to keep her. Luella explained the necessary papers were in a fanny pack and retrieved two documents, including a medical permission slip signed by the teenager's mother.

Cynthia stubbornly resisted removal, according to the policeman, saying she had talked with her father by telephone the previous night, but didn't know his whereabouts, and that her mother had no telephone.

When Kane questioned what sort of custodial paperwork was found, Hastings replied he was told the medical permit would allow the Binghams to take Cynthia to Spokane the very next day for an abortion. Ron Bingham, who was sitting behind Cynthia during that police questioning, answered when the girl was asked the identity of the man who impregnated her.

"Probably her boyfriend," he replied. When asked where the boyfriend was, Ron sneered, "I threw the no-good son of a bitch out of the house."

The cops huddled. The drug bust was a failure, a couple of minor arrests for equally minor possession charges, nothing like what they had expected. Instead, Hastings and the other officers swept the house and grounds again, looking for a different kind of evidence, something that would allow them to remove the underage Cynthia. "We searched the whole place for a reason to take her out of there," he told the court, although the kid was giving no sign whatsoever that she wanted to leave. In the end, he said, they found nothing on which to hinge such a decision.

Kane asked a pointed question. On national television, he said, it had been claimed that the police knew at the time of the raid that Cynthia was being abused. Hastings firmly denied that. "We didn't even know she was there!" he said.

The cops had to make a decision. It was about 6:30 in the morning, the sun was up and the search had turned up nothing that would let them remove the girl from the Bingham household. Instead, they had found a medical permission slip signed by her mother, she appeared to be safe and she had repeatedly said she wanted to stay. Since the fifteen-year-old was so firm in her decision and the Binghams had paperwork to back her up, the police decided to leave. Hastings had been working for twenty-four hours straight and was tired. After a long night, he was ready to go home.

At the defense table, Craig Mosman jotted some notes. Certainly, he felt, the policeman testifying about searching the house would open the questioning to what police found in the bedroom.

Hastings continued his testimony by recalling the events of April 20. A deputy sheriff telephoned him to say a woman was at the office, acting afraid and paranoid. A speakerphone setup was rigged and Hastings found he was talking again to the befuddled Patti Mahar Johnson. If anything, she was even more incoherent now than she was the previous night, carrying on overlapping conversations and at times even stalking out of the interview room, a screeching yell trailing behind her and over the telephone wires to Hastings. She was taken into protective custody, in hopes that she would be more understandable the next morning. Hastings saw that it was after midnight and groaned as he tried to get back to sleep.

The next morning, Patti was released from jail and submitted to another interview, admitting that she had been doing meth steadily for the past month. Hastings thought there was a touch of schizophrenia also at play, and the result was a rambling conversation, including more spectral references about the graveyard.

But when the conversation drifted away from drugs and onto sexual activity at the Bingham home, Hastings hit what he thought was some paydirt. The woman, fading in and out like a distant radio station, said Ron and Luella were having sex with young Cynthia Arrasmith. "I felt she was telling the truth," Hastings said on the stand.

That statement set in motion a series of seemingly unrelated actions that would eventually allow the defense lawyers to paint the police as being uncaring.

Hastings was trained in drug enforcement. Patti was

talking about a serious crime, sex with a minor, something that needed the attention of an expert. Luckily, the Asotin County Sheriff's Office had just such a person, Sergeant Tom White. Hastings immediately called him, only to find that White wasn't on the job. The call was transferred to Captain Jim Watkins, who came out to interview Patti.

Whatever her story, police were also wondering just what to do with this woman. Best, they thought, to call a relative, and they notified a sister in Oregon, who arranged for a plane ticket to Portland for Patti. They did not know at the time that there was an outstanding warrant for her arrest.

Hastings, having handed over the alleged sex offense to Watkins, resumed pumping her for drug information. Patti said she had a storage locker in Clarkston in which Ron hid some drugs, and led them right to it. As they prepared to pop the lock with giant bolt cutters, Hastings asked Patti if she was certain that the locker was hers. Well, she replied, actually, the rent was paid by her ex-boyfriend. The bolt cutters were lowered, and the cops, shorn of legal permission to invade the locker, once again went away empty-handed.

Patti was put on an airplane to fly to her sister's home and Hastings said he never saw her again. Meanwhile, he planned to lean on the two young men who had been arrested in the Bingham raid and coax them into trading lesser drug charges for testimony about sexual abuse. And that was that. Michael Kane and Denise Rosen had no further questions and turned the detective over to the defense for cross-examination.

Craig Mosman is not a big man, but as he stood with his arms crossed and attached with a firm voice, he immediately dominated the courtroom. He intended to put an entirely different twist to the detective's story, give the jury his view of police incompetence and mount an all-out challenge of Judge Leggett's order that barred bringing the past actions of Ron Bingham into court. Hastings would be nothing more than a stepping stone, since the Mosmans knew they had to trash the Bingham reputation to have any hope of winning this case.

Court orders or not, that was the goal. If they could paint a picture of Ken Arrasmith bumping off a couple of evil sexual predators, a couple of slimeballs that good upstanding members of socity probably would think needed killing, then there was a chance of acquittal.

Naturally, in preparing their defense, the Mosmans had talked to the sister of Patti Mahar Johnson. "Is it true," Mosman asked Hastings, "that you told Kathy Rudd (the sister) that Ron Bingham gets young guys out there and scares them to death? Did you tell her that Ron Bingham is crazy and the only chance for your sister is to get her out of there?"

Mosman started his cross-examination at 10:50 A.M., and only five minutes later Mike Kane jumped to his feet to object about what "this lawyer is trying to do." The judge called the first of what would be many private and frustrating conferences on the subject, and the jury left the courtroom while the legal point was argued.

"They want the jury to believe a lie," Mosman argued. The prosecution, he said, wanted the jurors to think police went into the Bingham house knowing nothing about Ron's background, when the records of previous rapes and his other problems, including a felony jail sentence, were certainly known. "We contend the information was there," he said. He further argued that the prosecution had opened the gate for such inquiries with their questions about the search for evidence that would allow them to remove Cynthia. "It's only fair," he said, to let the defense explore what else the officers might have known.

No way, responded Kane. "The fact that something

may have happened in the past is irrelevant'' to the murder charge, he argued.

The judge seemed indecisive as she sat silently for a few moments to consider the arguments. After all, it was her order that was being attacked, an order that she had wrestled with at great length before deciding to bar the Binghams' past. In an extraordinary comment, the jurist said that the lawyers ''may know more than the court'' about the issue at hand, but she was going to stick to the pretrial ruling, which was grounded in strong precedent and law.

Before long, she would not only be defending her order but would become a gatekeeper determining exactly how much information could be revealed about a search, and how much of a conversation or police interview could be heard in court. The result was a strange and truncated version of what had happened.

Craig Mosman turned his attention back to the policeman on the witness stand, quickly eliciting that the cop had believed ''a lot'' of what Patti had to say, and also believed the drug bust came up empty because Ron Bingham knew the police were coming.

Earlier on the night of the raid, a suspect had been followed to the Bingham place, where a second man in the car jumped out momentarily, went in and bought some drugs, then returned to the auto, which drove away. The two men in the car eventually delivered the drugs to an undercover policeman posing as a customer. They were quickly arrested and ready to make a deal that would provide a direct link to Ron Bingham's open-all-hours drugstore. A judge was called in the middle of the night, listened to the police plea for a warrant, granted it, and the Quad Cities Task Force swung into high gear.

However, any element of surprise had long been lost. Bingham, alerted by a telephone call from someone who knew of the arrests, spotted the unmarked police car which was hidden in the cemetery, from which a cop watched his house. Ron jumped into his own car and gave chase.

With a serious expression, Officer Hastings said the police car tried to get away, but Bingham easily got on its tail when the driver tapped his brakes at a corner. The policeman called for help and, although the Bingham car passed by without incident, a deputy sheriff soon pulled the Binghams over and got out to explain that the man in the mystery car wasn't really a cop, just a relative grieving at the grave of a recently deceased relative.

The police could not have done more to alert Bingham than if they had tacked a warning on his front door. By the time the cops burst into the house with guns drawn, Bingham had made certain that any drugs were removed.

Mosman couldn't have cared less about the comedy in the cemetery. He logically wanted to know if the police didn't find a major drug stash, did they find anything at all? Yes, replied Hastings, in the bedroom of Ron and Luella was a box of magazines and glossy photographs "of nude people and sex acts." Bingo. The sex pictures were in.

Mike Kane rocketed to his feet immediately to protest. The defense claimed the entire results of the police search should be admissible as evidence. Kane pointed to the court's order against bringing in material relating to the character of the Binghams. The judge sustained the motion and instructed the jury to ignore the question and the answer, and they nodded, promising to no longer think about a box of pornography that contained hundreds of pictures of naked people involved in sex acts.

The trial was only on its first witness and the Mosmans had already snuck in information that had been clearly barred by court order. With obvious frustration, Judge Leggett called a recess, told the jury to leave the room, then once again listened to arguments about the character issue.

"One of the fascinating things about the practice of law is how fast things change in court," Mosman told her, explaining that he wasn't really violating the court order, only following up on Denise Rosen's opening statement and Mike Kane's question. The policeman on the stand had said he was looking for something that would validate his concern for the welfare of the teen-aged girl in the house, and Mosman said the cops knew her age, found the photos and also a suitcase full of dildos and knew Ron Bingham had served time for rape. Mosman asked the judge the logical question: "My goodness, how could they not have concern?"

Kane responded that the sexual material found in the bedroom was not linked to Cynthia or any other young person. "They are trying to dump in character evidence," Kane declared. He pointed to Arrasmith. "The focus on this case is whether this man committed murder, not whether Ron Bingham served time twenty years ago . . . They're just trying to slip in some dirt that the court has already ruled on." He said the defense tactic was "making a farce" of the trial.

The judge's ruling was being pounded. To backtrack now would open the floodgates for the defense to bring in all sorts of questions about the Bingham's past and a string of witnesses who had been molested by the Binghams. To remain firm meant she had to almost stand in the bedroom door and chop off the search at an incomplete point. The court, she told the lawyers, would not change its stated reasoning, and the character evidence would not be allowed in this case, either. Stop it, she was saying, having made up her mind. Stop it now.

"I will not play games," she snapped. "Once I rule, I intend for that to be the ruling. I don't want to have to rule on this every three minutes."

Mosman submitted, but grumbled that there was "no possible way to have a fair trail if we're not allowed to cross-examine."

Tough. Once again, the judge had made it clear. The sex toys and photos would not be allowed into evidence. But turning to the prosecution, she told them to tread very carefully and not bring up the subject again, or the door might be thrown wide open.

"I guarantee," responded the obviously relieved Mike Kane, losing his urbanity for a moment. "I ain't bringing that up."

Everyone took a lunch break, gaining time for tempers to calm. The Mosmans went to a nearby restaurant and pondered their strategy. They were in an upbeat mood, although they knew that every time they would invite the jury to look at the Bingham's bedroom door, they were going to see a tiny black woman standing there, wearing a judge's robe with a single maroon stripe down the left side, and no smile. Leggett had made her point crystal clear. It would soon become just as clear that the defense team would not cease testing her, igniting the tempers of the prosecutors by slipping juicy tidbits about sex and drugs into the sterile world of the seven women and five men in the jury box.

After lunch, Craig Mosman resumed questioning Hastings and scored quickly when he asked if the police seized the box of pornographic photographs. Did you take pictures of it? Yes. Did you photograph other things that were seized?

The sandwiches of lunch were not yet digested and already Mosman was banging on that bedroom door again, indicating to the jury that something—they didn't yet know what—had been taken away by police. Kane objected, but the judge this time overruled him and allowed Hastings to answer. Yes, he said, they took pictures of other things that were seized. The response was the first crack in the dam. Mosman's drop-by-drop water torture had at last shown a sign of success. At the prosecution table, Denise Rosen scribbled furiously on her yellow notepad, her left hand almost flying across the page.

Throughout the trial, the Mosmans would carry out an odd strategy. Every time the prosecution veered from the straight and narrow of eliciting only a yes-or-no answer from a witness, the defense would strenuously object. But when they asked questions, they used awkward sentence structure such as, "Isn't it true that you did so-and-so?" The "so-and-so" part would turn into a statement by the defense lawyer to which the witness would respond, as if the witness himself had made the observation. The prosecution rarely objected to the leading questions, which were very effective in the hands of someone like Craig Mosman.

Mosman went back to the police interview of Patti Mahar Johnson, asking Hastings where she had gotten the drugs that had made her so high. "She said that she and (Ron) Bingham were involved in drugs together," the policeman said. And although she rambled on, you believed what she said about observing Ron and Luella having sex with Cynthia Arrasmith, Craig Mosman asked in one of his horse-before-the-cart questions. "For thirty seconds every five minutes, she would focus on something that appeared truthful," Hastings said. Mosman had him confirm that Patti's statement included the observation that Ron saved Cynthia's trimmed pubic hair in an envelope, a statement she had given police on April 21.

Leading to his main point, Mosman had Hastings confirm that on that date, when the molestation report was received, police did not intervene.

That point would be hammered home with every police officer who came to the stand—*Why didn't you do something more than you did to extricate an obviously underage girl from the clutches of Ron Bingham?* Mosman, well experienced in the laws governing child sexual abuse, gave the jury a quick tour of that seedy territory by questioning Hastings about the so-called "grooming process" through which a child molester will gain the victim's confidence and trust to such an extent that the child will willingly remain with the abuser.

Through Hastings' own comments, the jury learned that he had stayed primarily within his prescribed role as head of the Quad City Task Force raiders on the night that they found the underage Cynthia, but little else, at the Binghams. Then he turned the sex-abuse allegations over to Captain Watkins. Hastings said he made no attempt to personally contact Cynthia's parents, Ken Arrasmith or Linda Bartlett.

As the questioning of the first witness came to an end at 2:09 P.M., the strategy for the defense was on the table. They wanted to spin this case away from murder and focus instead on rape, child abuse and police errors. They had done a fine job of doing just that with the prosecution's first witness.

The prosecution knew the onslaught was coming and, except for objecting to the attempts to bring in character evidence, were content to let the cops tell their story. After all, this was just the first day of a long trial. Many days and many witnesses and much testimony would pass before the jury deliberations got underway, and by then, jurors' memories would dim. If the defense wanted to beat up on the cops, let them do it in the first part of the trial so the jury would have time to forget about it.

The next witness was Officer Tim Ottmar of the Clarkston Police Department, wearing his silver badge on the dark blue uniform. He was on the witness stand for only seven minutes.

For Special Prosecutor Mike Kane, the policeman said he stood guard in the living room and was in a position to observe Miss Arrasmith. Her behavior was "no big deal" and she "didn't seem concerned" about what was happening. At no point did Cynthia give any indication that she wanted or needed assistance or wanted to leave. Kane asked if Ottmar personally had found anything in the search and the cop said it was he who took the meth from Todd Reed.

Defense Attorney Craig Mosman totally ignored the comments about Cynthia, leaving an unspoken hint that her behavior on that night would be normal for a trapped child who had been trained well by her abusers. Instead, he tried to go through that bedroom door again. He wanted to focus on the box of photographs and the suitcase of sex toys. In your search, did you find anything in the other rooms?

Objection, protested a weary Mike Kane.

Sustained, said the judge.

For the record, Mosman protested Kane's objection and the judge's ruling. A veteran court watcher later said, "They can write the headline on this one right now: Arrasmith Loses in Trial, Wins on Appeal."

19

Patrick John Kelley, a deep-voiced detective from the Whitman County Sheriff's Office and part of the Quad Cities Task Force, was served up as the next witness. He had been the first one to interview Cynthia Arrasmith on the night of the raid, after taking her picture with a Polaroid camera, writing her birthdate of 9-6-79 on the back and her name and age on the front. To the officer, the girl appeared "unkempt and on the dirty side."

He testified that the girl was uncooperative with police and told him that she had been living at the Binghams for a month or two. He added that Cynthia told him she and her boyfriend had met Bingham in Spokane, where she had been "tooting up" on drugs and working as a prostitute. It was the second time that day that a policeman reported Cynthia had claimed to be a Spokane prostitute, something that she would vehemently deny outside the courtroom. After looming so large, so early in the trial, the subject was never raised again. Kane explained that the state was not trying to prove she was a prostitute, only that she was telling that to the police, and that they were doing this to demonstrate the contradictions in Cynthia's story.

Kelley was asked if the girl wanted to leave the house,

and he replied, "Absolutely not . . . She never indicated she was in danger or that she wanted to get out of the household."

He described how, when the talk turned to taking Cynthia away, Luella Bingham, in handcuffs, had police look in her black "fanny pack" strapped around her waist. There, they discovered the April 17 letter signed by Linda Bartlett giving Luella permission to oversee "any authorized medical treatment" Cynthia might require. The permission slip was needed for a planned abortion, the policeman said.

"There was no legal reason to remove her from the home," he said. "She seemed to be happy they (the Binghams) were there."

Craig Mosman, on cross-examination, moved to his expected point, asking the detective why he had decided Cynthia should be removed from the residence. It was a ricochet shot at getting him to talk about the sex toys and pictures the police had discovered in the bedroom, and Judge Leggett quickly cut him off.

Undeterred, Mosman pointed out that Linda Bartlett's letter was only a medical permission slip and did not sign over custody of the girl to the Binghams. Kelley agreed.

Then he managed to score a direct hit in his next attempt to break into the bedroom. After being turned away repeatedly, this time Leggett allowed the questions. Before the jury could blink, Mosman had the cop admitting that hundreds of pictures of men and women performing sexual acts had been discovered in the police search. A female juror's hand fluttered at her throat, as if trying to pull her blouse, already buttoned to the neck, closed even more.

With the jury's full attention now, Mosman pressed on, asking the policeman if he looked "at each and every one" of the hundreds of pictures? As many as possible, the witness said. Mosman wanted to know how many of the sexually explicit pictures were of children. None were under twenty-one, the witness replied. Then he hedged, saying the people in the pictures only appeared to him to be adults, all over twenty-one. That was far from the certainty of his first answers.

"So it was a guess?" Mosman needled.

"An accurate estimation," said Kelley.

Mosman followed up by asking if there were some pictures the detective did not view. The veteran cop, however, sidestepped and sought shelter behind the judge's earlier ruling. "I had no evidence to take Cynthia Arrasmith," he said.

"You didn't look at the pictures to see if Cynthia Arrasmith herself was pictured in any of those photographs?"

"Yes, I did," the witness said, nervously cutting his eyes toward Mike Kane, as if seeking guidance.

Only a moment before, Kelley had admitted that he had not viewed all of the photographs. "You can't have it both ways," shot back Mosman.

"She wasn't in the ones that I viewed," Kelley added.

"But you have no idea if she was in the ones you didn't view," Mosman declared. "Even though you didn't look, you left Cynthia Arrasmith there. Right?"

"Correct," replied the battered witness. Mosman also coaxed the witness into calling the photos "the most disgusting pictures anyone could imagine."

Mosman had made his point, then added to it by getting the detective to admit he had "a gut feeling" that Cynthia was being groomed by the Binghams to participate in their sexual lifestyle.

The attorney acted as if he were outraged. "Your gut feeling was that she was being sexually abused in that home," he said in one of his statement-questions. He delivered the line again, positioning himself beside the jury and repeating it almost in a whisper, making the jurors lean forward to hear. "Your gut feeling was that she was being sexually abused in that home."

"I can't answer that question, your honor," the witness replied, seeking help from the judge. Since he had gotten himself into this mess with his own words, she refused to throw him a lifeline, telling him to answer yes or no. "I had a gut feeling. Yes."

"Did you try to contact Cynthia Arrasmith's parents?"

"I did not."

"Did you try to contact Health and Welfare?"

"I did not."

"Did you try to contact Juvenile Services?"

"I did not."

Mike Kane tried a quick rescue effort on cross-examination and the weary officer said, "I did what I could." That only opened him up for one final swat from Craig Mosman.

"Did you look in the Clarkston-Lewiston telephone book for her parents' names?"

"No," the witness responded.

Mosman wrapped it up, almost as if he were tired of this person. He had plainly given the jury a show that the police on that night perhaps did not do everything they could to assist the fifteen-year-old girl. One final shot.

"You didn't even try, did you?"

"No."

At 3:35 P.M. on the opening day of the trial, Asotin County Sheriff's Department Captain James Watkins stepped to the witness stand in behalf of the prosecution. But with the exceptions of Cynthia Arrasmith and Ken Arrasmith, Jim Watkins would turn out to be the strongest witness the defense team had. To portray his testimony as stumbling would be inaccurate. He bobbled the first question—What is your name?—and went downhill from there.

Watkins is not a bad cop. He was just thrust into a complex web of explosive issues that blew up in his face. For twenty-one of the past thirty-five years, he had been in the law enforcement business, and his white hair and gravelly voice reflected the experience of such a career. At other times in his life, he had traveled with a country-western band, playing the pedal steel guitar and singing twangy songs about lost loves and horses that can't be rode and riders that can't be throwed.

With his varied experiences and his advanced rank, he might have been just the person to have handled the tricky early days of the case, when Patti Mahar Johnson and Cynthia Arrasmith finally began reporting the abuses at the hands of the Binghams. Instead, Watkins was at the time assigned to solving not-top-of-the-line mysteries. For the past six years, he had been handling crimes against property in Asotin County: burglaries, thefts and minor heists. He appeared totally unready for the Bingham-Arrasmith drama when it fell onto his lap on the morning of April 21, 1995, and admitted that he had been given no training in the area of sexual abuse crimes.

After Joel Hastings talked to Patti Mahar Johnson, he wanted to hand the case off to Sergeant Tom White, the department's expert on sex crimes, but White was still off the active duty roster, so Hastings, the drug investigator, gave the sticky ball to Watkins, the burglary guy. Watkins went to the jail to interview the wobbly Patti, whose rambling statements still defied logical interpretation. "She appeared to be coming down off a high," Watkins recalled. She also perhaps was calming down enough to realize that she was sitting in a police station and that other cops were still after her for a barroom brawl. The longer she stayed, the more likely that those pesky warrants would come to light. She was in a hurry to get to the airport and go to the home of her sister,

Watkins said, and they spoke for only ten to fifteen
minutes.

But on the subject of Cynthia Arrasmith, Patti Mahar
Johnson did have something to say. Watkins scribbled
notes as she described watching at the Quality Inn on
April 14 and 15 as Ron Bingham clipped and shaved
the pubic hairs from the teenager and Luella had oral
sex with the shaven girl. Then Patti went to Oregon, Jim
Watkins went back to his routine work and the Arrasmith incident seemed to get shelved.

"I didn't do anything that day," he testified. "I was
the duty deputy and had to answer the calls." Anyway,
he felt that just based upon the strange statement from
the obviously disturbed Patti Mahar Johnson, probable
cause did not exist to arrest the Binghams. More evidence was needed, so he did not go out to the Bingham
house at that point. After doing nothing more on the day
of the interview, a Friday, Watkins then cashed in a vacation day to take a long weekend off.

When he returned to work on Tuesday, he drove out
to the Quality Inn and obtained check-in records for the
days Patti mentioned. Sure enough, the chits showed the
Binghams had rented a room. Then, to the embarrass-
ment of the prosecuting attorneys, Watkins seemed to go
blank in his memory. Asked how he followed up that
lead, Watkins responded: "At that point, I don't recall."
He said he did not notify Cynthia's parents, nor did he
call Health and Welfare officers. "I was just holding the
fort until Sergeant White got back," he said, his voice
failing. "I was working my own theft and burglary
cases."

Craig and Roy Mosman somehow kept the smiles
from their faces, although they felt like dancing. This
guy was punching holes in the prosecution case as fast
as he could. The defense team had planned all along to
emphasize police incompetence, and Jim Watkins was
following that line of persuasion perfectly. He looked

like Captain Kangaroo up there, fumbling his answers enough to give the jury pause to wonder if the entire case might have been fumbled, too.

On May 9, Watkins continued, Ken Arrasmith and Linda Bartlett came by to see him and advise that Cynthia had been taken into detention at their request. The sheriff's captain advised the parents of what Patti had said and received permission to talk to Cynthia. When asked how Ken Arrasmith took the news of the shaved pubic hair and sex acts, Watkins again went blank. "I don't recall," he said. He should have stopped there, but he added, "I suppose he was going to be upset."

But Watkins did tell Arrasmith the case would be turned over to the sex crimes specialist as soon as possible.

Then he went across the river to the Juvenile Detention Center in Lewiston for an early afternoon interview with Cynthia Arrasmith and her mother, Linda Bartlett. Cynthia said she had known Ron Bingham for about two and a half months and had stayed at the Bingham house with her boyfriend, Ken Rathbone.

Concerning the April 14–15 incident at the Quality Inn, she said that after Ron shaved her, he joined her in taking a shower. When Ron and Patti left, she said, Lue had sex with her, and had used some sexual toys. Then Cynthia added new information, saying that there was a second visit to the Quality Inn, on Saturday, April 29. At that time, Bingham gave her a Valium "to help her rest" and an enema "to help her feel good," she said. Ron raped her and Lue "touched" her, the girl said. "She told them it hurt, to stop," Captain Watkins added, then with a pause, "That was it."

He returned to the Quality Inn and retrieved more records of Bingham having a room also on the weekend that began April 29, just as Cynthia had told him.

With Watkins self-destructing on the stand, the first day of court came mercifully to an end exactly at 4 P.M.

The day had clearly been an emotional win for the defense team, but the strategy of the prosecution was also doing well. Let the police take their lumps early on, let the Mosmans try to turn this into a case of sexual abuse, and give the jury time to forget about it when the evidence piles up on the real charges, two counts of first degree murder.

At least, that's about the only bright lining that Denise Rosen and Michael Kane would be able to find on that very cloudy day.

Watkins's agony was not yet at an end. As soon as court began on Wednesday, November 8, he was back on the stand, this time starting his testimony by admitting he was hard of hearing. Mike Kane lightly traced Watkins's actions during the early days of May, including conversations he had with Ken Arrasmith on May 9, 10 and 11. Arrasmith would call Watkins on the telephone four times a day. In later days, Arrasmith would tell the court he was outraged that twenty-five-year-old Ken Rathbone was dating the fifteen-year-old Cynthia, but on May 11, he escorted the young man to the police station, not to demand his arrest, but for a taped interview with Watkins.

Watkins apparently continued to do as little as possible, telling Arrasmith that he would turn the case over to another officer as soon as possible. Kane asked: "Did you explain any course of action?"

"Oh, I said I would try to find another victim or witness in the case."

"How were you going to do that?"

Blankness fell again over Watkins, and his glasses slipped to the end of his nose as he responded, "I didn't have a clue."

But Kane did pry a few points from the sheriff's captain when he said neither Ken Arrasmith nor Linda Bartlett had indicated any displeasure at the slow pace of the investigation.

That slight advance was erased in the next moment. As Watkins described one conversation with Arrasmith, he went so far as to tell the defendant that "he would possibly be able to get information a lot easier on the street" by working on his own. Street people, Watkins said, were reluctant to talk to police. The admission opened the door for the defense lawyers to now point at Watkins's testimony and say that a police captain had personally given Ken Arrasmith permission to conduct his own investigation—which would explain why he did many things that could seem otherwise quite peculiar, if not at least suspicious and possibly even criminal, under other circumstances.

Finally, Kane ended the questioning. There was no point in trying to make Watkins out to be an efficient cop. He looked like an old man, he talked like an old man and his odd police work was threatening to drive the Arrasmith case off a cliff.

Roy Mosman was ready for the cross-examination. Like Watkins, the silver-haired lawyer was on the distant side of fifty years of age, he also had a hearing problem and shared the same kind of cold that was plaguing the policeman. The jury had seen Craig Mosman in action but was now going to get a look at where the son had gone to school on questioning witnesses. Roy spoke softly, remaining seated at the table, telling Watkins, "We started our careers at about the same time." Friendly, utterly charming and murderously effective.

Of course, he didn't want to beat up on Watkins any more than necessary. After all, the man had been a terrific witness for the defense. He did not want to let the jury start sympathizing with this guy. But there were a few things that needed to be covered, so he asked Watkins if he gave more attention to one crime over another in pursuing his burglary investigations. The captain stepped neatly into the trap, answering that a "high-ticket" crime such as the theft of expensive jewelry would naturally rate harder police work.

Roy Mosman raised his eyebrows. "Would you say that child abuse and rape is a more serious crime?"

Watkins paused, trying to think his way out of this one, but there were no exits. "Yes," he admitted.

Mosman gently asked if he had looked into the stories of sexual abuse of Tiffany Calico and Tina Cole, names that Arrasmith had given Watkins. The policeman said he did not.

The surgical questioning continued, slowly and expertly, with Mosman finally asking the captain if, upon "looking back," he would have done anything differently. Taking his usual pause before answering, Watkins said that perhaps, "if he had the expertise" in sexual crimes, he might have handled the case some other way. It was all but a flat admission that he had blown the investigation.

Mike Kane had a last chance on recross examination and used it to show the thorough knowledge that a small town cop has of his area, and even provided a decent reason for Watkins not doing more, or doing things quicker. When asked why the delay, the policeman responded, "She (Cynthia) was out of harm's way. The Binghams lived in the valley and weren't going anywhere." That could easily be interpreted that the police had plenty of time to handle this case.

Mosman had also questioned Watkins about reports that Bingham had put a contract out for Arrasmith's death, and a comment by Cynthia that Ron Bingham once strapped packets of explosives beneath his shirt and threatened to blow up a building. Watkins said there was no information about a "contract" in any of the police reports he had read, leading him to think "it didn't happen." And as far as Cynthia, locked up in Juvenile Detention, still being afraid that Ron would walk in loaded with C4 explosives, Watkins insisted that she had said just the opposite during their interview. "She said she wasn't afraid of the Binghams, that they were probably more afraid of her because of what she could do."

On the issue of probable cause, why he hadn't moved quickly based on the information provided by Cynthia and Patti and the Quality Inn documents, Watkins said he had hoped to find another victim before going to a judge for the necessary arrest warrant.

Mosman had one last question. "In this case, you didn't give the judge a chance, did you?"

"No, sir," Watkins replied.

Finally, he was allowed to step down. The damage done to the prosecution case had been substantial, but Denise Rosen had known it was coming. There was no secret that the Mosmans wanted to make this case revolve around sexual abuse and police errors. Rosen breathed slightly easier now. Watkins was gone, and she hoped that any damage he had caused went with him.

Certainly, what was coming next would begin to drown out the jury's recall of the bumpy investigation. She and Kane had decided that if the cops were beaten up badly in court, she would rearrange the witness list. They were, she did, and it worked. By the end of the day, it would be hard for the jurors to remember anything about Captain Jim Watkins. Anything at all.

For when the trial's fifth witness was called, it wasn't another policeman to provide more cannon fodder for the Mosmans. It was Cynthia Arrasmith.

20

She was nervous, scooting between two reporters on the front row before her name was called as a witness. Neat in a black velveteen skirt, a black scoop-neck top and her denim jacket, her brown hair fell to her slight shoulders and bangs covered her forehead to her dark eyebrows. Cynthia Arrasmith was in a good mood, primarily because her incarcerated dad had given his permission to adopt the kitten with no name. Before court, she had been anxious to get to the stand and tell what *really* happened during her stay with the Binghams, and to particularly knock down police comments that she had been a Spokane streetwalker.

She moved quickly to the witness stand when her name was called, and Denise Rosen stood to carry on the questioning, brushing imaginary wrinkles from her patterned cream blouse and a brown pleated skirt that almost reached her ankles. Just as Roy Mosman dealt with the older policeman as an equal, Rosen would be able to question Cynthia much more harshly than a male prosecutor. For the moment, there was clearly a gender shift in Courtroom 3—the teenaged girl on the witness stand, the female prosecutor, the woman judge and a jury that contained more women than men. If sex was to be discussed, it would be handled on a female plateau.

As she arranged herself in her seat, Cynthia looked directly at her father and silently mouthed the words, "I love you." Rosen quickly took position between them.

The background came first, as Cynthia said she had moved out of her mother's home in September of 1994, had lived with her father for only four months in the past two years, had been with her boyfriend Ken Rathbone for a year and lived at the Binghams, both with and without Rathbone, from February 24 until May 7.

Rosen then hurled the first hard pitch. "You've given interviews to a lot of people," the prosecutor said to the girl whose face had been seen, and whose story read, by an audience of millions. Rosen pointed to the section of the *People* magazine article that declared Cynthia had had a difficult time since Ken and Linda's 1979 divorce, had used drugs and often run away from home. This would reveal Cynthia's troubled background, something the Mosmans wanted to avoid. "It's not true," she answered from the stand, and Craig Mosman objected, saying the girl could not be held responsible for what someone else had written. The judge agreed, and the entire media issue—which Arrasmith's supporters had manipulated to maximum advantage—ground to a halt. Whatever reporters and talk show hosts had been told became irrelevant.

Rosen moved on and had the teenager describe life at the Binghams. Cynthia said that after Ron and Luella kicked Ken off the property, "saying he wasn't doing enough work," both Binghams showered her with affection, gave her money and bought her clothes. "Luella said I was the daughter she never had," Cynthia said, her voice beginning to quaver.

She bit her lip and looked down. "Then one night we were in her room trying on clothes and she raped me." There was silence in the court.

Cynthia said the Binghams supplied her with Valium and crank (meth), and admitted that she had been using crank for several years before reaching the Binghams. "You were shooting up at one point?" Cynthia answered yes. Then, hurriedly, "I had quit for a long time before I went to the Binghams." A strand of hair fell across her left eye and she moved it away.

The subject went back to sex. "After Luella got done, Ron came into the room and raped me." According to her, that happened around the first of March, which would have been a week after she had moved into the trailer with her boyfriend. If that time line was accurate, Rathbone would still have been around. Rosen did not press to find out whether Cynthia had told her boyfriend about the attack.

The story got worse as the prosecutor, with a quiet and emotionless voice, led Cynthia to describe the Quality Inn assaults. She said Luella took her to the motel, where Ron and Patti had spent the night. "Ron had no clothes on, Luella took hers off and the other girl was lying on the bed," she said. "They made me take off my clothes, then Ron shaved the pubic hairs off me while Lue stood and watched. After that, Ron took a shower with me."

The tears came and Marshal Tommy Williams placed a box of tissues before her. At one moment in the courtroom, Judge Leggett was dabbing at her nose with a tissue because of a cold, Cynthia was wiping tears from her eyes and Roy Mosman was also using a tissue for his cold. With many female members of the audience suddenly pulling out hankies and tissues, the courtroom seemed ready to dissolve.

Matching Mosman's earlier ploy against Watkins, Denise Rosen softened her voice, almost as if she were in sympathy with the witness, and Cynthia continued her story. Ron and Patti left the room, and "Lue strapped on one of her dildos and came after me with it and raped me" again. She emphasized that she was frightened of

Ron Bingham and "I had to listen" to him. When he ordered her to strip, she did.

Rosen shifted gears, having the girl confirm that when she was arrested at her parents' request the morning of May 8, a drug test showed "opiates, crack and Valium" in her system.

Craig Mosman watched closely, almost hovering over this critical witness as Rosen took Cynthia through the next Quality Inn scene, eliciting more details. This time, she said, Ron gave her a Valium and a line of meth-amphetamines at the motel, then waited until she "couldn't stand up" without assistance. "They took me to the bathroom, took my clothes off, laid me on the sink on my stomach and Ron gave me an enema," she said. "Then they took me to bed and Ron had anal sex with me." A woman juror put a hand to her mouth, as if in shock.

The prosecutor pointed out that the first motel rape took place *before* the police drug raid found her at the Bingham home, and Cynthia protested that the cops never asked why she was there.

Two officers had testified, using almost the same words to describe that situation, Rosen said. "Ms. Arrasmith," Rosen said in a voice dripping with sarcasm. "Are you saying these officers lied?"

"No," Cynthia replied, her confidence and strength returning as she grew angry. She stared at Rosen. "All I'm saying is that I'm telling the truth."

"You did not tell them of any sexual contact or abuse by the Binghams?"

"No, I didn't," Cynthia admitted.

"You said you had a right to be there?"

"Yes." The jury would have to weigh that Cynthia said on one hand that the police had never asked why she was in the Bingham house, then they heard her describe almost immediately thereafter the permission slip that finally persuaded the cops to leave her where she was. The jurors also learned that Linda Bartlett had gone to the Binghams home herself to sign the medical authorization paper on April 17, and that on at least one occasion, Ken Arrasmith had driven her to the Bingham place. And she told neither about any sexual abuse.

However, she claimed to have told her mother on an earlier occasion that "You don't know what they are doing. They make me sleep with them."

Rosen jumped ahead to May 8 and the Hollywood Motel situation where Cynthia was picked up in the presence of her father by police who had been called by her mother. Time had changed the girl's recall of the incident, erasing any responsibility by her parents, who were telling the officers the girl was about to run away to California with her older boyfriend. "They came out there and arrested me," she declared in court, her mouth narrowing into a pout.

Finally, when she was in detention, her father came to see her and "I told him some of the things he (Ron) did," Cynthia said. "I was mad that they were running loose while I was locked up." On different days, Cynthia told Ken Arrasmith different things, but primarily that "they raped me." She added that she also gave her father the names of other girls who had been raped.

Then Rosen steered back to the drug problems, hoping to probe Cynthia's background. Mosman blocked it, but Rosen did get the girl to admit she willingly took drugs while she was with the Binghams.

The prosecutor asked if she had sex with the Binghams more times than she had already described. Cynthia said there had been more contact, all at their house except for the two motel visits. "Not every day," she said.

Rosen then wanted to show that if things were so bad for her there, Cynthia had plenty of opportunities to leave or ask for help. Under the relentless questioning, Cynthia admitted she was allowed to leave the house when she wanted, that she stayed even when Ron and

Luella were gone, that other people regularly visited the house, that she thought Josh was a "nice boy," and that she frequently talked on the telephone with her mother. The prosecutor's opinion was clear—that the girl could have left at almost any time if she felt abused or endangered.

Rosen ended the direct examination by having Cynthia give an important detail about the abortion. Her mother, the teenager said, not only signed the medical permission slip and allowed Lue to escort Cynthia to the abortion clinic, but also paid for part of the procedure. The prosecutor never asked the name of the father.

As the court took a lunch recess, Cynthia left with her team of supporters. She was steaming. "Denise has always been so mean. Now she stands up with the jury and is, like, so nice to me."

Craig Mosman began his cross-examination after lunch, hoping to mask a steely punch with a kid glove treatment of one of his key witnesses. He played an honesty card first, allowing a peek into Cynthia's background, by having her admit dropping out of school after the eighth grade, which explained some of her awkward use of the English language. She had scored high on GED tests, however, and planned to become a veterinarian. With a smile, she also admitted to some undefined "other problems."

She then described her initial meeting with Ron Bingham and said that once ensconced in the trailer, she really became fond of Lue. "We did really fun things. She'd be there to talk to . . . it was kind of like we were best friends, like I could trust her, no matter what. She would do special things for me. It was really nice."

But the ugly payback for all that kindness came soon enough, Cynthia would testify, when Lue coaxed her into the bedroom to try on some clothes. Cynthia had been wearing a top and a pair of shorts on that warm spring day, but soon stripped them off, along with her underclothes. She tried on a couple of black dresses, played with a long feather boa, then acquiesced when Lue had her model some sexy lingerie. After that, ''she pushed me onto the bed and strapped on her dildo,'' the teenager related, and later performed oral sex. When Luella was done, she called Ron into the room and ''he raped me.''

''It was disgusting and I was shocked. I couldn't believe she'd turn on me like that. She got me to trust her and like her so much,'' Cynthia testified softly. ''She hurt me really bad . . . I never knew there was [sic] people like that in a small town.''

And at the Quality Inn, Lue held her arms while Ron raped her. When she protested that it was hurting, Ron sneered, ''you like it when I hurt you.'' She added: ''They had no feelings. They didn't care.''

Mosman had wasted no time at all in getting the jury's attention, swinging the pendulum back to the sex angle of the case. He planned to make Ron and Luella appear as foul as possible, and eventually hoped to bring in the forbidden background items that Judge Leggett had thus far barred. Even under the judge's order, there was still plenty of room to move.

Ron paraded around the house in the nude and nobody said anything about it. Ron and Lue fed her methamphetamines up to ten times each day. Large quantities of drugs were stashed on the property. Ron bragged about the drugs he was trading.

It was time for a bombshell, and Mosman dropped it right on the jury. Under his quiet guiding questions, Cynthia testified that the shaving of her pubic hairs at the Quality Inn was not the first time it had happened. Ron had taken her into the bathroom at the house and said ''he wanted to give me a haircut, that he had done this before.''

Beginning to weep again, Cynthia described how Ron

put her on a stool, spread her legs, and using an electric razor first and then a normal shaving razor, carefully removed her pubic hair. While doing so, he laughed that since coming back from Vietnam, he only liked girls without pubic hair, the sort of women he slept with in Asia. The courtroom was absolutely silent except for her quite, little-girl voice and her sniffling into a tissue.

Then Mosman asked if Ron Bingham had a nickname, and Cynthia said he did. He had cut pubic hair so often that he was known as Ronnie Razorhands.

The shaven pubic hair was carefully picked up and placed in an envelope that Ron put in a book on his desk. After the Quality Inn incident, he added to his collection of Cynthia's hair and also showed her the pubic hair he had shaved from Patti Johnson. The Twin Cities jurors may have thought they were accustomed to being shocked in this trial, but now they had to take another disgusting step into the weird world of Ronnie Razorhands.

Having established from one of their victims that the Binghams were a sordid and sick couple, Mosman set out to show that Ron Bingham was something else, too—very dangerous.

Cynthia said he carried a gun most of the time and was constantly screaming at people, issuing uncaring threats, even at cops. "He didn't care," she said. "He said he had gotten away with it before and would get away with it now."

Then, as witnesses may do when they get wrapped up in their stories, Cynthia overstepped. In describing the police raid on the Bingham house, she said that she secretly welcomed their intrusion. "I thought that I would get to leave now," she said, sounding tiny and doubtful at the same time. "I thought, 'I'm a kid in a house full of drugs.' I thought the officers would take me home." It was in direct conflict with the police testimony and therefore might allow the jurors to question her credibility. Nothing the police had said indicated Cynthia, with a signed paper from her mother and apparently insistent on staying at the Binghams, had wanted any such thing. And if that important point was false, perhaps she might be fudging other important facts.

To recover the lost ground, Mosman steered her back to admitting a few more aching truths. Yes, Cynthia responded, she had been addicted to meth at the time of the police raid. Before the trial, in one of her many interviews, she told a television reporter she had been "as high as a kite" during the raid and didn't remember much about it. The jury would not hear that.

She also admitted going to Spokane with Lue and Josh for the abortion, and she sounded shamed when she described how Lue joked with the doctor who performed the operation, asking "how he liked my haircut."

As for finally leaving the Bingham house, Cynthia introduced a new element. Friends got her out of the house, she said, after she finally confided to her mother what was going on there. The friends were unnamed and the method of departure unexplained. There was no mention that she left the Bingham house to spend the night at a motel with her old boyfriend, Ken Rathbone, nor that it was her parents who then labeled her to police as a runaway.

Mosman skillfully had her talk about her interview with Captain Watkins at the Detention Center, and describe how she was disappointed because he seemed to want to talk more about his dogs than her predicament. "I was not in the mood to talk about animals," she said. "I wanted to talk and get it over with so he would go arrest them and I wouldn't have to be scared anymore." In fact, she even called for him to come back for a second interview and asked why he had not arrested the Binghams. "He had no answers," she replied with a shake of her head.

Certainly, Mosman probed, you must have told your

father something about what was happening? She had, she said, but it resulted in a tragic misunderstanding. She was talking about sex and he thought she was talking about her drug use.

When he drove her back to the Binghams one day in his truck, she confided that she didn't want to go back there, and her father replied, "Don't you think some of the things that happened are your fault?"

"I got mad," Cynthia testified. "He thought it was just drugs. He didn't know what had happened, that these people were raping me." Left unsaid, however, was why Cynthia didn't come right out and *tell* her father that.

It was only much later, during their meetings at the Detention Center, that she told him about her pubic hair being shaved and that other girls had also been raped, giving him the names of Tiffany Calico and Tina Cole. In the spectator section, Donnita Weddle wiped her eyes with a blue tissue.

Another powerful point was now extracted by Mosman, as Cynthia related how she also told her father in one of those meetings that she was frightened of Ron Bingham, although she was behind bars and in police custody. "I told him Ron would blow up the place," she said. In her version, Ron had once been to court in Clarkston and when he returned he grabbed her hand and ran it over the outside of his shirt. She had felt something and he told her that he was strapped with high explosives.

"He said, 'If I get in trouble, I won't serve time. I'd blow up the whole Asotin County Courthouse,' " Cynthia recalled, her eyes wide. "I was scared to death that he'd come after me and blow up the whole place. I was locked in a room and scared. . . . Everyone was afraid of him."

This was important information, for when Arrasmith had shot the Binghams, his daughter had been locked up and presumably out of harm's way, which would negate using her fear as part of his self-defense plea. By introducing a bomb-laced Ron Bingham into the mix, the defense could say Bingham had the ability to strike anywhere and at anytime.

A brief recess was called and during the break, Ken Arrasmith rose from his chair at the defense table and moved confidently around in a small area nearby. With the jury out of the room, he chatted amiably with Sergeant Jim Colvin, talked briefly with Cynthia, smiled at Donnita and exuded an air of confidence. The police witnesses had been badly battered and now his daughter was telling her extraordinary story. At that moment, he probably felt he had this thing whipped. His smiles reflected an inner glow of satisfaction, although his teenaged child was describing horrendous events that had happened to her.

When Cynthia resumed her testimony, she talked about her father's reaction. "My dad had always been a strong man. After he heard about me, he was hurt. He started crying," she said. "I had never seen him cry before. No one ever sees my dad that way. . . . He told me he was so sorry."

Denise Rosen responded with a few brief questions, attacking the bomb threat allegation. Did you tell Captain Watkins you did *not* feel threatened by the Binghams? she asked. The reply was yes, and Rosen read from the police report that Cynthia had stated the Binghams had more reason to be afraid of her than she of them. Further, she read from that interview that Cynthia had told Linda Bartlett at that time, "They never said they would kill me or kill you or anything."

Rosen repeated. "Did you tell Detective Watkins that you were not afraid of them?"

"Yes."

"Did you say: 'I'm not afraid of them because I

know they're afraid of me more. I can get them into trouble.' ''

Cynthia paused, and the jury paused with her. They had heard her say moments before that she had told Ken Arrasmith that Ron Bingham sometimes walked around like a human bomb, but her statements to investigators were just the opposite and painted a picture of an almost cocky youngster who was secure in holding a legal hammer over the Binghams. Something was out of focus with the picture and Cynthia didn't clear it up much with her answer. "Yes," she admitted. "I did say that."

At 3:05 P.M., after holding her audience spellbound for three and one-half hours, Cynthia Arrasmith stepped down and walked from the room, a paper cup of water in her hand.

Following Cynthia's dizzying, but powerful, testimony, the prosecution was at a crossroads. The few witnesses they had called to the stand, instead of presenting damning evidence against Ken Arrasmith, actually had fortified the defense position. Time was running out for the day, and a strong witness was needed before the jury went back to the Riverview Motel for the night. The prosecutors did not want the jurors to dwell too long on a tearful teenager's tales of predatory sex and the image of bumbling police.

It would not be known for some time, but at that moment, the legal pendulum had swung as far as it was going to go toward the defense.

The sixth witness of the trial came through the door, preceded by his name: Bingham.

Sixteen-year-old Josh Walter Bingham, the son of Luella and Ron, represented a stark contrast to his friend, Cynthia Arrasmith. He was neat and clean in a long-sleeved white shirt, open at the neck, with short, closely cut dark hair and an erect, almost military bearing. He wore pressed trousers.

The jury was surprised. After hearing the appalling litany of sins compiled by Ron and Luella Bingham, they may have been expecting someone who reflected a poor upbringing, a harried or arrogant youngster victimized by a rough childhood. This was not the case, and Josh, in his clear and firm young voice, soon explained why.

As Denise Rosen questioned him, he recalled that when his parents had found that he had a few marijuana cigarettes in his bedroom, they raised hell with him. It was astonishing behavior by Ron and Luella. They buried methamphetamine in the backyard and stacked marijuana bricks in the bus, dealt drugs on almost a convenience store basis, but blew up when finding their own boy had a couple of sticks of grass.

"Around our house, it was, 'Do as I say and not as I do.' They didn't want me to have any part of it," he said, although he confirmed that he knew that drugs were kept in his home. The result of the dual-edged upbringing by wild, but loving parents, was a boy who appeared well grounded, handsome and smart. Determination flashed in his eyes.

Answering Rosen's opening questions, he said he lifted weights to keep fit and was "pretty heavy" into mathematics, including a precalculus course, carrying a 3.3—3.4 grade point average at Clarkston High School and heading to college for engineering studies. All that from a kid whose parents had been killed without mercy.

The witness chair was only ten feet from the defense table, which meant that Josh Bingham was facing Ken Arrasmith, the man who coldly shot his parents to death. Josh paid him no attention whatsoever, focusing on Denise Rosen and the jury.

He said he liked his father, and that Ron spent a lot of quality time with him on fishing and camping trips, watching football on TV, going to car shows. "He always tried to find time to do stuff with me," Josh said. From the rows of spectators, his grandmother, Rilla Smith, watched him, trembling and worried, knowing that he had been "scared to death" prior to his court appearance.

Craig and Roy Mosman also were paying close attention to Josh. Surely, they thought, Rosen was about to drop some of the damning elements of the sexual behavior recited by Cynthia. Would she ask about Ron walking naked around the house all the time? Would she ask whether he had seen a box of porno pictures or a suitcase of sex toys?

Josh testified Cynthia came to stay at their house in the first part of the year, and spent time vacuuming the rugs and doing the laundry, doing chores "to pay for the room and board we were giving her, as best she could."

Rosen jacked up the heat, getting Josh to confirm that Cynthia's friends would come over frequently and take her out, often for overnight stays, and that her mother visited the Bingham house several times, even leaving the medical permission slip and a Medicare coupon.

His own relationship with Cynthia was that of "brother-sister," he said. When he, the good student, would come home from school, the girl, a junior high dropout, would give him a happy hug and ask about his day. But she slept a lot and their time together was limited. Sometimes, they would retreat from the adult world and hang out by themselves in the big bus in the front yard, joking and talking.

On the night of the police search, Josh related how there was a loud bang that woke him up at 2:10 A.M. as the cops charged in, yanked him from bed, handcuffed him and made him lie on the floor of the living room. "I wasn't paying too much attention to Cynthia at the time," he observed.

Finally, allowed to sit on the sofa, he saw that, "She was kind of anxious. She didn't want to go back to her mom. She wanted to stay there." It was a contradiction of Cynthia's story, that she had hoped to be swept up to safety by the police. Josh's comment was more in line with the police testimony.

Rosen pressed, giving the jury still another morsel to show that Cynthia wasn't really all alone on a dangerous iceberg, as she and the Mosmans insisted. Even her grandparents had been nearby when she was claiming to be almost held captive at the Bingham home. "Her grandparents live a quarter mile away," Josh said. They were neighbors, and Cynthia went down the hill several times to see them. Once, Luella took her down the street and snapped a photo of Cynthia and her father's new big truck, parked at the Arrasmith home. Hardly the stuff of emergency, but it didn't place an exact time, and Cynthia claimed the first weeks of her stay with the Binghams had been mostly pleasant.

The Mosmans were still expecting the sex bomb to fall. So far, Josh had said there were some pretty nice family-type times around the Bingham place when Cynthia was there, happy and sweeping floors and visiting her grandparents. But the picture was also emerging that young Josh was kept out of the loop as far as the evil side of the household was concerned.

Rosen knew she had to touch on the sex issue. Josh was not a participant, but he had been in the house much of the time that Cynthia was there and was able to show another side of the horror story the jury had heard earlier. He testified that his bedroom was next to his parents' bedroom, and that he had seen Cynthia in his parents' sleeping quarters several times, ranging from a few minutes to a few hours, and that she had never come out crying.

Rosen: Did Cynthia ever make remarks of inappropriate behavior?

Bingham: No.

Craig Mosman tensed. This could perhaps persuade a juror that Cynthia was a willing participant. Instead, Rosen let it die right there. Nothing about a naked Ron or a predatory Luella, nothing about the cache of sex material, nothing about Cynthia perhaps willingly having sex with them. Nothing. Mosman exhaled with obvious relief.

Rosen had Josh Bingham recall a time when he picked Cynthia up from her house, finding her furious and saying "she hated her parents," a statement not unusual for almost any troubled teenager. Finally, he said that within a week of his parents' deaths, he saw Ken Arrasmith drive up to the house in a pickup truck and have a discussion with Ron Bingham. Although he didn't know exactly what was said, he detected "some hostility in the air" and heard Arrasmith say he agreed with Ron about something.

Rosen said she had no further questions and turned Josh over to the defense, which didn't really want to deal with him. There was little for them to gain, and pounding him with questions might make him seem sympathetic to the jurors. Why rock the boat? Craig Mosman said he had no questions and Josh Bingham was dismissed.

The jury had spent the day listening to two young victims.

Cynthia was drugged and sexually assaulted. Josh was orphaned by gunfire. Both were only sixteen and both were trapped in a violent, perverse world.

As the second day of trial came to a close, the conclusion of court watchers was that the defense had, once again, made points on the prosecution's time. Cynthia's emotional and graphic testimony obviously dented the jury's feelings and had skewed the case sharply from the purely murder scenario.

Perhaps the prosecution's most important witness had

been brought on too early and had backfired. Whatever inconsistencies she may have had in her testimony—and there were a number—Cynthia walked away with the very important sympathy vote. Forced enemas and sodomy? Group rape? Drugged so heavily she couldn't walk by herself? Her exaggerations of fact seemed minor in comparison. Only someone with a strong stomach would have given a damn about the stumbles in her story.

The court adjourned and the Mosmans put the second day of testimony in their briefcases, alongside the unexpected victory of the first day. They were a perfect two-and-oh so far and weren't even approaching the starting line of their own case.

21

Thursday, November 9, began with a major surprise in the *Lewiston Morning Tribune*. A color photograph of a weeping Cynthia Arrasmith was played across most of the front page above the fold. Adjacent was the headline "Double Murder: Trial ends with a guilty plea." Readers who had closely followed the most celebrated case ever to hit the town were astonished until they read the story that went with the headline. It wasn't the Arrasmith case after all, but one in which a former University of Idaho graduate student, Wenkai Li, entered a plea in the stabbing deaths of two fellow Chinese. The other news of interest was that former General Colin Powell announced he would not run for president, and a story about the Militia of Montana urging its soldiers to buy waterproof barrels in which to store their weapons. But nothing compared with the ongoing coverage provided by reporter Joan Abrams of the Arrasmith trial, which she had fought for and she owned. The reporter knew everyone involved, cops and lawyers, family members on both sides of the case and witnesses. Ken Arrasmith regularly called her from jail, talking to her paternally. Her coverage was read by all, and people would approach her in the courthouse, the curious drawn to an information magnet, to critique what she had written each day, trying to determine if she was for or against anyone involved, not understanding that she was neutral, and letting the story roll on its own steam.

Craig Mosman opened the third day by taking still another stab at getting Bingham's background into the trial, hoping to follow up on the names that Cynthia testified she had given her father as other rape victims of Ron Bingham. Leggett blocked him again. But at the prosecution table, the tempers of Mike Kane and Denise Rosen grew short as the defense refused to let go of their game plan, no matter what the judge ruled. Before the day was over, the issue would detonate.

Police returned to the witness stand, and everyone braced for another assault by the Mosmans on their professionalism. But these two men were different from the earlier officers, for Patrolmen Nick Krakalia and David Meyers of the Lewiston Police Department would be testifying only about the incident at the Hollywood Motel, when Cynthia was taken into custody. They each spent only eighteen minutes on the stand.

Krakalia, a fourteen-year veteran of law enforcement, said that on May 8, he was working the day shift patrol of what was known as the Adam Beat in the north and western parts of the city, when a runaway report came in at 11:40 A.M. After, he spoke with Linda Bartlett at the police station, and she told him that her daughter was with an adult male and planned to get on a California-bound bus that morning at the Flying-J truck stop across the street from the motel. Krakalia radioed Meyers to meet him at the Hollywood, and they arrived at the same time, finding Ken Arrasmith already there, parked in the rear lot in his black Nissan extended cab pickup truck.

As Arrasmith walked over to the policemen, Cynthia emerged from the motel with Ken Rathbone. Krakalia interviewed Rathbone while Arrasmith stood there insisting the policeman arrest the boyfriend for rape. The officer determined that Rathbone was twenty-six years old, but that he denied having sex with Cynthia. The girl stood off to one side, apparently healthy and alert and obviously antagonistic toward her father. The cop saw no probable cause on which to hold Rathbone and "cut him loose" while he took Cynthia into custody.

In response to a question from Craig Mosman, the policeman replied, "Ken Arrasmith wanted his daughter picked up and arrested."

Meyers, with more than sixteen years of experience, repeated much of the same story. At the motel, he talked with Ken Arrasmith, who said his daughter may have had sex with the boyfriend and that he was worried she was going to leave the state with Rathbone. When Meyers questioned Cynthia, she denied that she had sex with Rathbone. Arrasmith's original game plan was for the cops to arrest Cynthia, take her to the police station and then release her to the custody of her mother and father.

Meyers told Cynthia what was happening as he arrested her and drove her back to the Lewiston Police Department, where her mother was waiting. But Cynthia did not cooperate with her parents' plan. "She was hostile," said Meyers. "She didn't want to go with her father or her mother."

With that, Arrasmith told police that he was now concerned that if she was released, she would run away again as soon as they left the police station. At his request, the officer said, she was placed under guard in Juvenile Detention.

Craig Mosman attacked Meyers, noting that an older male having sex with a teenaged girl was a crime serious enough in Idaho to merit a life term in the penitentiary. Using his questioning style of making statements, the attorney belittled the brief encounter of Meyers and Krakalia and the Arrasmiths that day at the motel. He

almost sneered that "the extent of the investigation by
the Lewiston Police Department into this serious crime"
was simply asking Cynthia if she had had sex with the
older man, then arresting her and letting Rathbone walk
away.

Krakalia was called back to the stand briefly to testify
again that a calm and cooperative Rathbone had insisted
he had not had sex with the girl. This time, Mosman
jumped him with the same accusations.

"Did you contact anyone to try and determine
whether they were in the motel all night?"

"No," replied the officer.

"And then you just let him walk across the street to
the bus station and head out of town."

"That is correct."

The episode may have led some jurors to wonder, if
this issue of sex between Rathbone and Cynthia had
been so important, why neither Arrasmith nor Linda
Bartlett told the police that Cynthia had only recently
had an abortion, and that Rathbone, her longtime boyfriend, was suspected of being the father. Bartlett had
even signed the permission slip for her underage daughter to have the abortion. Like many parts of this case,
things did not always make sense.

On May 9, some twenty-four hours after her parents had
her locked up, Cynthia Arrasmith remained defiant and
apparently under the influence of drugs. That was the
analysis not of a policeman, but of someone who knew
Cynthia well. Allen Johnson, a child protection worker
with the state Department of Health and Welfare, had
worked with Cynthia before when she was on drugs,
and, in fact, was her assigned caseworker.

The defense team would rather not have seen the middle-aged, quiet Johnson at all, but Denise Rosen had won
a fight to have him testify, with Judge Leggett knocking
down some of the secrecy that normally would surround

the interaction between caseworker and patient.

He had gone to see her the day after she was arrested and found her to still be an angry young girl who "did not want to be controlled." With his past contacts, Johnson was able to compare Cynthia's present condition with how he had observed her on other occasions. "I determined that it was not in her best interests to return home," he said. "She was likely to flee the area."

That weakened the defense picture that she was being held as punishment. In reality, she had been locked up at the request of her parents and then her caseworker found her too belligerent to send home. Johnson determined that the teenager needed to kick her drug habit before she could be released.

Later, on May 12, he talked with Ken Arrasmith about getting her into a treatment program. Arrasmith said Linda Bartlett's insurance could cover 80 percent of the cost of a hospital stay, and he would pick up the remaining 20 percent. Plans were laid to send Cynthia off on May 22 to a substance abuse treatment program at Mercy Hospital near Boise.

During the conversation, Johnson said, Arrasmith told him that Cynthia had been raped by the Binghams, that her pubic hairs had been shaved and that police hadn't yet moved on the case. But the father showed little emotion and was "very controlled" during their interview, which centered on getting the treatment program started.

On May 16, the day before the Binghams were killed, Johnson said he spoke again with Arrasmith about the treatment plan. This time, Arrasmith seemed upset with the police, his voice was louder and he was more animated as he explained how he was gathering evidence and "staying in touch" with the Binghams. Arrasmith claimed the police still had not taken action and wanted more evidence, apparently because they didn't totally believe Cynthia's story.

Craig Mosman's cross-examination brought out a few

more details, such as Arrasmith being "very concerned" about the rape during his first talk with the caseworker. Arrasmith also seemed very interested in the location of the shorn pubic hairs, saying that the police had either not found them or had not even looked for the envelope.

Mosman slid in another one of his statement-questions, asking: "Isn't it true, Mr. Johnson, that when Cynthia was here for her detention hearing . . . that you heard that Cynthia was afraid for her life?"

Johnson replied that he had, although he couldn't recall exactly who had said such a thing, because he had talked with so many people about the case. That, Mosman pressed, could have been one of the reasons for the continued detention. Yes, the caseworker said, it could have been one factor.

In his final moments on the witness stand, Johnson finally gave the Mosmans what they wanted. He said, at one point, Cynthia reported she was afraid to go back to the Binghams, that she had been sexually assaulted and that if she tried to return to her mother's home, Ron had threatened to kill both Cynthia and Linda Bartlett.

Asotin County Sheriff John Jeffers had been elected to office at the end of November 1994, less than six months before the Bingham murders, but he had a much longer association with the case and the valley. In fact, he had attended Clarkston High School, where he met a fellow student, Ken Arrasmith, and later worked at Potlatch with Arrasmith's mother. In the opening segment of his testimony, he made clear that he had not even seen his school acquaintance since then.

That distant link, however, would soon loom large. As the prosecution's tenth witness, the sheriff said that on the morning of May 11, he had seen Arrasmith circling the block and later found him, "quite upset" and waiting in the lobby of the sheriff's department. His face was tense and his eyes shone with moisture as he clutched his fists, his jaw muscles taut. Arrasmith asked if he could speak privately with the sheriff; Jeffers agreed.

Once seated in the office, Jeffers leaned back and listened as a sobbing Arrasmith muttered that he needed to talk to somebody. According to the sheriff, Arrasmith launched into a tale of how his sister died of a drug overdose and that he had decided to infiltrate the drug world "and fight against drug people." He even told the sheriff that he planned to bust a couple of people on drug charges in a few days, that he would have done so earlier, but the people involved had "helped get his daughter out of a situation" with the Binghams. Jeffers, concerned about lone wolf justice meted out by a civilian, offered that Ken didn't have to do that. The police could get them on their own.

Arrasmith continued to babble, saying he could understand why people might think that he was also doing drugs, because he was a long-haul truck driver, and when he was unable to stay awake, had actually purchased and taken drugs. Now, however, he wanted to help the police capture drug dealers. The sheriff politely declined, giving Arrasmith the telephone number of the experts, the Quad Cities Task Force, a unit that might contract with Arrasmith to be an undercover informant. The sheriff alerted a task force detective who said he would contact Arrasmith later.

The thirty-minute talk steered toward Arrasmith saying that "he needed to stay away from the Binghams," and by the time he quit talking, Arrasmith had calmed and "appeared satisfied" with the situation. Prosecutor Mike Kane asked if Arrasmith, at any point during that discussion less than a week before the murders, had made any comments whatsoever about being afraid for himself or for his daughter, or whether he was unhappy with any part of the police investigation. The sheriff shook his head and said, "He didn't make any requests."

When Craig Mosman had his chance for cross-examination, he was determined that the conversation needed deeper exploration. Yes, the sheriff said, he had heard "a rumor" of some vague death threat against Arrasmith.

Mosman attacked Captain Watkins again, this time to show that the sheriff had not been kept abreast of the developing situation involving Cynthia. He did not know that Watkins, waiting for Deputy White to return to work, had pushed the case aside after some preliminary investigation and turned his attention instead to his burglary cases. He didn't know that the child's pubic hairs had been shaved. He didn't know of oral sex involving Luella; or that there was a possible witness to child abuse, or that Watkins had the names of other potential victims. The defense attorney wasn't going to cut any cop a break in this case and now pressed the possibility that Watkins's actions may actually have constituted a neglect of his duties, a crime in the state of Washington.

And one last question, a zinger. Mosman asked if he had been aware of any threats by Ron Bingham against police officers. Again, he managed to inject one of those narrow slices of history about Ron Bingham. Jeffers said he knew about that. It was the final straw for the two prosecutors. They would not let Mosman continue to bring up past history unrelated to the murders!

The explosion finally came when the jury was asked to step out of the courtroom for a few minutes. For the first time in either of their legal careers, Denise Rosen and Mike Kane made a motion for a mistrial. "The people simply are not getting a fair trial!" Kane almost bellowed, claiming that the Mosmans were "deliberately and consistently" ignoring the court order about previous "bad acts" by Ron and Luella Bingham. At every opportunity, the defense attorneys were making comments about what despicable people the Binghams were, despite Leggett's repeated warnings and rulings.

Craig Mosman shot back that the motion was "crazy" and that he had done nothing "that rises to the level of a mistrial." He said the defense had only followed lines of inquiry raised by the witnesses themselves and that much of the information had come into testimony without objection from the prosecution.

Kane argued that comments such as Bingham making threats against cops had been done solely "to prejudice the jury."

Judge Leggett disagreed and overruled the motion. She said the state had gone around her order by deciding to put in evidence about drug use, and although she had sought to rein in much of the defense actions through orders from the bench, the Mosmans had the right to confront the witnesses on their testimony. Jeffers had spoken about drug activity, and the defense could probe that subject, which included Ron's reported threats against other cops. "I do not agree this court is tainted, and deny the motion for mistrial," the judge declared.

Craig Mosman turned his back to the judge and the prosecuting attorneys, rearranging pieces of paper on his table. He wore a broad grin on his face. He had scored three ways—he batted away the mistrial motion, introduced more "bad acts" of Bingham and, most of all, he had made the prosecutors mad enough to shout.

Detective Sergeant Tom White had a lot of explaining to do. If one was to believe the defense strategy, White had merely perpetuated the stumbling investigation from Captain Watkins, and together they had bungled the case so badly that Ken Arrasmith had no option, other than to take the law into his own hands.

But when Tom White walked into the courtroom to testify, he did not look like the kind of cop who would ignore a serious crime. A veteran of eighteen years in law enforcement, he had spent all but four of those years concentrating on the crimes of child abuse and rape. His brown hair and mustache matched his suit and his calm demeanor indicated a person who was deliberate and unswerving in his extraordinary job of dealing with some of society's most horrible crimes.

First, he was to account for why he was so late getting to the Cynthia Arrasmith case. He said he had been on vacation during the last part of April and, while working on security for the county fair, had damaged the sciatic nerve in his back. For the first two weeks of May, White was flat on his back in bed.

Even so, he was still able to begin working on the Arrasmith matter, because two days before he was able to go back to work, Watkins dropped the files off at his house. As White read the statement by Patti Johnson and Watkins's notes on his interview with Cynthia, White began to work out a game plan. He wanted a search warrant so he could check the clinic in Spokane where Cynthia had her abortion, and also planned to go to Lewiston and interview the girl again himself. Further, he intended to track down Patti Mahar Johnson and reinterview her.

There was another factor to be considered. Cynthia was in detention and could be assumed safe. He called the YWCA, which handles much of the sexual abuse counseling in the county, to determine if any of the women seen there claimed to be victims of the Binghams. They reported none.

Finally returning to work on May 15, sore back and all, White received a telephone call from Ken Arrasmith. Years ago, when White was starting out as an Asotin County deputy sheriff, Arrasmith was wrapping up his own tenure in law work. Arrasmith wanted to know where White was heading with Cynthia's case. They spent quite a bit of time talking about the allegations made by Cynthia and the work done by Watkins, and both expressed some frustration with the way the system operated at times.

White refused to give Arrasmith an exact time line, but said he planned to "shore some things up" before going out to interview the Binghams. In fact, he planned to save that meeting for the very end of his investigation, when he would have solid evidence that he could turn over to the prosecuting attorney.

The policeman testified that Arrasmith called him frequently during the next few days and was kept abreast of the plans. Sitting in the witness chair, the detective was only about fifteen feet from the man he had known for so many years, a man now accused of a double-murder. "I told him virtually everything," White said.

On the morning of May 17, Arrasmith called him again, about nine o'clock, with the usual request for news. White was able to tell him that things were falling nicely into place, and he was planning to talk to the prosecuting attorney. The detective explained he was encountering some legal snags in getting to the medical records in Spokane, and would probably have to use other law enforcement officers to find and reinterview Patti Johnson. But overall, there had been progress and he was ready to put the case before the prosecutor and seek the necessary warrants on the Binghams. Even if they were arrested, the detective reminded the ex-deputy, the Binghams probably would be released on bail. Arrasmith thanked him and hung up.

Under oath in court, however, White was able to fill in more of the picture. Cynthia Arrasmith wasn't the only child who needed protection from a sexual predator when the policeman returned to work from his injury. At least she was in a safe place, he thought. Unfortunately, he could not make the same judgment of the other two instances. One girl, who was developmentally disabled, still was in the home of the person suspected of molesting her. And a neighbor was the prime suspect in the molestation of another girl. "I needed to get statements from those other gals," White said. In his opinion, they were in much more immediate jeopardy than Cynthia.

"I don't recall him being real critical of our work," White recalled. "He did not criticize what I had done. He had some frustration, but he was not critical of Captain Watkins."

He was asked: "Was Mr. Arrasmith in fear of the Binghams?"

"No," White replied.

Mike Kane was asking the questions and he turned the subject to the reports that Ron Bingham had offered a "contract" to have Arrasmith killed. White said that Arrasmith himself had mentioned there was a contract out on Cynthia, and maybe one on him, with a bale of marijuana supposedly the payment for a killing. White was polite. He didn't believe Arrasmith's assertion, thinking that Bingham wasn't a big enough dealer to put together an entire bale of marijuana, much less give it away free. He checked the report with narcotics officers and they didn't believe it either, he said. He told Arrasmith that if there was such a contract, it was probably just Ron hollering again, trying to scare people.

Craig Mosman rose to question White and went out of his way to establish the policeman's credentials as an expert in sexual abuse with a thousand hours of post-academy training, including instruction at the Harvard Medical Center and the FBI. The jury was aware of his tactic now: Set up the police as knowing what they were doing and then show they had dropped the ball, an error that resulted in Ken Arrasmith having few choices in protecting his daughter.

Mosman immediately ran White through the entire laundry list, having him admit knowing about the sex toys, the reported names of other victims, the enema and anal sex and other shocking things contained in the reports White had read. Then the lawyer asked: "Is it true that Cynthia reported there were other victims?'' There was no objection to the question, although it left jurors to deduce that "other victims" meant sexual molestations by the Binghams.

Then the two experts on sexual misbehavior conducted a clinic in how a pedophile can "groom" a child to be obedient. By piling on gifts and friendship, they gain the child's trust and isolate them from parents and friends. Mosman continued to press the policeman, who admitted that he wouldn't be surprised if a teenaged girl chose to stay with the people who were grooming her as a sexual plaything.

Then, White tripped. As Mosman picked at his knowledge, the policeman blurted that he was not expert enough in child abuse to answer all of the questions. Harvard and the FBI and fourteen years on the job handling such cases? If he wasn't expert, then who was?

Still, Mosman wasn't satisfied. He needed to show that, not only was Cynthia under the Binghams control even when other people were present, but that she was in imminent danger.

Naturally, there was an objection from the prosecution. Only a short time before they had moved for a mistrial because of a similar tactic and now the defense was at it again. The judge put a stop to the questioning and sent the jury from the room.

Mosman told the judge his line of questions was to lay the foundation for a future development they planned to introduce, that a fourteen-year-old girl had moved in with the Binghams as soon as Cynthia moved out.

Mike Kane said that the information wasn't relevant to the "case in chief," meaning two murders.

Mosman replied that it all went to explain Arrasmith's state of mind. "It's only fair," Mosman said, to fully explore everything the witness knew related to the entire Bingham-Arrasmith situation.

Leggett, obviously tired of the wrangling over the

same issue, time and again, once more ruled against him. "Regardless of how unfair it seems, it is set by precedent," she snapped. "This court will not accept an invitation to rewrite Idaho law."

Then it was Mosman's turn to trip, by going one question too far. He had tried to imply that the police gave Arrasmith permission to investigate the matter on his own, and that White had told Arrasmith that he, too, was afraid of Ron Bingham.

"No," the cop replied. "I told (Deputy) Wade Ralston that I wouldn't turn my back on the Binghams." That remark may have indicated police prudence, but it was far from demonstrating that the cops were afraid to tangle with Ron.

In a brief response, Mike Kane asked White if he could name "a single officer who told you about a (murder) contract prior to the killings?" White simply said no.

Kane, with one hand in his pocket and the other slicing the air, had White explain the status of the Cynthia probe when it came to such an abrupt end. The detective said both Cynthia and Patti Johnson had been "shaky" in their facts, because both were on drugs when they made their reports, and that while elements of child abuse were present, more than accusations were needed to build a case that would stick.

"Did you ever indicate to the defendant any plan not to go forward with the investigation?"

"No," said White.

"Ever?"

"No."

Mosman made one last attempt to show the seriousness of the crime of child abuse and how unusual it was for the police to have an adult (Patti Mahar Johnson) witness the rape and come forward as a witness. Her statement, Cynthia's statement, combined with the Quality Inn receipts and the pubic hair allegation left an unspoken question hanging in the air: *"How much do the police really need to take a sex offender off the streets?"*

Unfortunately, White had been a solid witness for the prosecution. Mosman had been unable to shake the detective, who had begun working on the strange case even before he returned from sick leave. He had prepared enough material to take to the prosecuting attorney and had kept Ken Arrasmith informed every step of the way . . . right up until Ron and Luella Bingham were shot to death.

Tom White stepped from the stand having punched a big hole in Arrasmith's alibi that he had been forced to move because the police would not.

22

Twenty-four-year-old Paul Jason Sharrai ambled into the courtroom, lanky and seeming out of place. After the string of well-scrubbed police officers who had given testimony, Sharrai, who would soon admit to being a drug addict, instantly took the trial right into the gritty world where it belonged, for this was not a country club crime. He wore jeans, a denim shirt buttoned at the throat, dirty black-and-white Nike sneakers, and his long brown hair was tied back in a ponytail by a small pink elastic band. There was a fuzz of a goatee and pencil-thin mustache on the youthful face, his eyes were wide and his manner calm. Since the shootings in May, his life had progressed, but not far. Sharrai told prosecutor Denise Rosen that he was now living in Twin Falls, where he worked at a car wash. Across the room, the jurors, all of whom had been brought in from that same city, realized they were watching a home boy. Maybe this bizarre crime wasn't as far from their front doorsteps as they may have liked.

Back in May, Sharrai explained in a flat, quiet voice, he had been in the Lewiston area for a couple of months, hanging out with friends, one of whom introduced him to Ron Bingham, who offered him mechanical work.

Rosen knew this witness was a bit of a powder keg

as far as credibility, but it was better for her to bring out
the weak links rather than let the Mosmans surprise the
jury. The strong side of Sharrai's testimony was its pure
simplicity. He saw what he saw, and what he saw was
important.

Rosen had the young man describe the area, then
asked: "What happened?"

Sharrai leaned so far back in the witness chair that he
seemed about to topple over. He exhaled loudly and said,
"Phew! They got shot!"

A car guy, he was able to exactly describe the pickup
truck that had driven up that morning—black Toyota,
four-wheel-drive, '90s (model), extended cab, toolbox
and "some weird stripe going down the side." He said
it pulled up once, paused and drove away, returning a
short time later. In this laconic way, Sharrai had introduced new information, for no public report ever said
the truck was there twice. And if the driver had left once
and returned, the elapsed time could spell premeditation.

Sharrai said while he worked on a truck behind the
shop, someone walked past, "carrying what I thought
was a stack of car magazines." The stranger asked
where Ron was and someone pointed to Bingham, who
lay on the ground, halfway beneath a pickup truck on
which he was replacing a bumper. Luella Bingham,
standing near Sharrai in front of the line of parked
trucks, said nothing.

Then, Sharrai testified, he heard a series of popping
sounds. "I thought they were firecrackers, to be honest.
Somebody playing a joke."

He quickly realized it was no joke when he heard
Luella scream: "You son of a bitch! You shot him!"

When Luella began "freakin' out," Paul Sharrai decided it was time to leave. He dashed away and thought
Lue was "running right behind me." There were more
pops and Luella went down.

"Did you change your mind about the pops?" Rosen asked.

"Oh, yes," the itinerant mechanic replied.

"Were they continuous?"

"Oh, continuous."

"Were they gunshots?"

"Gunshots," he said, adding an emphatic nod. "Definitely gunshots."

He hid in a clump of bushes until the black truck drove away. "It was a relief to see it leaving," he said, but he did not leave his hiding place until a fire truck and police cars arrived. When he returned to the scene, he identified himself, was handcuffed and taken to the police station for a statement.

Rosen asked him to describe the driver of the truck. While exact on the vehicle, he was vague on the man's description, saying only that the driver was a "fairly tall, slender and clean-cut guy."

At the defense table, the Mosmans already knew Sharrai would not be able to exactly identify Ken Arrasmith. Describing a truck was one thing, being able to point out their client was another. In fact, Craig Mosman's first questions centered on that identification process. When asked if he saw the suspect clearly, Sharrai replied, "No. I didn't look back."

Mosman was determined that the jury know just who was on the witness stand, and he made Sharrai admit he had been using methamphetamines since he was about thirteen years old and was "hooked" on meth at the time of the slayings, even sharing some meth in the garage with Ron and another man the night before the killings, doing "one or two lines . . . through my nostril."

Could that have affected what he saw on the morning of May 17? Sharrai said it did not. "It is pretty concrete in my head what happened there," he vouched with a straight face.

Mosman attacked whether the Toyota really came to

the shop twice that morning but was unable to shake
Sharrai. The lawyer pointed out that the information
wasn't in the statement Sharrai gave the police. "The
question wasn't asked." The witness shrugged. "I didn't
tell the police a lot of things."

Mosman hammered, but to no avail. He had been able
to poke holes in the stories of previous witnesses with
ease, but Sharrai, who had nothing to hide, and therefore
nothing to lose, was as rugged as a rock. He saw what
he saw. Even if he couldn't put Arrasmith at the scene,
he was able to do one very important thing. Paul Sharrai,
the admitted meth addict, turned the trial away from the
hot button topics of child rape, sex abuse and police
incompetence, redirecting it back to murder.

The court adjourned for a long weekend, since Friday
was Veterans Day, and the jurors returned to the Riverside Inn for a three-day marathon of movies and bore-
dom. They had learned a lot in the first three days of the
trial, and the smooth defense lawyers had done a good
job of winning individual battles in the courtroom. The
trial had begun with Denise Rosen's opening statement
describing a vicious double-murder, and ended for the
week with Rosen cashing the Sharrai chip, a tactic that
returned the case to the murders of Ron and Luella Bingham. That was precisely where the prosecutor wanted
the jurors' minds to be during the long, sequestered
weekend.

Waiting on her desk back in the Brammer Building
were two dark red roses, sent by an anonymous sup-
porter. As she put on her long black coat and stepped
out into the early winter chill for a bit of family time
and another weekend of preparation for the next phase
of the trial, the diminutive prosecutor could feel satisfied.
The damage of police bobbles and Cynthia's tears were
behind. From here on, she intended to concentrate on
murder most foul.

*   *   *

Following the long, wet and dreary weekend, trial resumed on a chill, damp Monday morning at 9:05 A.M., when the baby-faced Robert Warnock, the young man who could place Ken Arrasmith at the murder scene, came to the witness stand. "He's a terrible witness," Donnita whispered to someone sitting beside her. The other side felt the same way. Warnock's testimony, from the beginning, had been inconsistent and jumpy. Today he wore jeans with a big cowboy buckle and a quasi-American flag shirt with white stars on a field of blue in front, and red and white stripes in the rear around the legend: "Rodeo Greatest Show On Dirt." Dark hair curled over his collar.

Denise Rosen opened by determining that while Warnock was currently without a job, he had been a mechanic back in May at Specialized Automotive on Shelter Road. On the morning of the shootings, he arrived at work at 8 A.M., talked with several people for a while, then drove to a motel to awaken the garage owner, Tony Adams. Back at Shelter Road, Warnock strolled over to the huge pile of tires in an adjacent field to visit a pal, returning to the shop about 11 A.M. when he saw a dark Toyota pickup truck stop and park.

"Can I help you?" he had asked. The driver responded, "Yes. Is Ron Bingham here?" Warnock answered, "Oh, yeah," and escorted the visitor to where Ron was beneath the Chevy pickup.

Rosen clipped a rough map of the garage layout, drawn on brown kraft paper, to a tripod in the middle of the room. Warnock carefully marked the locations of the Toyota, Ron Bingham and the path he had walked between the two. The jury studied it as though it contained directions to a treasure.

Warnock said they passed Paul Sharrai, who was under the hood of a truck repairing a master cylinder. Luella Bingham stood nearby.

"The guy said to her, 'Ron left this at my house,' "

Warnock reported, adding the stranger carried a red, white and blue box. "She ignored it, like it was nothing," he said. Then, the witness said, he heard the man tell Ron, "I got something for you."

"Oh, cool," Ron had responded.

Then Warnock heard the series of shots. "I ran," he said, first hiding in some bushes, then jumping into a truck and speeding away. When he returned, police were at the scene, and he was also questioned and handcuffed.

Now came a gamble for the prosecution. Warnock had screwed up the identification at the preliminary hearing when he couldn't distinguish the well-dressed Arrasmith from the other suit-clad lawyers in the courtroom. There was no choice but to run him through the exercise again. Warnock said the man he saw on May 17 had darkish blond, long hair and was wearing dark glasses.

A detective, he reported, later handed him the card containing six photographs and told him to take his time and "pick out the man you saw," but added that the man's photograph might not be among the six he was shown. Rosen put the photo card into evidence and Warnock said that the Number Five picture "was the person I saw that day."

"That was the person in the truck?" Yes, it was.

"That was the person carrying the box?" Yes, it was.

"That was the person you left with Ron Bingham?" Yes, it was.

The photo was of Ken Arrasmith.

Rosen, covering a weak point, addressed the difficult time Warnock had in picking Arrasmith out in court during the preliminary hearing. "I was scared," said Warnock. "The person looked different in a suit than he did that day."

And how about now, Rosen asked. Is he in court today? Without hesitation, Warnock pointed to Arrasmith.

Warnock had behaved like an upstanding witness to a crime, and even held his own when Craig Mosman sharply cross-examined him for five minutes. The defense attorney had Warnock admit that he didn't really know exactly what Ron Bingham had done during the fatal meeting, because he had turned and walked away. The lawyer asked if Warnock heard Ron swear at Arrasmith about Cynthia, and Warnock said he did not.

He also said he did not see any weapons and didn't remember noticing whether Arrasmith carried a stack of car magazines, as Sharrai had mentioned. It was a minor discrepancy. Mosman sat down, having done little with the witness.

But at the prosecution table, a blunder was shaping up as Mike Kane whispered to Denise Rosen. There is an axiom that lawyers should never ask questions for which they do not already know the answer. However, the prosecution wanted to show that Warnock had only just turned away from Ken and Ron when the shooting began and had therefore been present at the crucial moments. Rosen asked how much time elapsed between the time Warnock and Arrasmith walked up to Bingham and the time Warnock walked away.

The young man paused, then said, "Maybe one minute. Maybe two."

"Right away?" Rosen tried to interpret, but the damage was done, and Mosman slammed in an objection to stop Warnock from embellishing his answer.

The defense team had just been provided with two minutes of time that had not previously existed. They could plant the seed of doubt that an argument between Ron and Ken may have taken place prior to the shooting, perhaps words threatening enough to make Arrasmith open fire in fear of his life. A lot of argument can take place in two minutes.

The jinx of Robert Warnock had struck again. He got the identification right this time but had handed the defense an important time element. It was a classic instance of a lawyer asking one question too many.

*   *   *

A march of law enforcement officers and investigative officials came next, with Nez Perce County Deputy Don Taylor and Captain Scott Whitcomb describing what they found as the first officers arriving at the murder scene. In an exchange that was to reverberate loudly in coming months, Mosman had Whitcomb admit that his own son was employed at the Shelter Road repair shop.

A uniformed deputy, Corporal Guy Arnzin, testified about making a videotape of the scene and the bodies, and the prosecution played the cassette for the jury. It had a powerful effect, for it allowed them to view Ron and Luella Bingham not as abstract figures, but as real people. People who were dead.

Dr. Carl Koenen, a veteran pathologist who had the calm, concerned look of a family physician, told of performing the autopsies. In total, he said, Ron Bingham had forty-four wounds—ten on his right side, twenty-six on his left, six in the back, one grazing wound on his penis and one in the right buttock. Twenty-four were entrance wounds, the rest exit and grazing wounds. A line drawing of a male torso with a dot representing each wound was introduced as evidence, and the large number of heavy blue dots made the diagram more effective than a simple photograph.

The wounds caused horrendous damage, the pathologist said. One of the first shots hit the brain, fracturing the head, bringing instant death to Ron Bingham. The kidney was blown apart and most internal organs were lacerated—liver, heart and stomach. The adrenal gland could not even be found. "There are many fatal wounds here," the doctor observed.

He moved on to discuss the autopsy of Luella Bingham, whom he described as "a middle-aged lady," and Donnita Weddle whispered in disgust to an Arrasmith daughter, "A lady!" Koenen again described multiple gunshot wounds, fourteen in total—one through the right breast and into the left, three exit wounds in the right chest, five in the back causing "extreme" damage, one in the middle of her upper right leg and one exit wound in the right groin. Some jurors leaned forward in their chairs to follow the doctor's line drawing of a woman, on which the dots represented bullet holes. He said she was at a right angle to the shooter when attacked, with the first bullet hitting her in the right breast. She began to spin to the left, going down, and the next shot hit her in the back as she was in a stooped-over position. It dug through the right lung and ribs. The third went through the neck, the spinal column and lodged behind her right ear. She was going down fast, stumbling. Another bullet hit her left back and came out through the chest and another ripped her spleen, heart, stomach and diaphragm. "She was probably on the ground" and already dead from her massive wounds when the final bullet was fired into her back. Her arms were tucked neatly beneath her, meaning she made no effort to break her facedown fall.

Then came the tale of Clarkston Police Detective Ron Roberts, who arrested Arrasmith on May 17. A small man, only five-foot-seven, he had been with the police department for twenty-three years and had known Ken Arrasmith since grade school.

He described how he had been walking to his unmarked police car in the parking lot, ready to cruise around in search of the truck sought by police, when he spotted it driving slowly toward him. Roberts was astonished when Arrasmith climbed from behind the steering wheel and held out the ignition key. Roberts immediately asked if Arrasmith had been involved in the Shelter Road shootings, and when he received no reply, searched his old friend and took him into the police station to await Nez Perce County authorities. Other cops were assigned to guard the gun-laden truck parked outside police headquarters.

On cross-examination, Craig Mosman attempted to explore the suggestion that Ron Bingham had put out a contract to kill Arrasmith, offering a pound of methamphetamine for his death. Roberts said another policeman had told him that such an offer had been made, and Mosman had Roberts confirm the deal was "to take Ken Arrasmith's life."

The contract, however, was still only a rumor, since Roberts had no personal knowledge of it. It was only something that came to him through the police department grapevine. Words, not proof.

23

Laughter filtered into Courtroom 1 from behind the brown wooden door that led to the private jury room. "The jury seems to be having a good time," remarked Judge Leggett. On Day Five of the Kenneth Arrasmith trial, there was little reason for levity in a case that alternated between the sexual abuse of children and murder.

Detective Wade Ralston, the lead investigator, had spent a half hour on the stand, decribing the murder scene, the photo montage used for Robert Warnock to identify Ken Arrasmith, and the lucrative search of the truck, which turned up a variety of guns, binoculars, a cellular telephone, a police scanner radio and a paper containing the description of an automobile owned by Rilla Smtih.

Craig Mosman asked one of his patented nonquestions, whether Ralston thought the description of the car had been made, "Maybe so Ken Arrasmith would know when he was being followed by this vehicle?" The automatic objection by Kane was sustained, since this was Mosman rolling out an idea that might stick to the mind of some juror.

Deputy Don Taylor came on next and the trial almost came to a stop. Everyone had heard about the murder weapons, and the policeman actually brought them into the courtroom. It was one of those moments that moves a jury from speculation to reality, and when he unzipped a gray and blue gun bag and withdrew the Chinese-made SKS rifle—large, black and menacing—there was an audible gasp of surprise. "Man, look at that thing," whispered one spectator of the military-style rifle that seemed to almost fill the court. It was the first time the jury had seen a weapon in what, until now, had been a confusing and almost hypothetical case. Taylor said the weapon had been found in the toolbox of the pickup truck, fully loaded with one 7.62mm round in the chamber and thirty-four more in the clip.

The guns were inside paper bags, resembling a load of lethal groceries, and Taylor now ripped open a second bag to withdraw a big .357 Magnum revolver, also fully loaded with six bullets and found in the glove compartment.

Taylor's display continued when he loudly tore open another paper evidence bag and introduced a lithe .22 caliber pistol with wooden grips and a bare metal finish, which also had been discovered in the glove compartment. He brought out clips of bullets of different sizes that had been found under the seat and in nylon pouches.

Then came the 9mm Ruger semiautomatic pistol, found on the front seat of the truck. On the handle was a tiny band, which when squeezed, turned on a small laser sight mounted under the barrel. Taylor said it was empty when discovered.

Finally, the detective held up the lightweight Tec-9, its dull black finish making it seem more lethal than its small, almost pistollike size would indicate. The semiautomatic weapon's long and narrow clip was totally empty when it was picked off the front seat. Several jurors began to furiously scribble on their notepads.

Throughout the presentation of the weapons, including

the two guns used in the murders, there was a noticeable silence at the defense table. Where Craig Mosman had been quick to jump on the other police witnesses, objections were few as Taylor put into evidence the five guns found in the truck driven by Ken Arrasmith. Actually, the defense lawyers had been willing to stipulate that the weapons were discovered as police claimed, but the prosecution wanted the impact the firearms would have on the jury, seeing gun after gun after gun pulled from evidence bags. It was the exact opposite of the police performances earlier in the trial, and the jurors had to realize that no matter what had happened in the sexual abuse field, Taylor and Ralston knew what they were doing in the area of investigating a double-murder.

That was underlined now by Denise Rosen, whose almost awkward handling of the earlier attacks had suddenly been smoothed out. She had almost a word-by-word script typed on yellow legal paper and she carefully followed it, giving the entire episode of the guns the important flow of logic that was needed.

On cross-examination, Mosman used his knowledge of the West and the favor in which guns are held in the region, asking Taylor if it was illegal for a citizen to own any or all of them. No, the policeman replied.

Mosman also discussed the minicassette tape recorder that was found in the truck, asking if it was the kind police used ''to record important interviews.'' Taylor affirmed that it was. That was an important piece of the defense theory, indicating that Arrasmith had intended to only intimidate the Binghams into admitting their assaults on Cynthia and capturing their words on tape.

The lawyer then added another layer to this theory by picking up the Ruger 9mm pistol and gently squeezing the grip to activate the laser sighting system. Instantly, a narrow scarlet beam of light came from the device, ending as a bright red dot that danced on the courtroom's white wall, between the head of Judge Leggett and the

Idaho state flag. Every juror's eye followed the moving dot. He asked Taylor if such a laser dot, fastened to a weapon, "can be used to intimidate a person?"

"That depends on the situation," retorted the policeman.

The red dot scanned down the judge's bench and crossed over a water jug, giving the jury a good look at it. Mosman asked if someone could use the combination of the red dot, a pistol and a tape recorder to "get someone to make a statement." Denise Rosen immediately objected at the leap in logic and the judge sustained the motion. But it made no difference. The jury had heard it anyway and it was too powerful for them to ignore, no matter that the judge ordered them to forget what was just said.

Mosman tried again, couching the statement carefully this time, only to have Taylor respond that police would not use such a scare tactic to coerce a confession. "It's against the law," he said. In fact, it would be considered aggravated assault for a cop to use the device on a suspect.

The defense attorney asked if the moving red dot, to show where a bullet would go, is "used in prison settings" to suppress fights. Taylor said he didn't know. Although the policeman had successfully dodged all attempts to get him to agree with the defense statements, the jury had Mosman's theory firmly in their minds by the time Taylor left the witness stand.

It would be reinforced repeatedly in coming days, every time Craig Mosman would pick up the pistol and squeeze the grip. The red laser would flare out and the dot would dance. Onlookers could only imagine how it must feel to have such a thing pointed at them.

The prosecutors brought on two more witnesses—Deputy Doug McPherson and fingerprint expert Robert Kerchusky—to provide evidence pointing toward Ken

Arrasmith being the triggerman on May 17. McPherson introduced bullets and fragments of bullets gathered at the scene, the flat box Arrasmith carried that day, pictures and charts of the murder scene, along with autopsy photographs, noting that one bullet fell from the riddled body of Ron Bingham and another was found in Lue Bingham's shirt. Denise Rosen held up the Tec-9, showing without saying it, that the weapon was so small and light that even a tiny woman could wield it. She then placed the Tec-9 inside the box to show how it was completely hidden in the cardboard sandwich, and demonstrated how the weapon could be held and fired, even while in the container. Kerchusky was able to pull clearly identifiable prints from the ammunition clip in the Ruger pistol and on the box that had hidden the Tec-9. The prints belonged to Arrasmith.

Mosman was reduced to probing only whether any weapons were discovered at the site, and whether Ron Bingham was known to carry weapons. The police witnesses said they saw no guns at Shelter Road, only tools scattered around the area where Ron was working.

But the morning's testimony, as powerful as it was, soon was overshadowed. The jury was excused for lunch as the court handled a rather important matter.

Kyle Richardson was brought into the room, lumbering up to stand before the judge. He had decided to take a sweetheart deal that the state of Idaho was offering. By testifying against his old pal Ken Arrasmith, Richardson would escape the possible fate of life imprisonment himself as a coconspirator.

Instead, he would plead guilty to the charge of being an accessory to a felony. In exchange, he would receive a minimum of two years or a maximum of five years in prison and/or a fifty-thousand dollar fine. That alone would be better than risking life in prison, or a possible death sentence, for the conspiracy charge.

What made the deal particularly appealing, however, was that it would start with a 180-day term in a drug rehabilitation program in a miminum security facility. If he successfully completed the six months of rehab, the remainder of his sentence would be withheld and he would serve five years on probation.

He could receive the lenient treatment only if he testified fully and completely against Ken Arrasmith. It was an astonishing offer, with the state almost doing everything but buying Kyle Richardson a new car to get him on the witness stand against his buddy, Arrasmith.

Judge Leggett went over the terms of the agreement and Richardson acknowledged that he understood and accepted the deal. The judge knew the deal was too good for the young man to pass up. She said that if he didn't show up to testify, she would have to question his intelligence, adding that she would also be very "unhappy" if that happened. Richardson could clearly understand the little woman in the black robe would throw him to the wolves if he didn't do exactly what he had promised.

Later that day, an odd thing happened at the court clerk's office. When a copy of the state's agreement with Richardson was requested, it was refused. Since it had already been read in court, it was public record, and only after a protracted discussion was it provided. Court Administrator Steve Caylor appeared personally to make the point that although the deal had been agreed to by the prosecutors and Richardson, Judge Leggett had not yet signed off on it. The matter was viewed at the time as merely a piece of fresh paperwork awaiting Leggett's signature after Richardson lived up to his part of the bargain. But when the trial was done, the incident assumed a much greater importance.

Prosecutors went to lunch looking satisfied with their morning's work, while the Mosmans almost slumped in their chairs as Kyle Richardson agreed to sell out his chum, Ken Arrasmith. Leaving the court, even the usually-positive Donnita Weddle admitted that she was "a little depressed."

Actually, the evidence presented was sufficient to both put Arrasmith at the scene of the crime and to tie him directly to the murder weapons. Sharrai and Warnock had identified him as the driver of the truck, the cops had found the guns in the vehicle and forensics experts had discovered Arrasmith's fingerprints, both on the cardboard box that concealed the Tec-9 and on the ammunition clip of the Ruger pistol used in the shootings. There was no doubt now that Ken Arrasmith had killed Ron and Luella Bingham.

In fact, although he had never admitted doing so, there had been little doubt from the very beginning of the case back in May when he gave himself up to Ron Roberts.

The missing link, however, was not any of the hard evidence of the deaths, and both sides knew it. The legal waters were muddied by the *why* in the case, which was the reason that Denise Rosen and Mike Kane had to go far beyond just proving that Arrasmith had committed the crimes as charged. The clever use of the media, the advertising done by the defense fund, the forum of the national TV talk shows had painted a portrait of a father in agony over the molestation of his daughter, a father driven to do what he did because the cops would not do their jobs. If the Mosmans could still manage to sell that line to a jury, Ken Arrasmith could walk out of the court a free man. Rosen and Kane had to knock Arrasmith off his high horse of publicity.

There was no other reason to trace for the jury the bizarre history of the Tec-9 that ended up in the defendant's hands on May 17. But by doing so, the prosecution would uncover the one thing that would taint Arrasmith's golden image: drugs. Such knowledge was already on the street, and reporter Eric Sorensen of the

Spokesman-Review observed that "Arrasmith's public image has begun to slip from outraged father to methamphetamine-snorting, deadbeat dad." To let such testimony go before the jury would pose a major threat. Arrasmith's carefully cultivated media image could crack like a cheap mirror.

The defense launched a major battle before Judge Leggett on the Tec-9 issue, after Richardson had accepted his deal to become a state witness. Craig Mosman wanted to block any witness who might testify that Arrasmith used drugs and "tangentially participated" in a drug deal. He claimed it was "intellectually dishonest" to bring up that past history, when the defense was prohibited from introducing the dirty past of Ron Bingham.

Mike Kane responded that prosecutors would show there was a conspiracy to kill the Binghams, and that Arrasmith was a user of methamphetamines and was "an occasional business partner" of Richardson in drug deals.

Still out of the hearing of the jury, Kane dropped the bombshell news that Arrasmith had paid Richardson ten thousand dollars in one hundred dollar bills for use in a drug purchase. Richardson was supposed to pay back eighteen thousand dollars within thirty days. When Kyle spent the profits instead, Arrasmith claimed the collateral Richardson had put up for the loan, including the Tec-9. "Everyday, they used meth together," the prosecutor said.

In addition to talking repeatedly about stalking and wanting to kill the Binghams, Richardson would testify that Arrasmith actually left for Shelter Road the morning of the murders from Richardson's automobile shop. Kane's argument was lucid and clear and turned the tables on Mosman's earlier probings that went far beyond the murders of the Binghams. Kane said the defense brought in facts that had no relevancy to Arrasmith pulling the trigger, such as Ron Bingham doing drugs the night before being killed, and Cynthia testifying about things other than the murders. Fine, said Kane, then "let's get it all out. It brought this killing into some sort of focus." Drugs—not guns or motor cars—were the primary link, he insisted, between the young Richardson and the adult Arrasmith.

Mosman was coldly outraged and said he could not "find words to describe the gall of the People of the State of Idaho," but the judge cut off his sweeping protest and told him to get to the point. There were specific areas of law involved and she thought Kane had covered them all, she said.

Mosman countered that there was "no one in this courtroom so dull" as not to understand there was no reason for linking the defendant with drugs other than "to besmirch the character of Mr. Arrasmith."

Leggett sharply replied that "regardless of how dull I may be" she considered the legal points of how he obtained the weapon, his constant conversations with Richardson and "the drug debt" to be "part and parcel" of Arrasmith's ultimate actions.

The polite argument continued unabated for more than an hour as Mosman used every trick he knew to slow the momentum that was building for the prosecution. But the judge, who had seen so much straying from the course already in this trial, was in no mood to buy his package. She stuck by her decisions that the victims of the crime should not be the ones placed on trial, and ruled solidly against Mosman's two motions to block the looming juggernaut of evidence that was advancing on his client.

Afterward, she quipped that such fast-paced and intense drama is seldom seen in a real court. "Not since Perry Mason . . . has everything happened at once," she said.

When all was said and done, the prosecution had climbed the legal hill and stood on a sunny summit. Kyle

Richardson would be allowed to testify about everything, including the drug debt. It was the turning point of the trial because it stripped Ken Arrasmith of his shining robe of righteousness.

24

With the legal road now clear, the prosecutors were free to bring on the four witnesses who would be the appetizers leading to the Kyle Richardson main course. In order, the state served up Chris McFarland, Wes Rehm, Jerry Jobe and John Swett, and by doing so, plunged the jurors into the seedy underbelly of the Lewis-Clark Valley, a place in which a tough-guy brotherhood was fueled by drugs, cars and guns.

Chris McFarland, a twenty-nine-year-old construction worker, said he had known Kyle Richardson since about February of 1995, and had sold him "a bunch of Chevrolet parts." When Richardson was picking up his purchase at the home of McFarland's mother, he noticed that McFarland's father collected guns and had an arsenal that ranged from an AK-47 to an SKS to a Tec-9 to clips, bullets and reloading equipment.

Roy Mosman needled, attacked McFarland's credibility, asking if he did drugs. Yes, McFarland replied, some meth. Mosman asked if he used drugs with Kyle Richardson. Yes, came the answer. And did you steal something from Kyle Richardson? Yes, he said, "a couple of things" from the auto garage.

Drug-hammered thief or not, Richardson contacted

him a few days before the Bingham killings, asking if McFarland had an extra ammo clip for a Tec-9. Richardson seemed "stressed" and said he needed the clip immediately and did not even have time to drive to nearby Orofino and buy one legally at a gun shop.

According to McFarland, Richardson told him "a friend" had an emergency and that "a young girl had some misfortunate happenings." Richardson added ominously that McFarland would soon "read about two people in the paper." Apparently realizing he had talked too much, Richardson warned McFarland not to tell anyone. "He said if anybody crossed him, he had ways of taking care of them," the witness said. "I took him very seriously."

McFarland also offered the suggestion that Kyle see if he could get an extra Tec-9 clip from Jerry Jobe, who was going to be his brother-in-law. Jerry, he said, used to have a Tec-9.

Melvin Wesley "Wes" Rehm, a retired navy man, testified that, although he was not a "collector" of guns, he did own quite a number of pistols, rifles and shotguns. One item in his noncollection was a Tec-9 that he bought in January 1995, from a gun dealer in Oregon. He kept it in his basement, safe in its plastic carrying case, but late in March of 1995 he noticed that it was missing. He suspected either his girlfriend or her sixteen-year-old son, Curt Yates, and confronted them. But rather than get into a long squabble about it, he just let it go.

Mike Kane handed the Tec-9 that was already in evidence to Rehm and the former owner confirmed that it matched the serial number on the carrying case box that he had turned over to police.

Jerry Jobe, out of work since leaving his job as a Ramada Inn dishwasher months ago, testified that during the first part of March, a girl told him that Junior Yates had a Tec-9. The two men met and Jobe purchased the weapon for "a hundred bucks and a 'T' of meth."

Mike Kane wanted a translation. How much is a "T" of meth? Jobe answered in still more drug world lingo: "Half an eight-ball." He then had to explain that an eight-ball of methamphetamine has a street value of about two hundred dollars.

Jobe used a little steel wool to smooth down some rust spots on the gun and displayed it on a wall, resting on a set of deer antlers. He wanted the weapon to look good because he had a potential buyer. Kyle Richardson had heard talk about the weapon and told Jobe to get it. When Kyle examined the gun, he liked what he saw, gave Jobe three hundred dollars worth of meth and took the Tec-9 away in a black bag.

The relationship between the two was deeper than that single transaction. Jobe admitted that he "used to sell drugs" for Kyle and had charges pending against him for a drug delivery. He said he hoped his testimony today would help persuade a judge to give him probation in that case, but had been given no promises.

Jobe said drugs were always involved when he met with Kyle, usually at Richardson's car shop on Bridge Street in Clarkston. He added that once in March, he and his uncle, John Swett, were introduced to Arrasmith at the shop. Kyle took some meth from his toolbox, sliced it into equal portions, and each man snorted a line.

His last contact with Richardson, Jobe testified, was the day before the Binghams were killed. Kyle telephoned to ask if Jobe had found a Tec-9 clip, an item he had sought earlier, claiming "he didn't have time to wait, the guy needed it right now."

Jobe said that on the phone, "Kyle sounded kinda shook up, kinda scared a little bit."

Roy Mosman did not have much to work with on cross-examination because Jobe had already outlined his checkered past. But he did get the witness to admit he owed Richardson about a thousand dollars and would have been suspicious of anyone who didn't join them when invited to inhale a line of meth.

Then the old professional tripped up by asking the witness about Kyle's interest in guns. Jobe leaned forward and, before anyone could stop him, said, "I didn't know it was going to be used for a murder!" The answer drew an immediate objection and the judge told the jury to ignore the statement.

In a tone of utter contempt, Mosman used the usual shortcut of making a statement instead of posing a question, accusing Jobe of having held back the information on the gun until he was pressured enough by police on the drug charges to decide "you had something to tell." Jobe confirmed that he did not admit the transaction until October 7, only a month before the trial of Ken Arrasmith began. A few more weeks and he never would have been a witness.

The final player in the foursome was John Swett, the uncle of Jerry Jobe, and like his nephew, unemployed. He testified that he saw Junior sell the Tec-9 to Jerry Jobe and was present several days later when Kyle Richardson came over to "sell meth" and left after purchasing the Tec-9.

Yes, Swett said, he, too, was facing charges for the delivery of meth, with his trial scheduled for January 1996. No, he said, he made no deals with police about his testimony in the Arrasmith case.

Swett said he would meet with Richardson at Kyle's home in the Orchards, an area of Lewiston, and later at the shop, "drop money off and get drugs." He never sold meth for Kyle, but said, "I'd go over there and we'd do lines."

He met Ken Arrasmith at the garage a few days "before the murderings happened," said Swett. He would add later that "four lines (of meth) were made up, four lines disappeared."

Shortly before the killings, Swett said he and Jerry were at the shop with Kyle when the telephone rang in Kyle's restored black Chevrolet Camaro. The conversation was short, and afterward, Kyle hauled the big SKS from behind the car seat and held the rifle out to him, asking if. he would be willing to kill somebody for twenty-five hundred dollars. "I said I didn't want it," Swett testified.

Jobe, however, offered to carry out the hit. Richardson said since Jobe owned him a thousand dollars anyway, he would only pay Jobe fifteen hundred for the killing. Jobe handed the gun back, unwilling to agree to that cut-rate deal.

Roy Mosman had no use for John Swett, who actually used the defense lawyer's questions to advance the prosecution case. Swett, answering Mosman, said he was certain the weapon in evidence was the one Jobe bought and sold, identifying it by the rust marks. He also refused to say he would be suspicious if Arrasmith had not participated in snorting crank at the garage when they were all together.

But Roy Mosman wasn't about to let Swett go unchallenged. The man faced drug charges, and the case was yet to go to trial.

"Are you guilty of the offense of which you are being charged?" Mosman asked, turning away from the witness with a sly smile.

"Well . . ." Swett answered, paused and realized he had little room to maneuver. He could have refused to answer, based on his Constitutional right not to incriminate himself. But he had no lawyer at his side to coach him, so he blurted out: "Yes."

By doing so, he not only lowered his image in the eyes for the jury but threw away any chance he might have of forcing the state to actually prove he was guilty in his own court date.

Ken Arrasmith had received an interesting letter and during breaks in the trial family members distributed copies to the media. Another woman had come forward with being raped at gunpoint by the Binghams in 1977, while they were living in Colorado, and said she had seen the case portrayed on the *Leeza Show* and "had to write." Her letter said she had agonized for years about the crime and had not reported it to the police for fear they would not have helped. "I pray the jury accuits [*sic*] you because Ron and Lew [*sic*] are where they deserve to be—in Hell!"

The letter was dramatic and added still another victim to the Binghams' roster of violent conquests, but would never reach the light of day as evidence. Since it concerned one of those controversial "past bad acts" of the Binghams, the jury never saw it.

Bulky and overweight, Kyle Richardson lumbered to the witness stand at 9:50 A.M. on Wednesday, November 15, the sixth day of the trial and admitted immediately that he had been a meth dealer in the valley for about two years. He wore jeans and an open-neck, long-sleeved shirt of wide green and brown stripes that spread tightly around his big stomach as he sat. A beefy baby face, clean shaven, was notable only for the youthful features, a straight nose, small mouth and nervous blue eyes. His light brown hair hung over his collar in back, was short on the sides and long bangs fell over his forehead, almost to his eyebrows. He weighed about 240 pounds.

Mike Kane, making certain the jury knew the bad news about this key witness so the Mosmans could not expose it, had Richardson admit that he had been charged with conspiracy to commit murder in late October, after lying to police interviewers. Why did you lie? "I was scared, trying to protect myself and a friend, Ken," Richardson added, pointing the index finger of his left hand at the defendant. Instead of facing trial for that felony, Richardson explained that he had agreed to become a witness against his friend in exchange for a lighter sentence. Mike Kane finally established that if Kyle wavered or lied on the stand, then the plea agreement would be junked, and he would face the conspiracy charges as well as a new accusation of perjury. Understanding that, the jury realized the hard-breathing man in the witness chair was probably going to be telling the truth, no matter what his background.

The show finally began as Kyle Richardson said he met Ken Arrasmith in December 1994 and was introduced by Lynn Kohl, Arrasmith's second wife. "She sold drugs for me for six months prior to December," he said. The jurors were stoic as the stench of drug dealing in the case seemed to permeate the courtroom.

After the initial meeting, Richardson and Arrasmith saw each other "two or three times a month" over the next five months. The new buddies would "dink around with cars, b.s., and do things that normal people do," he said with a slight grin. The meeting places would be Lynn's house, Kyle's shop or Ken's home in Sunnyside, Washington.

Perhaps, Mike Kane goaded, you participated in a few other activities, too? "We did crank . . . everytime we were together," the former drug dealer said. "I was doing it every day. We'd be together doing something and casually . . . snort it."

Several jurors sat back heavily in their chairs, the looks changing from blank to resigned. Their opinion of Ken Arrasmith was sliding down a steep, slick slope paved with drugs. And there was more to come.

Arrasmith sat stiffly, with his fingers entwined and hands resting on the defense table. Unblinking eyes blazed in silent fury at the witness and his mouth was a tight line of disgust as Kyle Richardson told his story.

Over a strong objection by Craig Mosman, the judge allowed Mike Kane to ask Richardson about a "financial transaction" he had with Arrasmith about the first of March. "He loaned me ten thousand dollars," Richardson said in his slightly nasal twang. "I was going to pay him back eighteen thousand dollars at the end of the month. I was going to purchase methamphetamine, bring it back here, sell it and give him cash."

Arrasmith handed the ten thousand, in one hundred dollar bills, to Kyle in the presence of his second wife, Lynn. She then wrote out a note, dated February 20, 1995, that said the money was loaned at twenty percent interest for thirty days, and that Kyle put up his shop and equipment as collateral for the cash. "The note made it more legal," Richardson explained. "Meth is not something you would take to court."

Arrasmith was dressed in a suit in court, but no one was mistaking him for a lawyer now. The emerging image of a drug hustler loomed large.

Richardson said he sold the meth to customers around Pleasant Valley but spent most of the profit he had cleared, saying that he "reinvested" the funds, part of it going toward the purchase of still more meth.

Kane couldn't let that one slide by. "Reinvested? You didn't go down and play the futures market, did you?" Kyle's broad face remained blank. "You don't know what I'm talking about, do you?" Kane chided.

When it came time to settle the debt, Richardson didn't have more than a few thousand dollars to pay his original investor, so Arrasmith began laying claim to the shop's collateral: a front door key, automobile repair tools, stereo and electronic gear . . . and guns. Richardson kept a lot of weaponry around the place, including an SKS rifle, shotguns, the Tec-9 and old black powder rifles. Beneath the seat of his car, he kept a .45 caliber pistol.

Kane picked up the Tec-9 that was in evidence and put it in the hands of the fat man. Richardson said it "looked like" the one he used to own, that Arrasmith had seen at the shop and had taken it out and test fired.

The prosecutor moved the story ahead to Sunday, May 7, when Arrasmith called Richardson from his Sunnyside home and asked what Kyle knew about Cynthia and the Binghams. When Kyle would not discuss it on the telephone, Arrasmith said, "I've got to come down there," and he arrived at the shop about midnight.

The witness said he told Arrasmith that Lynn Kohl had told him that Cynthia had been raped by the Binghams and that they were feeding her drugs. "He was kind of overwhelmed, shocked," said Richardson. Arrasmith told him in a rambling predawn discussion that "he'd like to kill that motherfucker," Richardson said.

"Did you believe him?" Kane asked. "Yes. I understood how he would feel . . . We discussed what should happen to them on several occasions."

This part of the testimony marked an important change in Richardson's demeanor. He was still going to stick to his bargain with the court, but he lost his initial stage fright and would now come off as a person who still actually liked and admired Ken Arrasmith. That subtle change would not go unnoticed by the defense team nor the jury.

From May 7 until May 17, the day of the killings, Richardson said he saw Arrasmith every day, and that they snorted crank every day. "We talked a lot," the witness said. "I tried to keep his mind off things as best I could." One way they passed the time was to mount laser sights on their pistols, because Arrasmith had seen one that Kyle owned and thought it was "neat and very intimidating."

The day after Arrasmith drove down from Sunnyside, he returned to Kyle's shop and again said "something has to be done" about Ron Bingham. Thereafter, they talked not only in person, but frequently by telephone.

Richardson said that he met both Ron and Luella in the summer of 1994 when he asked Ron to build an engine for a Chevrolet Camaro Z28, and that he "became friends" and did drugs with Ron. He was at the Bingham place about once a week, mixing the car work with regular drug deals. While at the house, he had seen Cynthia several times, but insisted that he "didn't know what they were into" on the sex scene.

Therefore, when Ken asked questions about the Binghams, such as what kinds of cars they drove, Kyle was able to answer. The following Sunday, he would join Arrasmith in spying on the Bingham house with binoculars from the hillside.

As the days passed in the Clarkston shop, Richardson said Arrasmith told him that "he wanted to kill Ron and it would be nice to get Luella, too." When Kyle said that, a loud exhalation of breath from Donnita Weddle could be heard throughout the quiet courtroom. Richardson added that Arrasmith wanted to get Ron and Luella away from their house, because of a concern that Josh Bingham or Rilla Smith might inadvertently become involved.

There was another reason for caution, he testified. Arrasmith was concerned that a particularly tough character named Ken Stark was living on the property and serving as a bodyguard for Bingham. Because of that, Arrasmith "decided not to go and ask Ron for the pubic hairs" of his daughter. But retrieving the hairs was Arrasmith's overall goal, the witness said. "He said he didn't want that motherfucker to have his daughter's pubic hair as a trophy."

"Did he ever say he was doing this as part of a police investigation?" Kane asked. Richardson shrugged. "No."

Kane then turned to the allegation that he had offered Jobe and Swett twenty-five hundred dollars to "take care of a couple of people'' a few days before Ron and Luella Bingham were shot. ''I wasn't really being serious,'' the witness hedged, then calling the earlier witnesses liars. ''They both said: 'Hell, yes. I'll do it.' ''

Kane pinned him again, having Richardson confirm that he told Arrasmith around May 12 that he knew people in Los Angeles who would execute someone for only five hundred dollars. The prosecutor shot back, ''Who?'' and again Richardson hedged. ''I didn't know anyone specific,'' he said. ''People down there would do anything for me.''

However, back on his story, he said that Arrasmith rejected the contract-kill offer by his pal. ''He said: 'No, this is something I have to take care of myself.' ''

His friend started carrying more guns around with him and asking Richardson to hunt up extra clips and ammunition, Kyle said. But in response to a Mike Kane question, he said he ''wasn't sure'' of what was going to happen. Arrasmith never said he was in fear of his life, the witness recalled.

Kane then took Kyle Richardson to the morning of the murders, about nine o'clock on May 17. The witness said Arrasmith came in, wearing a shoulder holster containing a 9mm pistol, and said he knew where Ron Bingham was. He asked the large Richardson for a T-shirt from the stack at the far end of the shop, spread out the black garment and wrote on it with a marker: ''Save our daughters or protect our children or something.''

Arrasmith also found the cardboard box that had contained an automobile painting kit, got some red masking tape and made some cutouts in the box. Without explaining what he was doing, Arrasmith simply said, ''It's time.'' Richardson asked if he should go along, but Arrasmith refused the offer.

''I didn't see him again,'' the witness said. Shortly thereafter, the police scanner that Richardson was listening to began squawking about a shooting near Potlatch.

Richardson had kept his mouth shut about what had happened, choosing not to go to the police. "I didn't want to get involved and I was scared," he said. "I wanted to protect myself and Ken."

Even when the police began to question him, he lied to them, the witness said. Instead of telling the cops his story, he went to see Arrasmith in jail and told him what the police were asking.

The powerful prosecution questioning of Kyle Richardson ended just before lunchtime. Everyone was ready for a break in the intense action. As Richardson left the court, Ken Arrasmith turned around at the defense table and locked his eyes on his latest ex-wife, Donnita, and cocked a questioning eyebrow. If he had been silently asking for damage assessment, the answer would have had to have been: serious.

Naturally, the cross-examination was merciless, with Craig Mosman landing squarely on the deal the witness had made to save his own skin. Richardson confirmed that he never really believed he was guilty of a conspiracy and had never discussed with Arrasmith any plan to kill the Binghams.

"You were facing a death penalty, weren't you?"

"Yes."

"And now you got probation?"

"Yes."

The information was interesting, but the jury had already learned it from the prosecution, so it had minimal impact.

Mosman also used the lies Richardson had told police to plant the idea that he actually had been telling the truth at the time. The attorney pointed out that, at no time during the exhaustive interviews, had the witness claimed Arrasmith threatened to kill the Binghams. That did not come until the deal was made, Mosman said.

Once again, Mosman began to paint testimony from

his unique palette, by asking Richardson whether something was true rather than asking the witness to describe the event in detail. In this way, Kyle confirmed that it was his own idea to accompany Arrasmith on the surveillance of the Bingham home, primarily to protect his friend from being attacked by Bingham's imagined bodyguard. Indeed, after talking with Arrasmith on May 7, Kyle testified he personally went out to visit Ron Bingham, hoping Bingham would "slip up and say something" about the Cynthia matter. He would later admit he didn't know the alleged bodyguard and never saw him on the property.

Mosman also began to repeat a phrase that would, as the defense took over presenting its own case, become a mantra for him. The lawyer would ask himself, loud enough for the jury to hear, "I try to imagine how I would feel" if he had been in the shoes of a father tortured by the sexual abuse inflicted on his daughter.

Richardson was more than willing to be a friendly witness for Arrasmith and bought into Mosman's presentation wholeheartedly. "I told him that if it was me in his shoes, I'd kill the son of a bitch," he testified. Mosman nudged a little more with a statement: When Arrasmith responded, you took it the same way—as being a normal reaction of a parent? "Yes," said Kyle.

Kyle added the ominous note that Ron Bingham had gone by his shop several times and that he felt Bingham was watching both himself and Arrasmith. Then Mosman had the witness repeat that he wasn't being serious in making the offer to have Jobe or Swett kill someone, and said any such action would have been volunteered by him, not demanded by Arrasmith. "You did things for him like that because you knew how he would feel, and he seemed to be a pretty decent guy," Mosman said and Richardson affirmed. The witness had been reduced by the voluble lawyer to almost a monosyllabic parrot, answering yes when Mosman finished making his sweeping statements. The prosecution, however, made few attempts to object.

Mosman talked a while about the morning of May 17, when Arrasmith came to Kyle's shop, and the lawyer—drawing appropriate responses from the witness—described a scenario in which Arrasmith would take the laser-equipped pistol and the small tape recorder out to Shelter Road that morning to scare the Binghams into making a taped confession about Cynthia.

Asking about the T-shirt on which the defendant wrote with a marker, the lawyer was allowed to enhance his alternate theory. "He wanted a message to be sent if he didn't make it back alive?" Mosman queried. "Yes," said the obedient witness. Court observers were astonished at the free rein Mosman was given. No witness had made any such statement. Still, there were no objections, so he continued, having Kyle confirm Mosman's statements that "Ken was pretty disgusted" with "what was not being done" by the police.

Arrasmith's demeanor in court changed sharply. He was not exactly smiling at his old friend, but the earlier venom was gone from his expression, replaced by a mild, rather benign look that conveyed satisfaction with Kyle's performance.

Mosman, finding no resistance from the court, increased his attack, and with Richardson only answering yes three times, the attorney was able to introduce the idea that Arrasmith was "amazed" that the Binghams "had moved another teenage girl" into their house to replace Cynthia "and that child was strung out on drugs." Richardson had not testified to having personal knowledge of any such thing but was being casually used by the defense to put the whole theory before the jury. Ken Arrasmith nodded slightly in approval at the defense table.

*   *   *

Richardson was on thin ice now. He had agreed to help the prosecution and the prosecutors were very unhappy with his wishy-washy performance on the stand. Mike Kane verbally slapped him on his follow-up questioning, noting that Richardson had not told the police that he had said the Binghams should be killed.

Then Kane asked about the admission that Kyle volunteered to help spy on the Binghams. ''I didn't want to see Ken do something like that and spend the rest of his life in prison,'' the witness, now growing nervous, responded. He then waffled that he ''did and didn't'' believe that Arrasmith planned to attack the Binghams.

And about that message of the morning of May 17, Kane asked if the description that Arrasmith might not ''make it back alive'' were ''Mr. Mosman's words or Mr. Arrasmith's?''

''I don't remember for sure,'' the witness again waffled.

Richardson's testimony had been a mixed bag of results. The friendliness he exuded toward the defendant and his own drug-infested background helped Mosman's case. But the testimony that Arrasmith had lent him ten thousand dollars with which to buy drugs had been particularly damning.

Downstairs in the courthouse, Cynthia sipped a Diet Pepsi and gave the benediction on Kyle Richardson. ''He didn't hurt us,'' she said. She was wrong.

25

The prosecutors were nearing the end of their case as they called on Gaylen Warren, a forensic microscopist who tested the guns. The state had traced the purchase of the Tec-9, followed its path to Ken Arrasmith and established that such a gun was used in the murders. Warren, with scientific exactitude, was able to say that bullets taken from the bodies of Ron and Lue Bingham were fired by the P89 Ruger pistol and Tec-9 that were found in Arrasmith's truck.

Although Arrasmith still had never admitted shooting anyone, the evidence of the past days allowed no other conclusion.

Warren went through the list of various types of 9mm bullets that had been found—El Dorado Starfires, Federal Hydrastatics, two kinds of Winchester Silvertips and some other type that had been converted into hollowpoints, which cause massive damage.

His most important testimony was the brief mention that one of the bullets had been placed in the Tec-9 clip backward, meaning it would not fit into the chamber, causing the gun to jam. The shooter would have to pull a handle on the left side of the weapon to clear the blocked chamber and eject the backward shell before continuing to fire. And that would lead to the shooter pausing long enough to think about what he was doing. Premeditation.

Craig Mosman let the scientist describe the bullets and, using only one question on cross-examination, had Warren confirm for the jury that there was no law against an average citizen buying such ammunition.

On November 16, the seventh day of the trial, the courtroom was buzzing before the judge came in. The *Leeza Show*, one of the tabloid television journals, had just aired its version of the usual interviews with Cynthia Arrasmith and her troupe of supporters, obtaining tears and a one-sided story. The slanted television segment had long been outpaced by events and testimony. The defense supporters in the courtroom took the show as a good omen. That was a mirage, because the sequestered jurors, not allowed to watch television talk shows, were the only audience that really counted.

In criminal procedures, through a process known as "discovery," it is normal for each side to have access to the written material that the opposition will use in preparing its case. That point was about to become a major legal issue in the already tangled double-murder trial of Ken Arrasmith.

The defense team had hired a widely respected psychologist from Denver, Dr. Lenore Walker, to administer tests and conduct interviews with Arrasmith and be ready to testify as to his confused state of mind. If she could convince the jury that the defendant was not operating rationally because of the emotional turmoil caused by the molestation of Cynthia, then the jurors might weigh that in their deliberations and conclude he was acting on the spur of the moment and not with premeditation.

As the prosecution prepared to close its own case, the issue of Dr. Walker surfaced. Denise Rosen and Mike

Kane wanted to torpedo Walker, an expert in child abuse syndrome, before she ever set foot in court. With the jury out of the courtroom, Kane made a motion to eliminate Walker from the defense witness list. The reason, he said, was a "singular lack of success" in getting her to respond to prosecution inquiries. He further argued that the defense team had not turned over to the prosecution any of the documents upon which the doctor would base her conclusions.

Craig Mosman said that the law allowed for an expert to testify as to the defendant's state of mind, but Judge Leggett remained firm in her decision, saying no expert should usurp the place of a jury in determining such a thing.

Mosman, passionate in his argument, said the experience of Cynthia being "raped, sodomized and sexually tortured" and having her pubic hairs taken as a trophy had taken the experience far beyond the understanding of any ordinary juror. Walker, he said, interviewed Arrasmith for seven hours on August 2 and administered a number of tests.

Denise Rosen said the state twice requested, on discovery motions, and the court had even issued an order for all evidence to be turned over to them. "We have not received anything," she said. "The Mosmans stood in this court and said they had nothing."

Craig Mosman was stung by the direct rebuke. "We still have nothing," he said. "We don't have a single thing in reports from Dr. Walker." She had come, done her interviews and tests, and left again. Communication since then was only by telephone. Therefore, there were no documents to turn over. In addition, he said Walker was always hard to contact, even for them. For instance, her schedule immediately prior to coming to Idaho had her testifying in different cases in Kansas, New Hampshire, Florida and Mexico and lecturing lawyers in Virginia.

The defense team, by not producing the required documents, put at risk the crucial testimony they hoped Walker would provide. Judge Leggett flatly did not believe there was no documentation of Walker's work with Arrasmith. There had to be written tests, scoring and notes made of his verbal responses, she said, and the fact that those documents were not turned over, as per her earlier orders in two formal hearings and informal chats with the opposing lawyers, "cannot be justified."

The judge ruled that Dr. Walker was not needed to tell the jury how Arrasmith might have responded to events. The mystery witness upon whom the defense had pinned so much hope was scratched from the witness list.

Mosman wasn't through yet. He tried to have the judge throw out everything that had been mentioned that linked Arrasmith with drugs and drug transactions. He asked for a mistrial. He asked the judge to acquit Arrasmith of all charges, claiming the state hadn't proven its case. Both were standard motions. He lost them both.

The judge said the drugs showed the relationship between Richardson and Arrasmith, as well as documenting the path that put the Tec-9 in the hands of the defendant. And concerning the acquittal request, she said the evidence was clear that Arrasmith went to the scene with guns and when he left, "Ron and Luella Bingham are dead." The case, she ruled, was going to the jury.

With so many setbacks before even starting their own case, the Mosmans probably were wondering whether the judge was even going to let them call witnesses. Clearly, a major effort was going to be needed to regain the momentum needed for a favorable verdict.

At 10:16 A.M. on November 16, 1995, prosecuting attorney Denise Rosen told the court she had completed the primary case, and the state rested.

Roy Mosman, who had been quiet for most of the trial, moved to center stage, his white hair and soft, syrupy voice contrasting with his appearance. He looked like a bear in a suit and walked with a limp from an old football injury. He exuded Western ruggedness and charm as he began the opening statement for the defense.

He told the jury, softly, that much of the defense case had already been presented by the prosecution. He effortlessly shifted the spotlight from Ken Arrasmith to the "evil couple" named Ron and Luella Bingham, and Mosman would never ease up on blackening the reputations of the dead man and woman.

Cynthia, he said, "was not unfamiliar with drugs," but had no experience with Valium when it was fed to her by Ron Bingham. What followed was a nightmare of sexual exploitation in which Bingham raped the teenager and "the woman had her pleasure with oral sex." He did not dignify Luella with a name.

"We're not going to put on evidence that this was an all-American family," Mosman said of the Arrasmith clan, coasting over some rather sharp shoals. "But there was love."

When Cynthia was running away from the Bingham home and was picked up by police at the insistence of her parents, the child was "angry" at her father for not understanding what was happening to her. It was only later that Arrasmith "learned the details of her life with this awful couple." And, Mosman said, Ron had threatened to kill Cynthia and her mother if she didn't come back to him.

Once the authorities were involved, however, the case was almost ignored. "The system treated this as an ordinary case . . . like a shoplifter," Roy Mosman almost whispered to the jury which was falling under the spell of the courtroom veteran whose voice was as soft as falling snow.

Arrasmith, on May 8, "went out and found this perverted pair," Mosman recited, saying that Ron Bingham boasted that "I'm Rambo. I'm invincible. I've got night

vision and you can't sneak up on me." Then Ron
pointed his finger at Ken Arrasmith and warned, "You
come around here again and I'm going to kill you."

Arrasmith, the lawyer said, knew "these people"
from when he was a deputy sheriff and became "frustrated and scared" when he was a target of a contract
in which Ron offered killers a pound of meth, worth
about sixteen thousand dollars, for Arrasmith's life.

Mosman said that during May, Ken was staying at his
parents' home, just down the hill from the Binghams,
and nightly barricaded himself in a trailer parked in the
backyard because he was afraid of Bingham.

Cynthia, meanwhile, was in custody, asking, "Why
am I in jail?" when the Binghams were free. "She was
scared" because Ron Bingham was known to chase cops
and carry explosives. "She was not safe anyplace while
these people were out."

Then Arrasmith discovered that the Bingham "predators" had started grooming another young girl, just as
they had groomed Cynthia to be a sexual toy. Knowing
that child molesters "repeat and repeat and repeat" their
attacks, Arrasmith became frustrated when he could not
get police to speed up their investigation. "Their response was, 'We're working on it,' " the attorney said,
only to have days pass before they would inform Arrasmith of the status of the case, even while he fed them
details of the Binghams' victims.

Mosman dismissed the work of Captain Watkins,
claiming he bobbled a rape to which he had an eyewitness, Patti Mahar Johnson. "He was looking for a way
out of doing his job." Overall, the police were simply
"arrogant" in their handling of the Arrasmith incident.

"Imagine the frustration and anger," Mosman said,
his voice rising to the jury as he struck the heart of the
defense case. "We're going to be asking you . . . What
would you do?"

"Ken Arrasmith was a mental, emotional and physical

mess," he said, telling how this strong man "at his wits' end" wept in front of a sheriff as he asked for help in stopping the Binghams. And Arrasmith believed the police had indicated that he should do something.

Arrasmith went to the Binghams with weapons and a tape recorder, planning to use the laser beam on his pistol to intimidate Ron and Luella "to talk into the tape" and provide the police with the evidence they wanted. That would "force the police to do something."

He asked rhetorically, almost sorrowfully, whether the jurors thought such a bizarre scheme had any chance of succeeding. It just showed "the turmoil" in Arrasmith's mind, the lawyer said.

"If the police had done what they should have done, we wouldn't be here today," Mosman concluded, his voice now going so soft that several jurors leaned forward to catch his every word.

"We ask you to vote your conscience," Mosman said, and sat down.

26

The first defense witness was Patricia C. "Patti" Mahar Johnson, who was present when Cynthia Arrasmith was raped by Ron and Luella Bingham. The rotund, moon-faced woman had been brought in from the Portland, Oregon, area where she now lived with her sister, Kathy Rudd, and attended a community college in hopes of someday becoming a museum curator or an art teacher or the owner of a restaurant. The problem with her as a witness was her age: a weathered thirty-four, she would not be viewed as a tender child by a jury that had already heard policemen testify how she had been incomprehensible and high on drugs when she first came forward.

Nevertheless, Patti Mahar Johnson now appeared clean and sober and working to straighten out her life. She said she had stayed with Ron and Luella Bingham for only a week in the middle of April, but her story of drug deals, cops, guns, rape, weird sex, car chases and escape seemed to span a much longer time. A lot was crammed into those seven days.

There was no mention of how she had met the Binghams, while she was having delusions beside a grave, but Patti admitted being a meth user for about two years before she came to the Binghams, where Ron supplied her with crank, "very strong" marijuana and "some kind of blue pills."

Importantly, she testified that Ron also gave Cynthia a Valium tablet every day, and said Ron "always" walked around nude in his home. She also testified to hearing Ron Bingham call his drug-dealing pals and offering a thousand dollars or an ounce of crank to "secure" a person so Ron could "get to him," but she did not use the word *kill* nor could she remember the name of the person Ron wanted to "get" nor who Ron telephoned.

To demonstrate his violent side, Patti said that once she and Ron went to the house of a friend who was doing heroin, which Ron hated. Bingham pulled a gun and yelled, "I'll blow your goddam head off if you do any more!" But her own behavior came into question when she admitted that "we all carried guns." Actually, she said, she normally carried two of them and had instructions to "watch Ron's back."

The witness began to ramble as she tried to piece together the events of that exciting week, and several jury members averted their gaze, apparently finding it hard to follow her as she mixed times and subjects. Others scribbled furiously in their notebooks, trying to track her line of thought.

If Patti Mahar Johnson left the Binghams on April 20 and had only stayed for a week, then she would have come into the home on the previous Friday, April 14. Piecing together her testimony, it seemed that Ron almost immediately spirited her off to the Quality Inn Motel in Clarkston, claiming he was hiding her because her life was in danger.

Having been a frequent user of "speed," as she called meth, for several years, she had a strong reaction when Ron gave her a couple of Valium, or "downers," that evening, and she fell asleep in the motel room for at least fifteen hours. Lengthy periods of sleep are a normal reaction for people coming down from a meth high, a pattern repeated time and again by those involved in the Arrasmith saga.

She awoke Saturday afternoon, still feeling lethargic and "drugged out," when Luella and Cynthia brought some food, but also an electric razor with various attachments.

Patti said when she asked how old the childlike Cynthia was, Lue had replied, "Oh, eighteen or nineteen," while Ron was standing behind the teenager, holding up fingers for Patti to count—ten, then four—and laughing.

Ron said he had "a special present," and stripped Cynthia naked except for a T-shirt, put her on the couch and "shaved her."

This jogged the jurors' memories, because Cynthia's powerful testimony had been very specific—Ronnie Razorhands had shaved her groin in the bathroom on a stool, not on a couch, and she had stripped naked and took a shower with Ron, and was not wearing a T-shirt as Patti alleged.

"I didn't understand what was going on until I realized it was moving into something else," Patti continued.

Lue and Cynthia left for a while, and Ron used the time to also shave Patti's pubic hair. "He was quite mean about it. It hurt and he liked it," she testified. When Luella and Cynthia returned, Lue gathered the fallen hair and carefully saved it in a towel.

Then everyone proceeded to get high. In addition to marijuana, they broke the top off a light bulb, placed a rock of meth inside, cooked it with a cigarette lighter and sucked the smoke wafting above the broken edge.

"We all ended up on the bed in various stages of undress," Patti testified, describing how Lue began having oral sex with Cynthia. "I asked that I'd rather have Lue," she said, to get her off of Cynthia "because she was a little girl . . . and I didn't think she knew what she was getting into."

This was another significant departure from the testimony of Cynthia, who had precisely described doing a line of meth, being given an enema, showering with Ron, and how all of them were nude and how Lue held her arms while Ron sodomized her—none of which was mentioned by Patti.

"After the drugs and sex, both Luella and Ron fell asleep, but Cynthia and I talked all night long," she said, then "went back to the house."

The next day, Sunday, April 15, was Easter. Ron and Patti did not go to church that day, but instead set off on a wild motorcycle ride into a far stretch of prairie. It would become an exciting, car-switching meet with "two Mexican gentlemen" who gave them "two bread sacks" full of drugs. Since Ron was driving the motorcycle, Patti, hanging onto him, hid the bags in her shirt.

They returned to Clarkston on Monday morning, and that was the day Patti testified that she started packing guns. She said she also "tweaked" out that day, becoming confused and weepy, and Ron fed her two Valium to make her sleep. The prairie ride would not be the final time Patti Mahar Johnson motored around with Ron Bingham. She said he would regularly take her out late at night to "go on patrol and terrorize people." Sometimes, they would go to the house of another dealer and Ron would yell and scream, shout obscenities from his car or make threatening telephone calls. "Every day he was upset about something," the witness said.

The police drug bust followed the next day, Tuesday, April 18, and the action began when she heard a twig snap outside about nine o'clock at night. She, Luella and Ron jumped into their car and headed into the cemetery, with Lue flashing around a spotlight and both Patti and Lue packing weapons. When Ron spotted the suspect car, he took off after it, driving like a madman, she said.

They passed the automobile and realized it was a policeman and were soon stopped by another cop. Lue and Patti told the officer they had guns on them, and he gave them all the story about the mystery driver being merely a grieving relative visiting a grave. Ron, she said, argued with the cop, telling him "that SOB of yours is giving me grief and is spying on me."

When the three of them returned to the house, a police spotlight illuminated them and all three were handcuffed. They weren't concerned about drugs, because Ron had been tipped off about the potential raid and told others to hide "a big box" of drugs. She added that the police spent about ninety minutes in Ron and Lue's bedroom, with the door locked, going through the dirty pictures and the suitcase of sex toys.

Throughout her short stay with the Binghams, the sexual relations continued. She testified that at one point, Ron asked her: "Did I fuck you when you were a little girl?" Patti told him no, he hadn't, only to have him respond, "You sure?"

She finally left the Bingham house on the evening of Thursday, April 20, describing a harrowing sort of James Bond-style escape. Patti said she put on black pants, a black cap and a black leather coat and went outside on the pretext of "going to check around."

Once out the door, she ran "as fast as I could" down the shadowy road to the country club at the bottom of the hill. Dashing into the lounge, she called the police, only to be told that they would not dispatch a patrol unit until she explained "who you are, what is happening and who is after you."

Patti then ran down the golf course and sprawled prone in the shadows. She testified that Ron had threatened to cut her throat or put a bullet in her head if she went to the cops. Eventually, a police car came along and she jumped out, waving and throwing her black leather cap to make it stop. They would not let her into the car immediately, she said, but she coaxed them into taking her to the police station.

Once talking to the police, she testified, she discovered they were more interested in finding out about drugs at the Bingham house than they were in helping her. "I wanted them to get Cynthia out of there," she said, because the teenager was "too gone to leave" on her own.

Eventually, Officer Hastings took her to the airport and put her on the plane to Portland. There, but "still frightened," she immediately checked into a drug treatment program at the Oregon State University Hospital. A month later, her ex-husband telephoned to let her know that Ron and Luella Bingham had been murdered.

Feelings were running high that day in court, and right after lunch, Steve Caylor, the court administrator, rushed in before the session resumed. Reading license numbers and car makes from a slip of paper, he shouted at the Arrasmith clan to either remove their cars from the parking lot or have them towed. The autos in question, facing the jury's window, bore the "Free Ken Arrasmith" bumper stickers. The offending bumper strips were quickly peeled off and court continued.

There was a cursory cross-examination, in which Patti Mahar Johnson changed her statement that the police were only interested in drugs at the Bingham place. Instead, she now insisted that Captain Watkins did not want to talk about drugs, but "just Cynthia." The jury was well aware of how Mosman had painted Watkins as being uncaring, but the first defense witness claimed the policeman wasn't interested in anything but the plight of Cynthia Arrasmith.

She also finally admitted her peculiar fascination with the cemetery and the resting place of her former boyfriend, where she fantasized about cars coming in and out of graves.

That was only prelude, however, for the prosecution. As soon as everyone was through questioning Patti, Denise Rosen stood up and announced that she had a fistful of warrants for the arrest of the witness. Craig Mosman detonated. He had earlier told the court the witness had been harassed by police on the way into town for her court appearance, and now the authorities wanted to take her into custody. As a subpoenaed witness in such an important trial, "she should be immune" from arrest.

Rosen said a policeman was waiting downstairs to take charge of Patti Mahar Johnson. Involved were five outstanding misdemeanor charges, stemming from a Lewiston brawl on December 2, 1994, in which Patti was charged with possessing drug paraphernalia, frequenting a place where marijuana is used, resisting arrest, kicking and scratching two police officers and fleeing the scene of the investigation.

Judge Leggett told the lawyers to stop sniping at each other, then gave Patti, who was sitting frightened in the witness chair, a free pass out of Idaho. The charges were not important enough for extradition but are still outstanding if she ever comes back to the state.

Kathy Rudd, Patti's sister, followed her to the witness stand, and said her sister was "a mess" when she retrieved Patti from the Portland airport on April 21. "She was very fearful of her life," said Rudd, who began to cry as she described signing her sister into a "locked facility."

The police who had spoken to Rudd by telephone had told her there was a lot of strange sex going on with the Binghams, who brought girls and women into their circle by trading a place to stay for work.

Rudd said she telephoned Ron Bingham to "put him off the track" of Patti. Still, he questioned her about her sister's location and said he was "hurt by her betrayal." Then Rudd said she had spoken earlier with Bingham, who led her to believe he was some sort of protective service agent and that Patti was safe with him.

On cross-examination, Rudd, a mother of four, told

Mike Kane she "begged" police to help Patti. Hastings drove her to the airport, picked up a ticket that Rudd bought in his name, because Patti had no identification, and handed it to Patti.

The highly emotional witness, her eyes misty and her voice quaking, told Craig Mosman that if her sister had been unable to escape Ron Bingham's clutches, then she, too, may have chosen the vigilante route. "If she hadn't gotten out, I could be sitting there, too," she stated, nodding at the defendant.

27

Tara Lebold was a petite kid in a bright print sundress, whose long blond hair, held in place by a barrette, fell to below her shoulders. The most striking part of her appearance was her unlined, pale face, the face of a child, not a young woman. An observer would have to wonder why this girl was not in school, enjoying a normal life. Why was such an innocent-looking kid here, on the witness stand during a murder trial, swept up in this stroll through the sordid underbelly of the Lewis-Clark Valley drug world?

The answer was tragically simple. Tara Lebold, the third witness for the defense, was not quite as innocent as she seemed.

Tara testified that she was now fifteen years old, a sophomore at Clarkston High School and was currently living with an aunt. But her story really centered on a period a few months earlier, on May 11, 1995, her fifteenth birthday, when she was thrown out of the home of one of her mother's friends.

She said she had been having a "really rough time," was using "drugs, crank, pot, coke and heroin" and had been living with her eighteen-year-old boyfriend, Donnie, for about a year. The evicted young couple wasn't completely without alternatives for they knew of a place where a lot of people with similar problems occasionally crashed for a period of time. Before the sun set, Tara and Donnie and her dog, Shiek, ended up at the ramshackle hillside home of Ron and Luella Bingham.

The two young lost souls were apparently immediately put on the fast track to Ron Bingham's sexual carnival. Within two hours of their arrival, the three of them were in Ron's garage when he pulled some meth from a hiding place in the freezer and laid out three large lines on a mirror, after Donnie confirmed that Tara used the drug. "I only wanted half," she testified, but Ron insisted. "Come on, Tara, you can do it," he goaded. When the frail teenager joined Ron and Donnie in snorting a whole line, she "felt my head wanted to explode." She tottered outside and spent some time petting and talking to her dog.

Ron and Lue were "really nice" to her that first evening, going so far as to buy her a birthday cake. After Tara took a shower, Lue helped her cut Tara's "really gross" hair. Soon, Tara said, she was "really glad" to be among such welcoming friends.

The following morning, the young couple was taken to breakfast and Tara said, with a clear head, she began to get "really scared" about her situation. Having been sexually abused before, she started having "bad vibes" and being frightened of Ron Bingham. Her concern was not eased when it was discovered that "some dude" was following their car.

Tara said that Ron offered Donnie a job. The boyfriend turned him down at first, but later became a sort of messenger, running errands around town for Ron. The couple continued to hang out with the Binghams, use drugs and sleep in Donnie's automobile, until Ron insisted that they move into the bus.

The same early pattern the Binghams had used to snare Cynthia was easily visible through Tara's testimony.

At the breakfast table one morning, as she sat there with Rilla and Josh and Luella, Ron walked in naked. He went to the bedroom and put some clothes on when Tara turned her head away from him. "That really disgusted me," she said.

At one point, Luella took her into the bedroom and went through the closet. "Lue showed me some clothes," she testified, "some really skanky outfits . . . slinky, like a prostitute would wear."

Tara said she personally wore "really baggy clothes" or jeans and a T-shirt. Nevertheless, she said, Ron Bingham was constantly talking trash, saying things like "I had a really sexy body" and making sexual innuendoes. "It was really gross," she said, her face flushing pink on the witness stand as she described how Ron and Lue discussed penises. "It made me feel really uncomfortable," she testified.

As usual, Ron eventually had an argument with the boyfriend, and on May 16, he asked Donnie to leave. As usual also, he said Tara could stay, saying, "There's always a place open for you here."

Instead, Tara chose to stay with Donnie and they drifted down to the home of his stepfather, Otis Dixon. Passing a mirror, she noticed the ravages that drugs had made on her young life. Dark rings circled her eyes, she had lost weight and was milky pale. "I looked really sick," she said. During the day of May 16, she played with some kids, took a nap on the couch and watched television, then spent the night.

Mike Kane, not wanting to rock this particular boat, was quickly done with the witness. Even with all that had happened—the drugs, the argument, the threat of sex—he had Tara confirm that she wasn't very afraid of the Binghams. On the morning of May 17, only the day after they had left, Tara and Donnie went back to the Bingham home because Ron had mentioned he wanted Donnie to run an errand. They never saw him, because by the time they arrived, Ron and Luella had already been shot to death.

Tara's testimony was significant in that it offered still another glimpse into the sordid world of Ron and Luella Bingham, painting a clear picture of how a troubled young woman could be lured into their perverted world of drugs and sex. However, in giving her testimony, she was forced to undermine her own credibility by the admission that she was a heavy drug user, who had run away from her own home and lived with other people, including an older boyfriend, when she was only fourteen, and even returned to the Bingham home where she said she had felt so threatened. The verbal picture Tara offered contrasted sharply with the girlish innocence she radiated on the witness stand. She was unable to say that either Ron or Luella had ever touched her sexually or had physically abused her, she offered not a word about the killings, and—in a point that was soon to become very important—Tara Lebold had never exchanged a single word with Ken Arrasmith.

To bolster the proposition that Tara Lebold was in imminent danger, the defense attorneys needed to validate the danger through the eyes of a policeman. Detective Tom White, who had been so badly maligned earlier by Craig Mosman, was now called back to the witness stand to, in effect, testify on behalf of Ken Arrasmith.

Mosman reiterated White's impressive resume in the field of child abuse, and the detective confirmed that he had the power to remove a child who was in imminent danger from a hostile environment. The defense lawyer told the detective the story that Tara had laid before the court, emphasizing that after Tara and her boyfriend moved into the Bingham sphere of influence, Ron Bingham gave the girl drugs and dropped the heavy hints that she had a sexy body. Now, knowing all that, Mosman said, would the detective feel that a fifteen-year-old girl being so groomed in the Bingham home would be classified as being in imminent danger?

Mike Kane immediately objected that the entire idea was not based on testimony, but on the speculation of the lawyer, and the judge upheld his request to strike the question.

Mosman backed up and tried again, slightly rewording the scenario, and this time Detective White smoothly handled it, replying that there wasn't enough information. "I'd have to ask more questions," he replied, such as did the parents know she was there and what did they have to say about it. The use of illegal drugs alone was not enough to force a police removal. There were also the questions of whether she was a runaway, whether she was being forced to take the drugs and was she in fear that the Binghams would have come to get her had she run away. "All of these options would have to be looked at," the detective said.

Mosman was getting nowhere with this line, so he cut to the most important part. "Would you be concerned" about the situation as described? Detective White said that he would be concerned, and also acknowledged that previous reports of sexual abuse and rape on the premises in similar situations would be "something I would consider."

Special Prosecutor Mike Kane, on cross-examination, put the speculation of what might have happened to Tara into perspective. In quick succession, the policeman testified that he had not been told about Tara's presence at the Binghams until two days after the murders, that Ken Arrasmith never told him in any of their frequent conversations that another young girl was in jeopardy, and that Otis Dixon, the stepfather of Tara's boyfriend, also had never spoken of any jeopardy the girl might be facing.

The Tara Lebold thrust had been a waste of time for the defense. No matter how they painted it, nothing had happened to the girl, no warnings had been given to the police and, not only had she voluntarily moved into the Bingham bus, but the day that her boyfriend was supposedly thrown out by Ron, Tara left along with him. They spent the night at the home of Donnie's stepfather. Anything beyond that was pure speculation.

The defense case, however, was gathering steam and heading toward one of the pivotal points of the trial. From the very first, the Mosmans had planned to parade a long roster of Ron and Luella's rape victims past the jury. It was almost time to roll the dice and see if the judge would allow it. Craig Mosman made his motion to call Tina Cole Turner to the stand, which would result in the jury learning of Ron's earlier conviction and prison sentence for the rape of his niece. Without such knowledge, he argued, the jury would not be able to make "any kind of adequate judgment."

Mike Kane dismissed the idea as "impossible" because the past crime and prison term did not have anything to do with the murders with which Arrasmith was charged. The information would only provide "tidbits of information" about the victims. Judge Leggett acknowledged that Cole would only point toward "the old character issue," but stalled on making a final decision. Get on with your next witness, she ordered.

Twenty-two-year-old Tracy Anderson, the mother of a five-and-a-half-month-old baby, was sworn in. She said that she had met the Binghams while having a truck fixed, and from February until the week before the Binghams died, she had visited their place about twice a week. On some of those visits, she had encountered Cynthia, whom she already knew.

The usual pattern then unfolded. Tracy said that in April, she had a fight with her boyfriend and called Ron Bingham, asking for temporary shelter. Soon, she joined the transient crowd that crashed periodically in the bus, the trailer or the house. Once there, Ron's weird behavior soon surfaced. Asked once to come into the bedroom for a talk, she found Ron nude, but nevertheless sat beside him on the bed "and had a normal conversation."

Everybody out there did drugs, she testified, but she abstained because her pregnancy was nearing its end. Bingham seemed to ignore the fact that she was almost nine months pregnant and "came onto me," Tracy testified, flirting in a sexual way and telling her in the distant past, when she was only a child, they had had sex. Tracy thought the idea was too strange, because she had never even met Ron until recently. But he insisted. "He said he had fucked me when I was about thirteen or fourteen," she said. "He tried to convince me. It was bizarre." Adding to the peculiar behavior was Ron's offer of money if the pregnant girl would pose for photographs in the nude.

However shocking that might be, the reason that Tracy Anderson was on the witness stand was not to underline the ugliness of the behavior at the Bingham place. For despite the circumstances, she was another young woman on whom Ron and Lue Bingham never laid a hand. Tracy was testifying for the specific purpose of describing how difficult it was for Cynthia to escape the Bingham clutches.

She said that the day after she moved her belongings into the crash pad, Ron and Lue had checked into the motel again and that Cynthia, still at the Bingham home, started to experience chest pains, complaining that her "heart was hurting." Weeping, Cynthia telephoned the motel to let Ron and Lue know what was going on, and Tracy picked up an extension telephone to listen. Ron screamed that he knew what they were up to and didn't want Cynthia to return to Linda Bartlett's home because her boyfriend would be there. "He was very angry," she said. Ron almost immediately drove back to the house "and told us to stay there."

Later, the two girls began talking about leaving but "we were scared" about how to proceed and didn't want to risk Ron's explosive anger.

But soon, when Tracy had left the Binghams on her own, Cynthia turned up on her doorstep one day. "She was crying, scared and upset," Anderson testified. "She looked terrible."

Tracy decided that Ron would come looking for the girl, so she drove Cynthia to the Hollywood Motel and paid for it. The teenager told Anderson that she was planning to run away to California "to hide."

The two prosecutors had listened carefully to the testimony of Tracy Anderson and knew she had said not a single word about Ken Arrasmith, nor the deaths of Ron and Luella Bingham. The jury had heard more testimony about still another young woman who sought, and was given, shelter at the home of Ron and Luella Bingham, only to discover she had stepped into a situation that was over her head. Tracy Anderson's entire presentation was an immaterial sideshow. She offered no damaging testimony and there was no need to cross-examine the witness, so prosecution didn't, apparently saving their energy for the important battle that loomed on the immediate horizon as the trial neared the end of its seventh day.

"I assume," said Judge Leggett, "that Tina Turner is not Ike's wife."

She was correct. Turner was the niece of Ron and Luella Bingham whose rape at the age of eleven eventually resulted in Ron serving eighteen months in a state penitentiary. She had become an outspoken advocate of Ken Arrasmith's actions, joining in the media blitz to raise money for his defense. Her powerful story posed a significant threat to the prosecution.

With the jury dismissed for the day, Craig Mosman argued before Leggett that the prosecution had "beat the drum throughout the trial'' that Cynthia's own testimony lacked credibility because she stayed voluntarily at the Binghams. Turner, he said, would be a witness who could say "the same thing happened to me." The prosecution's questioning of why Cynthia had remained had opened the door for Turner as a witness, he said. Further, the defense lawyer said, it was "mentally a strange thing that a woman would be involved in raping a female child" and the jury should know Lue's assaults did not happen to Cynthia alone.

Mike Kane shrugged away the ploy, saying that Tina Turner and other rape victims were "simply not relevant . . . to any scenario" involving the matter before the court—a pair of vicious murders. He pointed out that, "despite the antichildren rhetoric," the prosecution had never said bad things didn't happen to Cynthia while she was with the Binghams.

But where in that equation, he wanted to know, could be found "a need for the defendant to go and kill two people in Idaho." The attempt to bring in the rape victims was just another defense try at "heaping more character evidence on the victims." Kane was bringing the trial back to its major point by asking just who was on trial here, a live Arrasmith or the dead Binghams?

Craig Mosman responded that Ken Arrasmith knew about the Tina Turner case because it took place while he was a deputy sheriff, and that was indeed relevant. "This is a capital case," Mosman told Judge Leggett. "We deserve the opportunity to present a full defense." And that meant the introduction of witness after witness who could describe the rotten things the Binghams had done to women and girls over two decades.

Judge Leggett, after her shaky start in the early hours of the trial, was more confident on the bench each day that the murder trial progressed. This time she was almost rude in chopping down Mosman's request. She said that "evidence of a twelve-year-old connection won't help explain what happened in this case'' and would only ''inflame the jury.''

''The rules of law are clear on this,'' she said, wearily going over the same opinion once again. ''I've stated them over and over, and written them over and over.'' The probable testimony of the witnesses sought by Mosman were ''not admissible and so prejudicial as to be unfair and I won't permit it.''

She sustained the prosecutor's objection. Tina Turner and the other witnesses, among the most important cards in the defense deck, would never reach the witness chair. Mosman had even argued out of court that he be allowed to simply call the names of each witness and be told that she would not be permitted to testify, thus letting the numbers speak silently to the jury. Leggett snuffed that one out, too. After trying for months to break through the judge's order, the Mosmans had failed.

Combined with the barring of Dr. Walker from testifying about Arrasmith's state of mind, the elimination of the rape victims was a devastating blow to the defense case. Ken Arrasmith's anticipated road to freedom had just run into a major roadblock. There would be no barrage of sexual abuse charges against Ron and Luella Bingham. All that was left before the jury was a couple of murder indictments against Arrasmith.

Linda Bartlett, the first and second wife of Ken Arrasmith and the mother of Cynthia, was the sixth defense witness. Both she and Ken would dodge the question of how many times they had been married and simply claim they had been wed for eleven years. To do otherwise would cast doubt upon the family's integrity in the eyes of the jury.

Wearing a dark green pantsuit and with her reddish hair cut short, the nervous witness still had to admit that her youngest daughter frequently caused problems. ''I was always concerned,'' the mother said, particularly after fifteen-year-old Cynthia moved in with her new boy-friend, the twenty-five-year-old Ken Rathbone.

Therefore, Bartlett said, she was somewhat relieved that Cynthia ended up at the Bingham residence, feeling she was at least safe there and was not roaming the streets, homeless. She testified that drugs had been used at the place Cynthia had previously stayed, and Bartlett testified she was happy the girl was out of that danger.

The mother actually talked to Cynthia by telephone and visited the Binghams to see her daughter, she said, and Luella served her coffee while they all had a chat. "She was convincing me that this was a nice place for her to be," Bartlett said. An additional factor of comfort was that Ken's parents lived only a short distance away.

Linda Bartlett was troubled when she would visit or call her daughter, she said, because Lue would never leave them alone to talk. When the mother would pick up the girl for a lunch or dinner, Cynthia always "told me she had to get back." Bartlett also said that Luella emphasized that drugs were not allowed at the Bing-hams' home, but also admitted that Cynthia never said anything about voluntarily taking drugs there.

Bartlett said she discussed with police her teenaged daughter running around with a man ten years her senior, and the authorities shrugged it off, telling the mother that "sometimes you just have to let them hit rock bottom."

"I didn't know what to do," Bartlett told the court. In April, her contacts with Cynthia faded as the Bingh-ams would tell her the girl wasn't home when Bartlett telephoned or went to visit.

Then came the pivotal visit home, when Cynthia slept hard "all day, all night and the next day." A telephone call from Luella was ignored, which made Cynthia angry when she awoke. Bartlett then testified that she told her youngest daughter she did not have to return to the Binghams if she didn't want to, that she could stay home.

"Mom, I can't," Cynthia replied, standing behind the living room couch and holding onto a rocking chair.

"Why?" asked her mother.

"I have to go back," Cynthia said. "You don't know what they do to me . . . They make me sleep with them."

Linda Bartlett was shocked. "You're not going back. You're staying here," she told her child, who was a chronic runaway.

Cynthia protested that would not work. "No. They'll kill me. They'll kill you and they'll kill Taylor (Bartlett's grandchild)." Cynthia telephoned Josh Bingham to come give her a ride back to the house beside the cemetery.

"She was so scared," the mother recalled. Cynthia said she could go back and then leave sometime when Ron and Luella didn't suspect anything. Bartlett said it was she who drove both Cynthia and Ken Rathbone over to Tracy Anderson's place, and Tracy took them to the Hollywood Motel, where the couple spent Sunday night.

Meanwhile, Bartlett said she filed a runaway report with the police to get Cynthia picked up on Monday morning. "I said they needed to get at this right away, that she was in danger," she testified. "She was going to leave town to get away from them."

After the police picked Cynthia up on Monday morning, the parents discussed the situation with a judge and agreed to put the teenager into a detention center. "She was upset that I filed the runaway report. She said she didn't do anything wrong, that they did it to her."

Bartlett, who was present when Captain Watkins questioned Cynthia, repeated the testimony that the girl had told him about the sexual abuse and that Patti Mahar Johnson had witnessed her degradation. Later, she said, other police officers confirmed they already knew about the assaults on Cynthia through the report filed concerning Patti.

In private conversations between the mother and

daughter, Bartlett said Cynthia told her of how Ron had wired himself with explosives, which she had felt beneath his shirt, and that she was frightened staying in the detention center because police had done ''nothing'' to solve the problem.

Before Ken visited his daughter, however, he met with Bartlett at the Dairy Queen across the street from the jail, and she told him of the sexual atrocities endured by their child. ''He just kind of sat there,'' Bartlett said. The bewildered father promised he would retrieve the pubic hair that Bingham had shaved from his daughter and from the ''rest of the girls.''

Once he returned to town, Bartlett said she and Arrasmith were in contact every day, until the May 17 shootings.

''Did he ever say, one single time, that he was going to kill the Binghams?'' asked Craig Mosman.

Bartlett, her eyes misty, shook her head. ''No,'' she replied.

As Bartlett gallantly defended the man who divorced her twice and owed her tens of thousands of dollars in delinquent child support, Arrasmith rested his chin on cupped hands and leaned forward to hear her every word. She said Ken had actually told her that the police were ''going to make an arrest, sometime.'' Meanwhile, Bartlett said, she had lived in a state of perpetual fear for her daughter, for Ken and for herself.

On the afternoon of May 17, after hearing of the shootings and that Ken had turned himself in to police, Bartlett went to the detention center, but was barred from seeing Cynthia until two policemen finished interviewing the girl about the incident. When she was finally ushered in, Cynthia was relieved beyond measure, Bartlett said. ''She had thought it was her dad and I'' who had been killed.

Once again, Denise Rosen and Mike Kane had no questions for a defense witness. Bartlett was excused from the stand and took a seat in the audience, at the end of the third row. Donnita Weddle turned and squeezed Bartlett's hand.

The judge agreed with the prosecutors and said she had "difficulty seeing the relevance of Mrs. Bartlett's testimony," since most of it had already come into evidence through other witnesses. Mosman said that it was important for the jury to realize Bartlett had "hid" Cynthia in her home.

That was beside the point. Tears were the reason she had been on the stand. The jury might have been perplexed about why Linda Bartlett had testified, for she had not a word to say about the murders, but jurors could relate to a mother's tears.

28

At 10:02 A.M. on November 17, 1995, as a light valley fog enshrouded the courthouse and the smell of wood products hung in the outside air, Ken Arrasmith walked to the witness stand, with a cup of water in his hand and a cocky grin on his face. Almost exactly six months to the hour after he shot Ron and Luella Bingham to death, Arrasmith was finally getting his chance to place his version of events on the record.

He had a Constitutional right to remain silent, but the man who had caused his name and situation to be played out in front of the national media by talking to everyone who would listen had no intention of not speaking to the jury. He had had six months to prepare and he was ready. Since the defendant makes the choice on such matters, there was nothing the Mosmans could do or say to dissuade him. Arrasmith demanded his moment in the sun. He felt that all the jurors had to do was listen, and surely they would declare him innocent. Ken Arrasmith planned to be home, among his family, for Thanksgiving.

He was a truck driver, he said. Loved it. Hauled the rigs from California to Tacoma and Seattle and Portland and back to his current hometown of Sunnyside, Washington, as well as the Clarkston-Lewiston area. He en-

joyed hunting and fishing, but even those hobbies didn't
compare with being in the big Kenworth cab, jacking
through the gears, driving his truck. And of all the car-
goes he handled, he liked moving cattle best, because a
live cargo meant that he had to work with much more
care. Anyway, he loved dealing with the people he met
on the road, and he said they were the salt of the earth
types, "a hardworking bunch." He had fallen in love
with trucks when he was only a kid, back when his father
drove the road, and he had been driving trucks "all my
life," no matter what other job he might have.

Graduating from high school in 1969, he had worked
first for Asotin County, driving a dump truck. Then for
three years, from 1975–78, Arrasmith said he was a deputy sheriff in Asotin County. He "loved" that job, too,
but moved back into trucking when it ended.

With a smile, he tiptoed into his personal background,
telling the jurors he was married to Linda Bartlett, Cynthia's mother, in 1970, and they were divorced in 1981.
Actually, he and Linda had been married twice and divorced twice, but such an admission might have ripped
the picture of domestic tranquility Ken and Linda were
projecting. There is always a reason for a divorce, and
more reasons for a double divorce.

"Did you ever intend to kill Ron and Luella Bingham?" asked Craig Mosman.

"Never," responded the witness in a firm, sure voice.
The jurors might have wondered somewhat about that
statement. If he didn't intend to kill them, why carry five
different fully loaded weapons up to Shelter Road?

Mosman steered the testimony toward Cynthia, and
Arrasmith acknowleged his relationship with his daugh-
ter was "kind of tough," since his ultimate divorce from
Linda came when she was still a baby. Later, however,
Cynthia "spent a lot of time at my house when I re-
married." Since he hadn't mentioned he had remarried

twice since leaving Linda, it was unclear to which home he referred. The jury didn't know either.

The girls—Cynthia and her sister, Jennifer—"bickered like sisters do" when they were home, but "not at Dad's home. That was the fun place." He said he "coached" them to come and stay with his latest wife, Donnita, but they were growing up and resisted that idea, he said. Cynthia did live with them for one four-month period in Sunnyside, and Ken remembered that as a "fabulous" time, because when he came home from a driving trip, "my puppy would be waiting for you at the doorstep" and she would hug him and sit on his lap. "I enjoyed it," said Arrasmith.

The telephone connection was strong between him and his daughters, because he kept a cellular phone in his truck and bought the girls telephone credit cards they could use. Further, he said, he looked up Cynthia every time he returned to the valley and would take her shopping or out to eat. "I'd search her out to do something bonding," he said. "And if she heard I was around, I couldn't hide from her." Arrasmith smiled again.

Mosman steered him to the time when Cynthia moved into the Bingham home, and Ken said he didn't know about it until around the middle of April. Jurors might have wondered if contact was so close, why did it take the father a month and a half to learn where his daughter was living?

But all wasn't perfect, he admitted, although Cynthia and Jennifer had grown up "as perfect angels." Since Jennifer was older, she got a car first and had some freedom that led her to rebel against her parents. "Cynthia learned from her," he said. "She put her mother through the paces." There was not a word about discipline.

The father-daughter relationship was demonstrated again as he described meeting her at a telephone booth in Lewiston, accompanied by her older boyfriend, Ken Rathbone. They asked for money and Cynthia told her dad that she would rather have money than go to dinner with him. "She got ten bucks out of me," he said. Again, something seemed amiss. It had been demonstrated during the trial that Arrasmith had a burning dislike for Rathbone being with his young daughter, to the point of wanting him arrested after police found them together at the Hollywood Motel. But he did nothing at their first meeting to separate them.

Again, Arrasmith testified that "I didn't know about the Binghams" and was unaware for a long time that Cynthia was living with them. But when he found out, he knew the house was only "two minutes from my parents" and felt she would be safe, or at least "a lot better than running off to California."

Instead of being clear with his messages to her, Arrasmith indicated he had pretty much given up on her. "I can't grab her and haul her back to school," he said. "I tried to keep a neutral place (because) I wanted her to stay." Only a few minutes after admitting he had lost track of Cynthia for a month and a half, Arrasmith told the jury that he wouldn't have known "how to deal with not knowing where she was."

With his hands waving before him in explanation, or his fingers laced tightly together, Ken Arrasmith said that she had been her normal playful self during a meeting at the home of his parents. "She wanted to hang onto me," he said. "She looked fine." That evening, he drove her back up the hill to the Binghams' home, thinking that her staying with them and living with Rathbone was "a lot better" than the child being homeless and drifting on the streets, running "in the gutter" with other drug users.

Meanwhile, Cynthia was frequently calling both him and her mother "for no reason at all" and he said that he could not recall her ever saying that she had a problem.

* * *

It was time to discuss the main subject, and Mosman steered the testimony to Saturday, May 6. Arrasmith said he had been on his way to Sunnyside from a California run when Jennifer telephoned him, while he was in the truck, with the abrupt disclosure that "there seems to be a problem with Cynthia," including the possibility of sexual assault. "I wasn't really positive what it was," he said. Once back home in Sunnyside, Arrasmith talked with both Jennifer and Linda Bartlett and they confirmed that Cynthia had "blurted out" that she didn't want to return to the Binghams because of what they had done to her.

Arrasmith worked the phone and in talks with contacts in the area, including Kyle Richardson, discovered that "a lot of information was going around the community, and apparently something was coming to a head. They didn't know what it was, but it wasn't good."

Kyle was reluctant to discuss the matter on the telephone, other than confirming that he had "heard some things." A short time later, Ken Arrasmith drove out of Sunnyside, feeling "pretty sick" and, as he hurried toward the valley, he fretted about whether "as a father, I had fed my daughter to a predator."

Then, he said, he began to review exactly who the Binghams might be, recalling that Lue had told someone that Ron said "he knew me and we were friends." In later testimony, he would say that Ron Bingham once told him, while working on a car engine, that "I remember you from when you were a deputy."

That brought an immediate objection from the prosecution, which said that line of questioning was "only going in the direction of prior convictions." Mosman didn't disagree, but argued that Arrasmith would have realized that Ron Bingham was once a convicted rapist and should be allowed to testify as to his reaction to that fact. It was relevant, he said, and the judge agreed to take a recess to think over whether Arrasmith could answer questions that would bring in Bingham's past.

After the brief halt in the proceedings, with the jury still out of the court and laughing in their sequestered room so loudly that they could be heard through the door, Judge Leggett once again shot down the defense attempt to squeeze Bingham's past acts into the current proceedings. Even if Arrasmith did know about the rape conviction, the judge said it would not negate the state's evidence on the murders. Such testimony about the defendant's state of mind might confuse the jury into believing that Idaho law gives permission "to confront and kill a person because of previous bad acts," Leggett said, reading from a law book. "It's immaterial."

It was perhaps the judge's finest moment. After her soft start in handling her first murder case, she had come full circle and was now running the trial firmly, ever more comfortable in her decision to block the prior acts. Her rule was grounded in the law, and she pointed out that there was "no attack" on the accused from 11:30 until noon on the day of the murders. That was what was to be considered, not what the Binghams may have done in years gone by. Ironically, another loud burst of juror laughter came through the closed door just as she was making her ruling.

The court, she said, would be negligent in allowing the testimony about the Binghams' character issues. That also included any plans to call women to the stand to testify about "alleged" previous sexual abuse, the damning letter from Ron Bingham's raped niece, Laura, or police statements about previous bad acts. As far as Leggett was concerned, the law was crystal clear, she had ruled on it again and again and now she was fed up with the issue. "I don't want to hear this again," she snapped at Craig Mosman.

Arrasmith's monologue continued, moving back to his arrival in Clarkston after Jennifer's shocking call and

Kyle Richardson's comments. For one of the few times in the trial, and almost throughout the months of the story, he finally mentioned his second wife, Lynn Kohl, and the two children they had. It was only a passing reference, however, since Kyle had already spelled out that Lynn was in on the ten thousand dollar loan arrangement for drugs. Arrasmith said that he went to Lynn's house to see the kids and also hear her confirmation that Cynthia had been raped by the Binghams, not only at the Bingham's home, but also at a motel.

Of the information that Arrasmith was receiving about his daughter, he said he "was somewhat overwhelmed" and felt the episode was "bizarre." The next day he talked with his own mother and with Linda Bartlett to find out more information, and learned Cynthia was at the motel with her boyfriend. He said he was "going to get her . . . not to ask her to go, but tell her she had to go or have her locked up."

They were outside the motel in the parking lot when he drove up that morning, and upon seeing her, Cynthia's father said, "I felt like I'd been kicked in the stomach." The pretty child he remembered had become an image of "walking death," underweight and with sunken eyes. He motioned for her to get into the truck, and she did, but was "kind of defensive" when they began to talk, telling him she was leaving with Ken Rathbone for California.

Then came one of the stranger parts of his testimony, where a defendant who tries to piece things together too neatly usually stumbles. Arrasmith got his time line mixed up.

"I said, 'Cynthia, don't you think some of this is your fault?' " Arrasmith said he asked. Cynthia became offended and was hurt and their conversation "went from bad to worse." Finally, he told her that he was having her picked up as a runaway. Arrasmith then testified that he was referring only to her drug use as being partially

her own fault. However, he already had been notified on
May 6 by his other daughter of the sexual abuse and had
heard the same stories from Kyle Richardson, Lynn Kohl
and Linda Bartlett on May 7, before he drove to the
motel on the morning of May 8. To say that he was
referring to drugs alone at that point was difficult for
jurors to believe. He complicated things when he added,
"I really didn't believe it all." Immediately after their
conversation in the truck, he called the police on his
cellular telephone and told them he believed "she'd
been raped" and needed to be picked up.

Soon, the police arrived and Cynthia was in a squad
car. Arrasmith finally turned his attention to Ken Rathbone and told the cops to arrest him, too, because he
was twenty-five and had been with his daughter. He said
the police said Linda Bartlett was aware of the relationship, and Arrasmith responded, "I don't care. I want him
arrested." Of course, he had known of the relationship,
too, and had made no move to separate the lovers.

Then came a shock, he said, for the police at the station told Linda and Ken they were going to release Cynthia into their parental custody because "this was kind
of a parent thing." Arrasmith spread his hands and
looked at the jury as if he couldn't believe what the cops
told them. *"Say what?"* he declared in a frantic voice,
a term he would use repeatedly. He told the cops that
"she'll run" as soon as she is out the front door, and
after some pleading, the police agreed to call the child
protection services and "put her in lockup." When Ken
and Linda left the police station, their youngest daughter
was in juvenile detention, at their request.

Mosman then shifted the focus to the premise of police irresponsibility. Arrasmith testified that only forty-
five minutes after the lockup in Lewiston, which is in
Nez Perce County, he telephoned the Asotin County
Sheriff's Department and spoke to Captain Watkins to
make an appointment for an interview. In a gratuitous

slur, he added, "I think they woke him from his nap."
The next day, there was a court hearing for Cynthia at
8 A.M., and Watkins saw Linda Bartlett and Ken Arrasmith two hours later. Arrasmith introduced a mystery
element, claiming he was followed to the courthouse by
two long-haired men. During the hearing, at which Cynthia appeared in handcuffs and leg shackles—standard
for any prisoner in similar circumstances—Arrasmith
said he explained "all my fears," including the unnamed
guys waiting in the ominous car outside the courthouse,
and said he was afraid for the life of his daughter if she
were released.

The judge said he would do whatever was requested
and agreed to keep her in detention. Arrasmith again
showed his strange view of the situation. He had fought
strongly to have his daughter arrested and then kept in
custody, but blurted out that it was unfair for the authorities to give her the message: "You've been raped,
but we're going to put you in jail. Imagine how she
felt." Of course, the reason she was in jail was her parents did everything they could to keep her there because
she planned to run away to California.

While Arrasmith was being expressive on the witness
stand, something strange was happening in the jury box.
Several jurors were fiddling with their fingers, none were
taking notes, one yawned, another plucked at a strand of
hair, a third examined her fingernails and one actually
leaned back in his chair and closed his eyes. They were
hardly absorbed by Arrasmith's long-awaited testimony
and apparently were not buying it. The story just wasn't
washing with them.

Arrasmith described the "investigation" that he believed Captain Watkins had authorized him to conduct.
Watkins, he said, showed him the report he had taken
from Patti Mahar Johnson about Cynthia's assault, and
when Arrasmith noted it was dated two weeks before he
heard about the incident, he said, "I can't describe how

I felt." Anyway, he testified that Watkins felt Arrasmith should pursue his own line of inquiry.

And that, he said, was the sole reason that he was involved in some drug activity. To gain the confidence of street people, he was forced to enter their dirty world. Everywhere, he said, sources were "sick to their stomachs" and appalled by what the Binghams had done to Cynthia, telling Arrasmith that "you might sell drugs, buy drugs, use drugs, okay, but you don't rape children. Even the worst of people don't rape children." All of his new friends wanted to help, including one tough biker who volunteered to get some friends, barge into the Bingham home and retrieve Cynthia. It was an interesting offer to be put forth, since at the time he was describing, Cynthia was no longer with the Binghams, but already in juvenile detention.

Still, Arrasmith said, he was strangely flattered by the proposal from the tough guy. "I'm just a cowboy," Arrasmith pleaded before the jury. "I'm a truck driver . . . He doesn't know me. Why would he do this for me?" Juror eyes drifted toward the ceiling at the outpouring of self-pity.

While he was working the underbelly world of Clarkston and Lewiston, he continued to wonder "where are the flashing lights and sirens" of police cars rushing to pick up the Binghams? However, he also acknowledged that his own previous law enforcement experience provided him with some insight, that cops "just can't wave a wand and make things happen. They have to go through channels."

In another interesting revelation, Arrasmith then told the jury that one of his sisters had died of drug-related causes the previous year. So just because someone does drugs, "I don't condemn them." In Arrasmith's view, he would not even condemn the people who deal in drugs, as long as they don't force people to consume the product. Like the biker, the druggies rallied to him in his time of need, he said. "They came to help me, wanting to do for me what the police should be doing."

Then he touched on something that may have been the critical piece of the puzzle for him. He was determined, he said, to retrieve the pubic hairs that Ron Bingham had shaved from Cynthia. "I wanted those back, whatever the cost," he said. The lost pubic hair became a grail that he could pursue and changed the equation. Instead of the story being about Cynthia's sexual abuse, it shifted somewhat to Ken being unwilling to let Ron keep the pubic hair "as a trophy." That made it more of a man-to-man challenge, and made it more about him than about his daughter, because in reality, the shaven hairs were of minor consequence when compared to the much bigger issue of rape and abuse of a child. "I had to have that back," he told the jurors.

He was coming to the end of his lengthy presentation on direct examination and had not touched at all on the actual killings. With time running out, the Mosmans wanted to end the week's testimony on a strong and positive note—something the jury could consider over the weekend. Mosman edged Arrasmith toward the crime scene, ever so carefully, asking how he felt about what had happened.

Arrasmith fell back into his protective swamp of self-pity, a place where he did not have to take responsibility for anything, and sought juror sympathy. The defendant was playing the victim. "It is like a nightmare, but you wake up from nightmares," he pleaded. "I haven't woke up. It won't go away."

He said he wouldn't wish his dire situation "on my worst enemy," but added, somewhat philosophically, that "you can't unscramble eggs." He said he couldn't truly describe how sick and hurt he felt about the matter. Looking directly at the jury, however, he made it clear that the hurt he was describing was the hurt of a parent having "your child violated by two animals." There was no hurt, or sickness, about his assigning himself the role of judge, jury and executioner and shooting two defenseless people to death exactly six months earlier. To him, Luella and Ron Bingham were merely a couple of eggs that were accidentally scrambled.

After an uneventful weekend, all the players gathered in the courtroom on Monday morning, awaiting Arrasmith's continued peculiar recitation.

But first, the defense called another witness to the stand, Bob Hough, Ken's brother-in-law, who testified that he had seen Ken test firing the Tec-9 on Easter Sunday in April 1995, and that Arrasmith had owned guns ever since Hough had known him. If the object was to show there was nothing odd about Arrasmith having a Tec-9, the plan backfired, badly.

Over the objection of Craig Mosman, Mike Kane asked Hough if Arrasmith ever said, "The Binghams are going to be taken care of one way or another." Arrasmith's brother-in-law, under oath to tell the truth, answered yes.

Ken Arrasmith was back on the stand at 9:11 A.M., carrying another cup of water, smiling at the judge and joking, "It's surprising how dry I get."

Things got down to cases quickly, with Arrasmith recounting how he "had to run the same hours of the night crowd, the party crowd" as he conducted his own investigation into Cynthia's mistreatment. Usually, he would return to his temporary abode, a trailer parked in the backyard of his parents' home, about 3 A.M., when the "undesirables" were "wasted" and no longer functioning. The eighteen-foot-long trailer became a small fort because he feared Ron Bingham or one of his cronies might attack at any time. Arrasmith barricaded the windows and doors and, remembering his daughter's claim about Ron having explosives, forbade his parents

to enter the trailer because it might be booby-trapped.
His hands windmilling with excitement as he spoke, he
said he was convinced Bingham would do anything to
avoid going back to prison on another rape charge.
"This thing was more than I could possibly handle or
understand," he said.

"I would wake up in a cold sweat, absolutely positive
that he was out there with night binoculars," Arrasmith
said. And when he thought how scared he was, he could
only imagine how frightened a young girl would be of
Ron Bingham.

Despite the danger, however, he went to the Bingham
place on May 8—two days after learning of the assault
and the day he locked Cynthia up in juvenile detention—
"to collect her belongings." Arriving there after lunch,
he was invited inside by Luella. He sat down in the
living room where Rilla Smith was seated, and Ron
came out from a bedroom to join them. Everyone
seemed nervous, as if "knowing this was going to be
kind of a bombshell."

He confronted them, he said. "My daughter has made
accusations" that she was forced to sleep, perform sex
acts and do drugs with them, he charged, and Ron went
into a fit, denying it all. Bingham was like a kid caught
in the cookie jar and all three of them—Ron, Lue and
Rilla—wore looks of "absolute fear." Then, he said, he
realized that infuriating Bingham in his lair might not
be a good idea, so he softened his approach. While Ron
and Lue squealed about Cynthia's betrayal, Arrasmith
asked for and was given her clothing. Ron then started
talking about how Cynthia was angry at her mother and
father.

Out of the blue, Ken asked to see Ron's shop. Lue
was crying about Cynthia, and Ron started strutting to
show how tough he was. "I said I was trying to find out
what happened; I didn't want to fight," Arrasmith said.
But he told Bingham that if the accusations proved true,

Arrasmith would return with the sheriff and watch Ron and Lue be dragged away by the law, "kicking and screaming."

Bingham began shouting. "You come back here and you won't be leaving. I'll kill you. I'm Rambo. I'm invincible. I can see in the dark."

Arrasmith said he resumed interviewing his daughter, whenever possible, on visiting days at the detention center. "I wanted, needed to know everything that happened to her," and her graphic answers left him stunned. "There was nothing I could comfort her with."

Meanwhile, his own fear of Ron Bingham trailed him like a bad dream. He wouldn't start his truck if anyone was near it for fear it might blow up. He thought he was being followed. Then things got worse when his ex-wife, Linda Bartlett, told him that drugs had been offered by Bingham as payment for killing Arrasmith and Linda. He listened constantly to the police scanner to learn when the Bingham arrest was imminent so he could be present.

By Mother's Day, Sunday, May 14, Arrasmith had been in town for a week. He said during that time he had provided police with "name after name" of other Bingham victims, but nothing was happening, just as Ron had taunted him. "I was actually losing it by then," Arrasmith admitted. He found himself crying at times, including breaking down in front of Sheriff Jeffers, because he had no idea what to do. "The police were asleep and having donuts," he said.

"If nothing else, they're not going to have the trophy of my daughter's pubic hairs," Arrasmith said again, emphasizing the importance he placed on the item. So on that Mother's Day, he and Kyle Richardson drove up to Valley View Road to spy down on the Binghams. Kyle was along only to watch out for the bodyguard and to "make sure I didn't get shot in the back." At one point, he was going to knock on the door again, but changed his mind, because trouble might develop and endanger innocent bystanders, such as Josh Bingham and Rilla Smith.

Judge Leggett told Mosman to provide "some questions and answers and less storytelling."

The relationship with Kyle was critical because it linked Arrasmith to drugs. The defendant said he thought methamphetamines had "some lifting qualities," but did not do it every day, as Kyle had claimed, adding, "It was not a preferred drug by me." He did not identify his preferred drug. The reason he took the few sniffs of meth was quite simple, he told the jury. He had to in order to be accepted by the drug crowd in his investigation. Knowing they would be suspicious if he didn't join their habit, he "damn well" had to do at least a little bit.

He now explored his relationship with Kyle Richardson in more depth, and told an entirely different story, one that kept him clean and righteous. They had met around Christmas of 1994 and Arrasmith became enamoured with Kyle's "heaven" of an automobile repair shop. Kyle said he knew where he could get a "cool Mustang" that needed some work, but was short on cash. "He asked for money" and promised to return the amount within thirty days, and Lynn Kohl drew up the paper introduced into evidence. "Kyle said he could turn the Mustang in a week, that he had a customer. I wasn't worried, because he gave the shop as collateral," Arrasmith said. So that was it. The money was for a car deal, not drugs!

In fact, Arrasmith said, drug dealing simply wasn't smart. "Name me one drug dealer who's not broke or not in jail," he joked. Anyway, another reason for the loan was that Kyle "wanted to get out" of the drug business and Ken's money might help him do so. He had taken nine thousand dollars from the bank, with the intention of buying a twenty-foot flatbed trailer in Seattle, but that didn't work, so he still had the money lying around idle when Kyle asked for the loan.

"Kyle said you threatened to kill Ron Bingham," Mosman prodded. "I never said it and I never meant it," Arrasmith replied muddily, claiming he never really meant something he didn't say.

The reason for not wanting to again confront Bingham at his home was to remove Rilla and Josh from any potential problems, he testified. "I wanted to get Ron away by himself and get his statement on tape" and force the police to act on Cynthia's behalf. "I wanted him to tell something. I didn't care if it was under duress with the laser site pointed at his forehead. I was out of things to do."

The laser idea came about, he said, because "it's known to make prisoners wet their pants." He dramatically pointed his finger toward the jury, imitating the ruby beam of the laser sight. "The next thing coming is a bullet. It's very intimidating."

He dismissed any importance in his relationship with Kyle Richardson, saying the big guy was stupid. "He's twenty-five going on fifteen," Arrasmith testified. So when Arrasmith felt he was "having trouble holding my emotions back," he sought out a talk with an adult, Sheriff John Jeffers, when words "just drained out of me."

Again he referred to his deceased sister, saying she had been on drugs most of her adult life and he wanted to be able to write on her gravestone that he had fought back, that her brother had taken down a drug dealer. "If that's a nervous breakdown, then I had one," he proclaimed.

Then, he said, Sheriff Jeffers surprised him by agreeing, telling him: "Ken, somebody's got to take those Binghams out. But you know, Ken, you can't do it because we'd have to arrest you."

The self-righteous tone accelerated as Arrasmith built toward the climax of his story and his encounter with

Otis Dixon on May 16 at Kyle's shop. The tall, lean Dixon told Arrasmith he had spotted Ron Bingham at a shop in Lewiston, and later, at Dixon's home, Arrasmith met Dixon's stepson and saw the boy's girlfriend.

The boy said he worked for Bingham as a mechanic but had been told to leave because of some disagreement and Ken pumped him for information about Cynthia, without mentioning her by name. Then Arrasmith asked Otis if the stepson had a girlfriend and Dixon pointed to a girl sleeping on a nearby bed in a fetal position, and identified her as Tara Lebold. In a moment of perception, Arrasmith said he replied, "She was next. She was going to go through the hell my daughter went through."

Arrasmith said he couldn't handle the idea and went home about eleven o'clock that night. The following morning, his mother awoke him and he called Detective Tom White about ten o'clock and told him, "Tom, you know they have moved another girl into Cynthia's place." Arrasmith testified that White replied: "I wouldn't be a bit surprised."

"I couldn't get Tara out of my mind," he said, and decided to return to see Otis Dixon. When Dixon climbed into the pickup truck, he told Ken, "I know where Ron is at. I just saw him." Otis sketched a map of Shelter Road and got out of the truck.

Driving to Richardson's shop, Ken told Kyle that he knew Ron's location and discussed the Tara situation, then clipped an ammunition pack to his belt. "I was going over there and I was going to get a taped statement from him," Arrasmith said. Kyle handed Ken a T-shirt to wear over his shoulder holster and Arrasmith took a marking pen and wrote on it: "Don't Touch Our Daughters." The black T-shirt with the Bad Boys logo on it was shown to the jury.

With the small tape recorder in his pocket, he prepared to drive away with his loaded guns. The weaponry was necessary, he said, because he thought Ron might have a bodyguard and Ken would have "to get the drop" on them to make his plan work. Kyle Richardson offered to go along, but Ken declined, giving the young man his wristwatch as a reward "for being someone you can count on."

And then he drove away toward an uncertain rendezvous. "I didn't think I was coming back," he declared.

He found people working at the site on Shelter Road and he was sitting there feeling "sick and scared," when a young man approached to ask if he could help, and he was led up toward the work pad. When he saw Luella, he told her: "I need to see Ron." As he moved farther onto the property, he overheard Luella tell someone, "No, no. Just let Ron take care of it." When he saw Paul Sharrai working on an engine, Ken thought he was the fearsome bodyguard. Suddenly he felt surrounded and endangered. "I didn't know if there was a shotgun leaning against the car or what," he said. Luella was behind him and he saw Ron Bingham "getting on his hands and knees" and working on a bumper.

"I have something to talk to you about, Ron," Arrasmith quoted himself. Bingham ignored him and Ken thought Ron was stalling for time. He had not expected so many people to be around, and that perhaps Ron would draw courage from their presence and not be intimidated enough to talk. But perhaps if Ron saw the gun, he would talk. "I was terrified," Ken Arrasmith said.

"Ron, this is important for my daughter and important to you," Arrasmith said, gripping the Tec-9 in the cardboard box. "Fuck you and fuck your daughter," Bingham shot back.

Arrasmith thought Ron muttered something about a weapon and "reached for something shiny" that Ken thought was a gun. "Then I heard shots. I was wondering, 'Why don't they hurt? Why don't these bullets sting? It must be the adrenaline because I'm not feeling anything.' "

Then the scene went to slow motion, as if they were encased in heavy water, and he realized it was he who had been firing. "I know I did it, but I don't remember. Not at all." For the first time, Ken Arrasmith admitted pulling the trigger.

His movements sluggish and unreal, Arrasmith began walking away to find Luella and explain to her what had happened, how "it had all gone wrong" as his mind swirled wildly. He walked into the dark garage, unaware that he had also pulled out the laser-sighted Ruger pistol from beneath his shirt.

"Luella," he called, "it's over with. Come out. Don't do anything." Arrasmith testified that, although he knew Lue "always had a gun," he moved through the darkened garage with his eyes closed and soon was out through the door again, behind Luella, where he saw her "hunched down against the wall, looking around the corner, waiting for me." She stood and turned toward him and "I saw a gun and I heard shots . . . I don't remember pulling the trigger. I heard shots and she fell."

"This isn't what I want," he recalled thinking of that moment. "It had to come from me, I guess." His mind was doing something "weird" and telling him to get in the truck and escape. As he drove away from the scene, he used his cellular telephone to call Detective White, to arrange his surrender to a law officer whom he knew. "I just wanted to get into custody. I was worried somebody was going to get hurt," he said. White did not answer the calls and Arrasmith decided to give himself up at the Clarkston police station.

So, dialing his daughter Jennifer, he told her that "I loved her and to tell her sister that no matter what happened, it wasn't her fault."

At 11:20 A.M., Ken Arrasmith ended his testimony, sniffling.

29

Mike Kane and Denise Rosen were totally unimpressed with Arrasmith's long, rambling account. They had suffered, mostly in silence, throughout the presentation, and now Kane stood to begin the cross-examination and put the defendant's tangled tale into clearer focus.

Kane was almost contemptuous of Arrasmith saying he didn't know who fired the shots on Shelter Road, and when he questioned that, Arrasmith answered: "I just heard shots. My first instinct was they came from somewhere else." Only reluctantly did the defendant even admit firing "some" of the bullets. Kane handed Arrasmith the unloaded Tec-9 to give the jury a visual image of the killer with the murder weapon and told him to "show the jury what you did." Arrasmith dodged it. "I don't know . . . I don't remember pulling the trigger." Some more probing by Kane and Arrasmith added, "It was quite evident" that he had fired the gun.

The special prosecutor asked what Ron Bingham was doing beneath the truck to make Arrasmith feel he was in danger. The defendant answered that he saw Ron reach for "something silver" then heard the shots. Arrasmith nodded affirmatively when asked if he knew

Ron was "dead or dying" at his feet. "I knew he was shot," Arrasmith said.

When he was walking away, Arrasmith said he was talking to himself about the perceived danger from Luella, whispering, "For God's sake don't be comin' around that corner with a gun." Arrasmith said he thought he could still get a statement from Lue on his tape recorder, so he went to look for her. He confirmed he had the Tec-9 in one hand, but that he again "didn't remember" pulling the Ruger with the ruby laser sight from the shoulder holster. "It was dark inside the shed," he explained.

"You were going to use it as a flashlight?" Kane was incredulous. "No," Arrasmith quickly replied. Kane moved ahead, bringing out the coroner's chart again, showing the wounds of Luella Bingham and pointing out, "The shots are all in the back . . . You were in fear of your life?"

"Yes, absolutely," Arrasmith said. "She was standing sideways. She had something in her hand and I still say it was a gun." He paused, then fell back to his base line. "I don't remember telling myself to pull the trigger." He embellished, identifying Luella's gun as "a small automatic, not a revolver" and that he saw it as she began to turn toward him, crouched.

Kane scored a neat point, noting that if someone with a gun in their hand turned toward another person, "a normal everyday person would flee." Arrasmith indicated he had no choice because "she was laying in wait for me to come out of the shed."

Fine, said Kane. Suppose you explain why police found no firearm anywhere on the Shelter Road lot when they searched. "I don't have an explanation," Arrasmith said.

The prosecutor touched briefly upon the physical condition of Arrasmith at the time, and the defendant denied using either drugs or alcohol the day of the shootings.

The last time he had done meth was "maybe a day earlier." Kane wondered if Arrasmith knew meth was sometimes used to keep people awake and the defendant confirmed he had heard of such a thing. And what happened to you after your surrender in Clarkston? Arrasmith said he slept heavily, more than twenty hours a day for five days straight. "I'd think about what happened and go to sleep."

Then Arrasmith dodged a series of statements Kane alleged were made to other people, including telling a radio interviewer that Ron Bingham had finally "picked the wrong man" to challenge and that "I regret nothing." Arrasmith shrugged it off, saying he actually "felt pretty bad" about the deaths and that at times afterward "my mouth was going and my brain not."

Now about that tape recorded statement that you wanted so badly, Kane asked, why wasn't the tape recorder even turned on? Even when he went in search of Luella to get her words on tape, the little machine remained in his pocket, unused. Arrasmith made a minor concession. "It was a stupid idea," he said.

Following a short lunch break, the riveting exchange continued between Ken Arrasmith and the prosecutors who were trying to put him in prison, as Mike Kane asked what Arrasmith intended when he told Kyle Richardson that he might not be coming back on the morning he set out for Shelter Road. "Did you mean it was kill or be killed?" Arrasmith said simply, "No."

Kane asked why the box was assembled to hide the Tec-9. "Was it to get the drop on Ron?" The defendant parried, "No, it was so he couldn't get the drop on me." So, Kane wanted to know, why didn't he remove the gun from the box, and openly display it to force Ron into making a statement? "I didn't have a chance. Things were out of control," Arrasmith said.

The prosecutor asked how Ron might have caught a bullet in his upper thigh, as if he were trying to roll away from the gunfire. "I didn't look at each and every bullet hole," was the cold answer. "I don't know how he got shot in that position."

Changing direction suddenly, Kane probed Arrasmith's drug connection. Ken said that Kyle Richardson was lying; the ten thousand dollars was nothing but a legitimate loan, although his name did not appear on the questionable loan document; and that any report that he was more than thirty thousand dollars delinquent in child support payments was wrong, even if it did appear in court records. Again, Arrasmith said that "some drug dealers are okay people."

Kyle, he said, "was mistaken" about the amount of meth Ken used. It was only "once or twice a day, every other day." He gave his self-deprecating grin when he added that he didn't even like meth because it made his nose burn. "My buzz comes from Bud Lite." Not only Kyle, but everyone else who also testified that they saw him taking drugs were also liars, he said, contradicting his own testimony given moments earlier.

Moving ahead to the tearful meeting with Sheriff Jeffers, Kane wanted to know who Arrasmith was promising the sheriff, out of memory to his dead sister, that he would turn in as part of his personal war against drug dealers. Arrasmith asked the judge if he had to answer that question and she said he did, and Arrasmith said he was going to give the police both his ex-wife, Lynn Kohl, and his pal, Kyle Richardson.

Kane raised an eyebrow. "These were the people who were helping you?" The defendant admitted that they were.

But on the day of the killings, he telephoned both Lynn and Kyle, although he said he didn't remember why. Kane wanted to know what the hurry was on May 17, why Arrasmith felt he had to act instantly. He responded that he had been spurred to act by knowing the young girl he had seen the night before, Tara Lebold, was the Bingham's "next victim."

You did it for Tara? Kane asked. Yes, Arrasmith said, "That had to be done." Under further questioning, however, he admitted that he did not warn Otis Dixon, the stepson or Tara about the perceived danger, and did nothing to stop the girl from returning to the Bingham home if she wished. So, Kane continued, you went to Idaho to rescue Tara and get her out of the Bingham house? Arrasmith said that was correct.

What about the plan to get statements from Ron and Lue, pressed Kane—which was your real purpose? Arrasmith regrouped, saying the original plan was to get a statement, but he also wanted "to save her (Tara) . . . without question."

Kane dialed Arrasmith back to his training to be a deputy sheriff, particularly on the subjects of when to use a firearm. Arrasmith said the training emphasized "don't shoot anyone" unless absolutely necessary. "Pointing a weapon is a crime?" asked Kane. Yes, Arrasmith replied.

Kane questioned whether Luella had ever threatened Arrasmith and was told that she hadn't, but he was still concerned "about what she might do." As for Ron, Arrasmith said, he would still have been fearful, even if Ron had been taken to jail.

Then the prosecutor wanted to know about some statements Arrasmith had made to the media, particularly that "no one ever should be forced to take the law into their own hands." Since such a statement would be a clear admission of premeditation, Arrasmith hedged, saying he was talking about the judicial system, and anyway, that wasn't what he said. "I believe I was forced to investigate, to bring information to the police, forced into almost a nervous breakdown because of the lack of police effort," he declared on the stand.

Kane peppered him with a series of fast questions and

Arrasmith straddled the fence again, refusing to be pinned down. So you were very angry at law enforcement? No, he said, "I believe in it." You knew Detective White was going to work the case? "Yes, but I didn't have a good feeling that he was going to do anything with it."

Knowing the police were about to act, you still went up to Shelter Road. Why not wait another day? "I could have waited a year, or twenty-five years, like we already waited," Arrasmith said, his voice rising.

Kane moved to the murder site and noted twenty-three shots were fired into Ron Bingham. "I am sorry for the whole mess," Arrasmith said, adding that he had only wanted to see Ron "drug to a police car."

And Luella? Shot in the back six times, shot even when she was flat on the ground? Arrasmith was plainly nervous and responded in the third person: "Knowing Ken Arrasmith, if somebody was shot down on the ground . . . I would not shoot somebody on the ground. There's just no way."

On the second bench among the spectators, Donnita Weddle whispered, "I agree."

Kane again showed Arrasmith and the jurors the coroner's chart depicting the massive wounds to Luella. "Did you do anything wrong?" he asked. A simple, pointed and powerful question for it went to the sense of responsibility.

"Yeah," Arrasmith responded. "I never should have gone up there." That was the mistake from his point of view, not pulling the trigger. "There is no way to measure what has happened," he continued. "It'll continue to be a nightmare. No matter how bad Ron and Luella were . . ."

"Is it Ron's fault that you shot him?"

"Yes."

"Is it Lue's fault that you shot her?"

"Yes, because they were raping and torturing children. They set the stage.'' Had they not committed such acts, ''nothing would have happened'' to them, and nothing would have happened to the other twenty-five women they assaulted.

Ken Arrasmith finally left the witness stand, still wearing the cocky grin, unaware that the jurors didn't believe him.

There was one final piece of housework to be done. Craig Mosman filed a two and one-half page affidavit in an effort to at least get the qualifications of Dr. Lenore Walker, the Denver psychologist, before the jury. Judge Leggett said it would provide no help to the jury and would not change her ruling.

The defense, at 2:55 P.M., rested its case.

The prosecution had two rebuttal witnesses, both for brief and specific reasons—Detective Tom White and Sheriff John Jeffers.

Kane asked White if Arrasmith had ever mentioned to him either the name of Tara Lebolt or the idea that a fourteen-year-old girl was in the hands of the Binghams. The detective said he had no recollection of any such information.

Mosman pushed the detective to admit he had no notes of his conversations with Arrasmith, but that Ken did call him on the morning of May 17 and then the defense lawyer stumbled, for White stuck to his story. He didn't remember Tara's name being brought up and Arrasmith didn't talk about ''anybody being in danger.''

On a critical point, the detective was calling the defendant a liar.

Jeffers did the same thing, denying ever telling Arrasmith anything like the defendant's claim that the sheriff told him, ''Someone needs to take out the Binghams.'' The sheriff said he would never make such a statement. As for having Arrasmith help arrest drug people, the sheriff said he specifically told Arrasmith his help was not needed because the police would "catch them if they continued." Further, the sheriff said, Arrasmith told him that just because he drove a truck, some people thought he was hauling drugs. The sheriff related another Arrasmith admission that he once bought "a quantity" of drugs and sold them to a friend, and that the defendant wept, "I could have been busted."

Mosman's only point in response was to get Jeffers to say Arrasmith claimed he wanted to put drug dealers through the courts and to "put them away."

Ten minutes after the defense rested, the prosecution did the same thing. The evidence and the testimony was done. It was time for closing arguments.

30

With a sip of water and two quiet coughs to clear her throat, Denise Rosen began the final stage of the complex trial, the set of closing statments. She would rather not have been in court that day, because her six-year-old son, Jake, had been coughing up blood during the night. She had to leave him in the care of his father and drive to the courthouse, where she would spend the morning closing the prosecution side of this case. Then the defense attorneys would speak, and Mike Kane would respond for the state.

Rosen began her thirty-three minute statement at exactly 10:06 A.M., telling the jurors that the sexual attacks on Cynthia Arrasmith or any other minor child "is wrong and a crime," adding that part of Rosen's job was to send such perpetrators to jail. She had no sympathy for child molesters and told them that the state had never once in the trial said that the incidents related by Cynthia didn't happen.

Then she laid out the iron rule of the matter at hand. "This case is not about sexual abuse, but about murder," Rosen declared. "The defendant said he had to do it, that he was forced to go out to Shelter Road and shoot the Binghams, that it's okay to kill bad people." She said the defendant was about as wrong in that as he could be.

Kyle Richardson, she said, was a drug dealer and "not my friend." He was simply a person with information, and she urged the jurors not to be swayed because he appeared in the witness box after agreeing to a deal that promised him an exit from the heavy charge of conspiracy to commit murder. Rosen's tone was confident and she spoke clearly and quickly. Indeed, she said, it was not law enforcement, but Ken Arrasmith himself who was hanging out at Richardson's shop. "He hung out with a drug dealer."

"This case is about murder, simply murder," she underlined again, belittling Arrasmith's claim that he went to Shelter Road, carrying five loaded guns and clips of extra ammunition, wanting to intimidate Ron Bingham, and that "every time he pulled the trigger, it was self-defense."

Denise Rosen, a quiet person by nature, was showing new colors, pacing the courtroom like a petite cheetah. "Keep your eye on the ball," she told the jury. There were five things to focus upon—the day of the shootings was May 17; the place it happened was in Nez Perce County; that Ron and Luella Bingham were indeed killed; that there was malice aforethought ("A fancy word for intent to kill"), as illustrated by the repeated shots into both unarmed victims; and premeditation, demonstrated by the fact that Arrasmith not only "pulled the trigger" but took time to clear a jammed gun, shift position, open fire again, and "hunt down" and kill Luella Bingham.

That was it, she said. "The elements that the state has to prove have been shown."

Then she turned to attacking specific points of the defense version of events, showing a bit of actress in her presentation by putting both hands on her heart as she described Arrasmith's testimony that he thought the bul-

lets being fired were striking him. "A convenient argument . . . It's real easy to say that, to let it hang" in the
air, an unproven idea.

But this, Rosen argued, could not be considered self-
defense because Ron Bingham was without a weapon
and partially under a truck when he was killed. She told
the jurors to look at the physical evidence closely and
they would see that Arrasmith's "actions speak louder
than words." With a tone of disbelief, she said that the
defendant, carrying a Tec-9 hidden in a box and a laser-
equipped pistol out of sight in a shoulder holster, "was
afraid" of Ron Bingham, who was flat on his back and
not expecting the visit.

Then, "he wants you to really believe he was afraid
of Luella Bingham" and stalked her carrying two weapons. "Was there a gun in her hand?" Rosen asked.
"Where is it? There was nothing there. She was shot in
the back . . . it was not self-defense.

"It is wrong to kill," she stated. "It is wrong to murder." Rosen asked the jurors to consider what a society
would be in which everyone metes out individual justice.

She then raised the subject that had made this case so
famous. "Vigilante justice is wrong, simply wrong," she
said. "Where is it going to stop? Would Josh (Bingham)
be justified for shooting this defendant for killing his
parents?"

The Nez Perce prosecutor said she was certain that,
had Ron and Luella Bingham been brought to trial, they
would have been convicted. But there were some "problems" surrounding the story told by Cynthia: She did
not tell police the night of the raid that she lived in fear,
she told the cops she wanted to stay at the Bingham
house, and the only eyewitness to the assault was so
spaced out on drugs that she told police that cars were
driving in and out of graves.

Then, when Detective White finally got onto the case,

Arrasmith struck even though he had been told police were about to take care of things.

As for the report of Ron Bingham packing C4 explosives beneath his shirt, Rosen said, "We don't know that really happened." The only report of the C4 came from Cynthia to her parents, and not to the police. Cynthia never actually saw any packets, but only claimed that she felt something beneath Bingham's shirt.

The contract from Bingham to kill the family was also suspect, Rosen said. Arrasmith had mentioned it to Tom White, but importantly, "Not one person came into court and told you they heard that from the mouth of Ron Bingham," Rosen said. In her view, it was only another convenient excuse.

She then brought to light a fact that had emerged but had not been clearly stated. The only time that Ken Arrasmith had any direct contact with Ron Bingham was "when the defendant goes to him." Ron Bingham did not seek out Arrasmith, Rosen said.

The lawyer in Rosen was handed a plum in the testimony by and about Tara Lebold, and now she cooly plucked it from the evidence vine. "What a pretty young lady," she said of the teenager who looked like an innocent lamb when she testified. Rosen said the things, such as drugs, in the child's past were "horrible." But she discarded the idea that Arrasmith, once he saw her, had to go shoot Ron and Luella to save Tara from being a new sexual plaything. She pointed out that Arrasmith wanted the jury to believe the notion that "he went to Shelter Road and acted in self-defense of Tara, who he hasn't even talked to!" Leaving unspoken was the point that if Arrasmith thought the kid was in such danger, why didn't he at least warn her?

Rosen said the issue was accountability, for we are all accountable for our actions, and the defendant "is accountable for his actions on Shelter Road."

Correctly, she noted that the world was watching the

small courthouse in the small town of Lewiston, Idaho. The verdict of the jury would send a message to "other people in the future" about right and wrong. "Vigilante justice doesn't work in our society," she proclaimed. Even if Ron and Luella had been convicted of every crime they allegedly committed, every single rape and assault, they would not have been sentenced to death in any state in the union.

Arrasmith didn't go to Shelter Road to protect anyone, Rosen said. "He went out there to get his vengeance. He murdered them." Looking squarely at the jurors, she closed, saying: "Hold him accountable for his murders."

Only the week before, Craig Mosman had been called for jury duty in nearby Moscow, but had been excused, partially so he could address the jury in the Arrasmith double-murder case. Now he stood, buttoned his coat and crossed his arms before the jury, appearing almost to be standing guard over his client. He had fought hard with an idea because he had few facts, but he knew the idea—the sexual abuse of a child—remained a powerful weapon. He played the "parent" card, putting the jurors in the role of a mother or father forced to resort to drastic measures to save their child.

Mosman softly told the women and men who had sat through the trial that their duty was "to vote your conscience and what you believe to be fair and right." It was the start of a pattern that would be repeated so often it could have been the defense mantra.

In a louder voice, Mosman attacked the police performance. "Cops like these are why we have a jury system in the first place," he said, for they are "ordinary people" who can shield an individual citizen like Ken Arrasmith from "the power of government."

And there was no doubt the system was culpable, just as Arrasmith had described, for it "turned its back on women and children who were raped and sodomized by this evil couple'' and ''allowed a reign of terror on this family.''

''You must put yourself in Ken Arrasmith's shoes,'' Mosman declared, ''you must see what he saw.''

The Binghams had ''bragged'' that the law wouldn't touch them, the system had turned its back on Arrasmith and sent him out on the street to find information, because the police could not get it on their own. He pointed out that no one, at any time, testified that Arrasmith had threatened to kill Ron and Luella Bingham.

''He was doing what any parent would do. You can decide to end this family's nightmare today and that's what we are going to ask you to do. Vote your conscience,'' Mosman said. ''Do what I would do.''

The defense lawyer's voice slid lower, almost to a mumble, making the jurors strain to hear, to focus their attention exactly on what he was describing. He said he, too, had a daughter, and pointed her out, sitting in the courtroom. When he read about Arrasmith's situation, long before he got involved, Mosman said he wondered: ''What on earth would I do'' in a similar circumstance. When he learned that Cynthia had been molested, raped and sodomized, Mosman again wondered: ''What on earth would I do?'' Almost like the prince in the fairy tale of Cinderella, Mosman was trying to put Arrasmith's shoes on the feet of the jurors.

''This madman had explosives and he was going to get me,'' he continued, making the subject as personal as possible. ''Would I go up to the man and confront him? You bet I would.'' The threats and bragging by Bingham, the claim of being an invincible Rambo, the ability to keep another adult confined. It was hard to believe, but ''the police did nothing.''

Their lack of effort allowed the Binghams to take Cynthia back to the motel and rape her again. He brought in his own thoughts: ''How long am I going to

wait? How many are going to be sacrificed to their in-
satiable lust?'' His voice rose to thunder. ''Whose
daughter is going to be next?''

''These people declared war on Ken Arrasmith and
his family,'' a war with explosives and guns. ''They
were going to kill them. That was going to happen.''

The outraged Mosman had no doubt that he would
have reacted if the Binghams ''kept the pubic hair from
my daughter as a damned trophy.'' He looked into the
eyes of the jury. ''Would you become obsessed with
that? Would it have angered your every waking hour?''

Mosman took a look at Detective Watkins, who
''didn't have a clue'' about what to do and turned the
case over to the victim's father to investigate the allegations of drugs and rape. And, slapping the table, Mosman added, Arrasmith did give police evidence, then
drove to Shelter Road to get even more. ''He went out
there to obtain evidence!'' the lawyer said.

''I've concluded, as most parents would, that I'd do
anything to remove the threat from my family,'' he said.
''Snort methamphetamine? Absolutely. If that made a
difference, I'd do it in a heartbeat.'' He snapped his
fingers. ''So would you, so would any parent.''

The speech was well-crafted and emotional, but the
jurors sat still and stone-faced. No hankies were out, no
tears were shed, no nervousness showed.

Mosman told them it all came down to how they each
viewed the evidence that had been presented. The state,
he said, had to prove beyond a reasonable doubt that the
killings were not in self-defense or in the defense of
others. And the state failed, he claimed, inviting the jurors to see whether that evidence caused them to ''hes-
itate and pause.''

''This has never been a Who Done It. It's a Why,''
he said.

It wasn't just Ron Bingham. ''The Binghams acted as
a team,'' Mosman said. They would use drugs and other

methods to ensnare their victims, then both would commit sodomy and rape. Both carried guns and both went out at night to "terrorize" other people, as witnesses had said, so whether or not weapons were found at Shelter Road, Ken Arrasmith certainly had reason to think the Binghams would be armed. Both of the Binghams participated in shaving the pubic hair from women and girls and both would benefit by the presence of a bodyguard, such as the one Arrasmith had claimed was protecting them. "That's a fact and it's unshakable." It was a neat turn, since he did not specify which was the fact—that Arrasmith *thought* there was a bodyguard, or the unproven allegation that there was one.

Patti Mahar Johnson emerged from the Bingham hell "terrified" and "Tara was the next victim . . . They were going to begin their foul deeds again" and the police were not going to intervene, he said.

Mosman retreated to his personal life, trying to draw the jury out of the courtroom and back into their own private lives. He remembered once when his father was the Nez Perce prosecutor and an anonymous caller told Craig, who was only a child at the time, that his father was going to be killed. Police surrounded the house, but the threats didn't stop until a friend put word on the street that he personally was going looking for the "madman" frightening the family. The perpetrator became so scared of a possible vigilante payback that he turned himself in.

"Put yourself in the shoes of Ken Arrasmith. A madman was going to kill your wife, your child and you and the police don't stop him. What on earth are you going to do?" Mosman demanded. "Ken Arrasmith acted in self-defense or the defense of others."

Craig Mosman let the story evolve to Arrasmith's plan to get a statement from the Binghams on tape, and painted it as a "crazy and desperate" attempt by a desperate man who was driven by fear. "Ken has said it was a stupid plan," he noted, but it was "absolutely not" mapped out as a murder.

But once in the situation, it only made sense that he took along some guns for protection. Mosman picked up the Ruger pistol, squeezed the laser band to turn it on and once again the red dot danced on the creamy wall of the courtroom. Arrasmith wanted to use the laser to "intimidate" the Binghams, to make them react by talking.

Suddenly, Arrasmith had found himself standing in the middle of a number of people on Shelter Road, thinking they were packing guns, too. "He believed he was in danger." The cardboard box around the Tec-9 was nothing more than a ploy to allow Arrasmith to get close enough to Ron "to survive" if trouble erupted.

In fact, Mosman claimed, the plan was so suicidal in its conception that Arrasmith had written the plaintive message on his shirt, convinced that "he wasn't going to be able to make it back," but would be able to leave a message behind.

To this point in his closing statement, Mosman had tiptoed around actually mentioning Luella Bingham by name, always lumping her together with Ron. Since she had been shot so many times in the back, she was a weak point in the case.

He let the jurors imagine a mind-tortured Ken Arrasmith during those ten days of May. He was a man who knew "the highest duty" was to protect his family, but "there had been times in Ken's life when he hadn't been there" for Cynthia, and finally he realized that he had "fed his daughter to predators." He had held her as a baby and had thought he was always going to be there for her. Instead, he ended up wrapped in "his wildest nightmare . . . and was pushed too far."

"Ken Arrasmith is not guilty. Ask yourself this question: What would I do? Look in your heart," he said, once again in a soft voice, and you will conclude that

Ken Arrasmith's actions were actually a "reasonable" response to the impossible situation.

Roy Mosman can dominate a courtroom just by sitting in a chair, doing nothing. Now it was time for the old bear to bestir himself and he rose slowly, all eyes on his deliberate movements. He had gone to the funeral of a friend over the weekend, an outstanding fellow, an example to kids, he told the jury. And while others eulogized the deceased, citing his devotion to children, Roy Mosman sat in a church pew and scribbled notes for his closing speech in the Arrasmith trial.

And what he wrote was dynamite. The Binghams were "disgusting, degrading, despicable" and the jury had not been permitted to hear all of the atrocities they had committed. And Ken Arrasmith's reaction? Mosman was unequivocal. "It is a father's *right* to protect his family, his daughter!" he declared. "It's fundamental in our society!"

The jury wasn't just sitting on a murder case, they were there as "the conscience of the people of this state" and, as such, he said, "You must acquit."

Actually, the trial wasn't all bad. "There's a sense of relief here, even among law enforcement," Roy Mosman said. Because of the trial, at least Tara Lebold would never undergo the humiliation of sexual assault at the hands of the Binghams.

Tara had been in clear danger, but the police sat on their hands, he said, and then they lied to the jury. The investigating detective denied that Arrasmith told him Tara was being groomed as the new Bingham victim, and denied that Arrasmith told him "a girl named Tara" was at the Bingham place. Two lies, Mosman said.

That kind of police sloppiness cannot be tolerated today, he said. "They'll keep failing to do their duty unless you send them a message. Are you fed up with that?" Mosman's voice was full of contempt. "If the police had done their job, we wouldn't be here.''

He ridiculed the idea that Arrasmith planned anything at all, because nothing in the deck was in his favor should he carry out such an act, which at minimum would expose him to "great danger." Mosman's manner and tone and brevity were powerful and his message was short and clear. The former prosecutor, who had stood in this very courtroom so many times sending criminals to jail, was saying there was nothing to these charges against an anguished father forced to act because the police would not.

"The heart of our case, from the very beginning, was for you to put yourselves in Ken Arrasmith's shoes," Mosman said.

Promptly at noon, he returned to his seat, the closing statements by the defense concluded.

There was one lawyer left who had not been heard from during the long morning session, and he belonged to the other side. Ken Arrasmith, despite the impassioned oratory by his counsel, waited grim-faced at the defense table, almost as if he could envision the dark cloud over his head, a cloud that bore the name of Luella.

Mike Kane had been taking a shower when the idea came to him, the idea that would spin the trial, which had been dry, to a dramatic closing. The tall and quiet prosecutor would have been the last lawyer in the room expected to put on the best show of the entire sordid episode, which only made it more impressive.

His start was the usual slow and efficient presentation as he talked about the "incredibly sensitive and important case" that had put the eyes of the world on tiny Lewiston, Idaho, where the question had to be answered: "Do we ever say it is okay to kill, to take a human life?"

Kane asked the jury to sweep aside the emotion and take a cold look "at what they talked about," of how Ron and Luella should have been convicted of sex abuse. "They want you to look off in that direction" and not at what happened on Shelter Road.

Want to call the Binghams bad names? Kane said they were vermin, they were evil, they were animals and it was easy to feel anger and hatred toward them. In fact, he would personally have loved to have had the chance to prosecute them and put them in jail for their continuous attacks on women and girls.

"Sexual abuse is a dirty business," said Kane, getting the trial back on track. "But so too is murder, and that is what the evidence shows happened here."

He had picked up on the flaw in the Mosman arguments, that "they never mentioned" Luella by name. Kane began his tour of what happened at Shelter Road, picking up both the Tec-9 and the Ruger and describing how the heavily armed Arrasmith went into the shop "to get a statement from her after shooting to death her husband."

Then Kane launched his idea, an emotional show-and-tell depiction of the murders.

He did what the defense had asked the jury to do, and put himself in Arrasmith's shoes. He pointed the Tec-9 at the floor of the courtroom, aiming at an imaginary target, and explained that when Arrasmith opened fire on the prone Ron Bingham, he only pumped out four rounds in the first fusillade. Kane counted out loud, pretending to squeeze the trigger. ONE TWO THREE FOUR!

Then, he said, the Tec-9 jammed, and Kane pretended to clear the weapon. Then he moved a few steps, to depict Arrasmith changing position, from the right to the left side of the mortally wounded Ron Bingham, and pretended to resume firing: FIVE SIX SEVEN EIGHT NINE TEN ELEVEN TWELVE THIRTEEN FOURTEEN . . . he paused to take a breath . . . *FIFTEEN SIXTEEN SEVENTEEN EIGHTEEN NINETEEN TWENTY TWENTY-ONE*. Kane's voice increased in volume as he continued his mock murder. *TWENTY-TWO, TWENTY-THREE*. And those were just the bullets that struck the victim, he reminded, not all that were fired. There were thirty bullets in the clip, twenty-nine were fired and Ron Bingham had forty-four entrance and exit wounds. "That is murder. That is not self-defense," Kane said.

He ridiculed the idea that someone could walk up to another person, carrying a fully loaded Tec-9, and "if that person moves, I shoot." The law doesn't work that way, he said, and picked up a law book to read the relevant statute. "He moved and he died. It is that simple," Kane said. "Ron had no gun."

And if Luella had indeed had a gun that day, Kane said, she would have been within her rights in shooting Ken Arrasmith. "She had no gun," he said. Instead, she ran into the shop and "this man flushed her out."

Kane waved the Ruger and asked what was Luella supposed to think when she saw the shadowy Arrasmith coming after her. "She got her butt out of there, and he came out and shot her in the back six times," he said, pointing the Ruger and the glowing laser sight at an imaginary, falling Luella, and once again counting. *ONE TWO THREE . . . FOUR FIVE SIX*. "Folks," he said, "That is murder."

Despite the Binghams' background and their reputation and their repeated acts, even if convicted, they would not have been executed for their crimes. "They did not deserve to die. Society doesn't have that right and this man didn't have that right." Then he, too, dropped his voice to a pleading whisper: "Please, please, please, don't say to this man, to these people, that it would be okay to kill when you get mad enough."

Arrasmith was "out of his league" in the situation and only knew what he had been told by Cynthia, who had changed her story from when she told police she was not afraid of the Binghams and did not want to leave their house. Detective White was on the job and told

Arrasmith the morning of the murders that he was ready with evidence against the Binghams. "There was no need for him to go up there with his guns," said the special prosecutor. "The police were going to do their job."

He mocked the defense argument that asked the jury to put themselves in Arrasmith's shoes. "What would you do?" he asked. "We wouldn't do it and you wouldn't do it." Arrasmith acted irresponsibly and "cut the system out" of the process with his dual executions, said Kane.

"I ask, like they have, for you to vote your conscience. We all know what is right and wrong. You don't kill two human beings because you are angry with the system."

Even if the jurors felt that Ron's death was deserved, Kane asked them to "remember the forgotten victim," Luella. Despite their background, "They were not vermin. They were not animals. They were human beings . . . and they were entitled to the same rights as the defendant."

Mike Kane said there was only one "honest and responsible verdict" and that would be for the jury to return two counts of first degree murder.

31

Judge Leggett read the jury a lengthy set of instructions after hearing an argument in her chambers in which the prosecution asked for voluntary manslaughter to be included as an option. Back in court, she heard a defense request for involuntary manslaughter to be included. It was clear that neither side was certain which way the jury was going to jump and wanted as many options as possible for their cause.

Before the case began, both sides had opted for a straight up-or-down vote on first degree murder, and now both were trying to hedge their bets. Leggett's only concession was to instruct the jury that it could include second degree murder as a possible verdict, still another blow to the defense from the diminutive judge.

The benches were full as fourteen attentive jurors listened carefully to Leggett, their faces blank, their body language giving no hint as to their feelings. Ken Arrasmith sat at the defense table, picking his teeth.

Once the jury was given the case, Marshal Tommy Williams escorted them to their room, hung his coat on the back of a chair in front of the door, and sat. His imposing presence spoke volumes. The case was out of the hands of everyone except the people behind that door.

At 11 A.M., the courtroom emptied and the long vigil began, a silent countdown of unknown duration that would determine the fate of Arrasmith and the conclusion of a bizarre case that had captured national attention. Television personality Geraldo Rivera had been carrying live updates daily throughout the trial and stations in Idaho and Washington had played the story big on the evening news.

Lunch passed and the gathered crowd on the first floor of the courthouse settled in for an unknown length of stay. Would they come back soon? Would they take all night? Did they want to wrap it up in a hurry and hit the road for Thanksgiving with their families in Twin Falls? There were many questions, and no answers, only speculation.

There was no word before dinner, but the people waiting for the final decision ran out to grab a snack and hurry back. Craig and Roy Mosman sat on the stairs to the second floor courtroom, chatting with media representatives. Denise Rosen and Mike Kane were in their offices across the parking lot. Donnita was on the first floor pay telephone, tearfully talking to Ken Arrasmith, on the pay phone in the jail two floors above her. Cynthia nervously moved from group to group, trying to be brave, telling everyone her dad promised he would be home for Thanksgiving. Rilla Smith did not stay, for the numbers of the Arrasmith clan were simply too overwhelming. Once old friends, they were now forever divided.

About nine o'clock, the jury decided to adjourn for the night, and a wave of relief and disappointment swept the spectators as they filtered into the darkness to get a night's sleep.

The next morning, the deliberations resumed and there was still no hint as to what was being decided. Spirited arguments were made both ways as the hours stretched on.

At 11 A.M., the jurors were back, about twenty-four hours after they had been handed the case, and the courtroom quickly filled, with the Arrasmith family occupying the first two rows on the left side of the courtroom, behind the prosecuting attorneys. Rilla Smith sat on the other side, accompanied by a few relatives and friends. Arrasmith was brought down from the jail, blowing kisses to his family.

One juror in the front row was weeping, but nobody knew why. The tension was almost electric in its intensity.

The verdict was stunning. Guilty of murder in the second degree for the death of Ron Bingham; Guilty of murder in the first degree for the death of Luella Bingham. In interviews later, the jurors said their decision for a "guilty" verdict was never really in doubt and that they had only spent the hours discussing the extent of the guilt, reducing the charge concerning Ron Bingham by a notch from first to second degree.

Arrasmith looked down at the table, his face an emotionless mask, blank as a stone. The Arrasmith family was jolted and a number of them broke into tears, hugging each other, disbelief in their eyes. Audible sighs of satisfaction came from the other side of the courtroom.

The deputy sheriffs cleared the room quickly, and the Arrasmith family and friends gathered outside in the parking lot, against the court's rules, but the trial was over and they didn't care. The sobbing Donnita was lost in fury and screamed almost incoherently to the narrow windows of the jury room on the second floor: "Jury! I want you to know people have been killed! This is not right! They were murderers!"

Three deputies saw the crowd and escorted Rilla Smith, her sister and closest friend out another entrance, all the way to their automobile, then gave them directions on how to drive away without encountering the shocked Arrasmith tribe.

EPILOGUE

I was over, but it was not over. Years will pass before the final act is written in this disturbing and complex case.

The day after the verdict was Thanksgiving 1995, and Kell Arrasmith ate his turkey dinner in the Nez Perce County Jail, awaiting his February sentencing. The bird probably tasted somewhat like crow, because the idea that had bolstered him throughout the long months awaiting trial was his steadfast belief that people would *believe* what he said. The TV audiences might have, but the jury, by a unanimous vote, did not.

That did not mean that the media drumbeat was going to subside. True, the very next time Arrasmith was on the telephone to Geraldo Rivera, the mustachioed talk-meister actually asked a hard question, wondering aloud to Arrasmith: Who made you judge, jury and executioner? The now-convicted double-murderer had no answer. By keeping up with the trial on his nightly show, Rivera had been the only national media figure to realize Arrasmith was not as he seemed. The TV star had already begun making stinging remarks about Arrasmith's drug involvement.

But there were other shows on which the producers and the highly paid stars were unable or unwilling to grasp the details of the case. They apparently preferred to feed a dramatic story to the astonishing people who sit in such audiences and react in almost idiotic fashion. Cynthia was showcased on *Donahue*, where the audience hooted the first appearance by Rilla and Josh Smith. Cynthia was on *Oprah*, and the hostess retreated to the old story instead of presenting a full version of what had happened. The *Leeza Show*, which had flubbed its first attempt by broadcasting the Arrasmith version of the story during the trial, took another crack at it, becoming the first to attempt to balance the picture by interviewing Denise Rosen. Unfortunately, they allowed Arrasmith—a convicted double-murderer—to have the last word from jail. As a final insult, money was stolen from Rosen's purse in a dressing room while she appeared on camera. The show later made restitution.

If the case did anything, it pinpointed a major weakness of the media, particularly on television. The story defied brevity, but TV went for it in a big way. The chase resulted in chaos and a good reason for viewers to carefully weigh the content of any alleged TV news program to determine if the show is out to prove a point rather than report a story. In this case, what was left out was just as important as what was included.

Cynthia was a genuine victim, tearful and pretty and young, the answer to a producer's prayer. She endured a nightmare.

A few months after the trial, the country was shocked that a fourteen-year-old girl in Texas was pregnant by her twenty-two-year-old boyfriend. Yet no one had dared question Cynthia about her own pregnancy at the age of fifteen, allegedly by a boyfriend who was twenty-five, and the ensuing abortion. Her own troubled background was chronicled in an eighty-page Lewiston Police Department report, but was hardly mentioned, and rarely criticized. The woman-child who never finished junior high school received off-limits, prom queen treatment throughout.

The protective wall of publicity, however, did not shield Cynthia from some critics. Rilla and Josh Smith maintained that they never heard her so much as complain or cry out for help. A nineteen-year-old woman who knew her said, "You can't rape the willing." Another critic added, "A fifteen-year-old girl that had been living with her older boyfriend? Sex isn't new to her. And she just had an abortion? I mean . . . meth? So if anything happened, she went along with it. She was a fifteen-year-old sexually active child." None of those comments, however, refuted the law—she was a minor and she was assaulted.

Several jurors said their decision was influenced by the lack of credibility they assigned to Cynthia's testimony. It seemed that tears could cut both ways. The girl had not asked to be turned into a media darling, and one could only feel sorry for her by the time the verdict was handed down, for she was shouldering a burden that would have been too heavy for even a much stronger person to carry.

Drugged or not, she had gone through a horrific experience and then was caught in the glare of the public spotlight. Instead of being given time to recover in private, she was constantly paraded before the cameras and national television audiences.

Kyle Richardson reaped a whirlwind. Judge Leggett was dissatisfied both with his willingness to testify and with the sweetheart deal that he had made with authorities. She refused to accept the agreement and ordered that he be tried on the original conspiracy counts. New negotiations began to arrive at a compromise that was sure to include jail time. His reluctant testimony against Arrasmith had backfired.

* * *

For the same reason that the Binghams' violent past could not be brought into the court, neither could the records that charted the turbulent life of Ken Arrasmith. In hindsight, his violent temper, combined with drugs, had led to the showdown with Ron Bingham. Certainly, amassing more than thirty thousand dollars in child support debt while hiding a growing fortune behind a wall of legal paper clearly demonstrated the man's contempt and arrogance. Ken Arrasmith had ten thousand dollars in cash for a drug deal but was far behind in court-ordered support for his four children and one stepson.

The police did not cover themselves in glory on this one, although the most serious error was not in failing to pursue the Bingham assault on Cynthia with more vigor. In fact, prosecutors would later say that the evidence against the Binghams, primarily the unreliability of Patti Mahar Johnson and Cynthia's testimony, may not have been sufficient for an arrest that would put the Binghams in jail.

A much more substantive police error, a true Perry Mason Moment, took place in early February 1996, only a few weeks before Arrasmith was to be sentenced.

The telephone rang in the Mosman law offices. It was the girlfriend of Tony Adams, owner of the infamous auto shop on Shelter Road. Adams had been picked up by police and, angry at being arrested, decided to tell a very interesting story: Police indeed had found two guns at the shop on the day of the killings.

Craig and Roy Mosman, who had been paid $115,000 by the county for their spirited defense of Arrasmith, lost no time in seeing the significance of the claim. Much of the state's case against Arrasmith had been pinned to the absence of any weaponry around the Binghams, although Arrasmith insisted on the stand he thought he saw Ron reach for something and believed Lue was carrying a pistol. But the discovery of the guns at the shop had been kept secret from both lead detective Wade

Ralston and the prosecutors, Denise Rosen and Mike Kane.

The law enforcement team that had been accused by the Mosmans throughout the trial of being Keystone Kops were now accused of covering up vital evidence and lying about it. In a rare news release on February 6, Sheriff Ron Koeper of Nez Perce County was forced to acknowledge "that a nine mm handgun was found in the shop building" on the day of the killings.

"Deputy Jim Colvin was approached by a nearby resident who stated that a weapon may have been kept in the shop. Deputy Colvin found a handgun in a drawer on the north wall of the shop. It was located in a bench drawer behind some tools. A determination was made by Captain Scott Whitcomb and Sergeant Jim Colvin that the weapon had not been fired recently. Based upon their experience it was determined the weapon was of no evidentiary value to the murders. The handgun was not taken as evidence nor was its existence revealed to prosecutors," the news release stated.

"Based upon the experience and training of the sheriff's deputies involved, this weapon has no bearing on the case of State of Idaho vs. Ken Arrasmith."

While the development is likely not to change the outcome of the case, there could be no question that the presence of a firearm of any sort, found any place in or around the shop, would have strengthened the defense team's hand during the trial. The actions of Colvin and Whitcomb were questionable. Equally startling was the nonacknowledgment of the fact, by the sheriff in his public statement, that the gun in the shop belonged not to some ordinary citizen, but to Whitcomb's son, and that Whitcomb gave it to the boy to take home! A second pistol, obviously not used, had been discovered beneath the seat of a truck. In a case where firearms were to play such an important role, the discovery of guns anywhere around the crime scene should have been handled more again rejected the defense motions for dismissal of charges or a new trial. But it had been a close call.

Rilla Smith was also a victim in this story. Her devotion to her daughter plunged her into the untenable position of having to tolerate her son-in-law. As a result, not only has her name been sullied, but she has lost everything. Ron, choosing not to pay the insurance premiums in their last financial bargain, guaranteed the final insult of Rilla losing the little house that she and her late beloved husband, Walter, had lived in for years. Ironically, the property had suddenly increased in value as work began on a massive apartment project right next door.

For the appeals, the state agreed to continue paying Arrasmith's private lawyers instead of summoning a public defender. Meanwhile, Donnita Weddle built an expensive new home in Clarkston.

The idea of earning money from the case—through television, movies or books—never left Arrasmith's mind. Nez Perce County authorities would monitor any such transaction and try to seize the profits in repayment for the lawyers' fees. Tentative plans were discussed for Cynthia to write a book instead, authorities said.

* * *